Bar Code →

Jerry Lewis
IN PERSON

JERRY LEWIS

WITH

HERB GLUCK

Jerry Lewis
IN PERSON

New York ATHENEUM 1982

Library of Congress Cataloging in Publication Data

Lewis, Jerry, 1926–
    Jerry Lewis, in person.

    1. Lewis, Jerry, 1926–   2. Comedians—United
States—Biography. I. Gluck, Herb.   II. Title.
PN2287.L435A34   1982   791.43'028'0924 [B]   81-70109
ISBN 0-689-11290-4   AACR2

What better gift could one receive than the gift of life?
But I don't dedicate this book to them for that . . .
but because they earned it . . .

Jerry Lewis
IN PERSON

BOOK ONE

S POTLIGHT.

Then a short, electrifying silence as the announcement came: *"Ladies and Gentlemen, the Copacabana proudly presents . . . Martin and Lewis!"*

We started our run to the stage. A huge roar followed us, swirling all around, growing louder and louder and crackling over our heads like gunfire. The whole room shook. We brushed past a tangle of reaching hands, all those ringside celebrities—Eddie Cantor, Jack Benny, Jackie Gleason, Maurice Chevalier, Milton Berle, Victor Borge, Sammy Davis—name them, they were giving us the greatest welcome of our lives here at the Copa, this closing night of July 25, 1956.

Exactly ten years had passed since Dean and I first put the act together. Ten years to the day! A shaky beginning at the 500 Club in Atlantic City, then—wham!—we sky-rocketed out of there like two blazing comets, the thrust taking us straight up to unbelievable stardom. And the ride was filled with a million laughs, guided by a special kind of love that I thought two guys had for each other. But now it was ending. We were coming down fast, so fast I could hardly breathe.

I hit the stage and glanced at Dean. His face was a mask; nothing showed beyond that. He stood there peering into the lights, seemingly relaxed, almost languid as he flicked an imaginary piece of lint off his jacket sleeve. The same old game—same pattern—he would play it cool even if it killed him.

Automatically I nodded. Dick Stabile cued the band; on his downswing we moved out at full throttle and kept the momentum going for well over an hour, switching jokes and routines, ad-libbing, mugging, dancing and singing our heads off, and putting every ounce of energy into this one last performance. I didn't want it to stop. Not now or ever.

The applause rolled toward us in giant waves, ripping loose and rising to a sustained crescendo at the finish of "Pardners," the title song from our latest movie. I could hear a distant swell of music, saw Dean's hand come up over his head, then felt the lasso go around my shoulders. He pulled me to him. We hugged good. There were some tears, warm and useless.

There would be no coming back for an encore, or even a bow. We stumbled off the stage as if it were on fire.

Dean took one aisle leading to the rear of the club. I took the other—a wobbly dash into chaos, an overlapping of faces and bodies and voices hammering again and again in the air: "Stay together!" "We love you guys!" "Jerry! Jerry! Jerry!"

I buckled on the steps, gasping as though a rock had slammed into the pit of my stomach. The next thing I knew two captains had hooked my arms and were hauling me into the kitchen.

I sat there for a minute, catching my breath, staring vacantly into a dim, gentle kind of darkness, remembering the sound of surf breaking on the Atlantic City beach at the moment of sudden discovery: *Dean was hunched over a rail, his hands framing orange-blue clouds billowing up from the ocean, and saying, "We're gonna have lots of good times together, pallie. You wait and see. . . ."*

"Listen, kid, anything you want—say the word and it's yours." I heard the sandpaper voice of Copa boss Julie Podell. Gruff and street-wise as they come, but he had a generous heart for the people he liked, especially entertainers. Still, he couldn't give me what I needed most. My wife Patti was at home, three thousand miles away in California.

I got up and went to my dressing room suite above the Copa and flopped on the bed. I had no idea what I would be doing the next day or any day after that. There was only a foreboding sense of failure, of my life emptying away and becoming an absolute blank.

I closed my eyes. I felt myself falling, tumbling over and over in space like a feather—down into a trackless desert. . . . *No sign of life anywhere. Not a solitary bird crosses the sky. Even the stars are gone. I struggle forward, engulfed in a wide river of sand.*

Suddenly the desert spreads open. A highway shimmers before me. I'm walking on it—to where? Then the movie marquee!—It straddles the highway; ornate, gilded, the lights flashing round and round.

There, appearing in bulging, silvery brightness is the most enormous word I have ever seen:

A L O N E

I stagger, sink to my knees. I'm screaming at the top of my lungs:
"ONE! ONE! ONE ALONE!"

I was staring at the phone, trying to remember the time difference in Los Angeles. It was nearly one in the morning back there. I fumbled for a cigarette, took a deep drag, then dialed my number at home.

Patti answered the first ring. "I was about to call you. Are you OK?"

I began to tremble. "It's over, Momma."

"I know. It isn't easy. You've got ten years to cry away."

The tears came. Short, gulping sobs that wrenched every nerve in my body.

That little child again. When he hurts himself, he looks at Momma with squinty, innocent eyes and stutters, "I h-h-hurt my f-f-finger on the desk." And if she says, "Is my baby all right?"—you'll hear wailing like you've never heard. As though at any second the kid is ready to gush up the Pacific Ocean.

The phone sat on my lap for countless moments. When the tears stopped, I said, "Tell me what to do, honey."

"Come home. We're going to scrub our faces and meet you at the airport."

I saw her and the children, saw the glimmer of recognition, the wave of hands, all that sweetness in front of me. . . .

Nothing but a soft pillow and my head sinking into it as the switchboard operator connected me to Dean. To me, he was always Paul. And he always called me pallie, or Jew, or pardner.

"Hello, pallie, how're ya holdin' up?"

"I don't know yet. I just want to say . . . we've had some good times, Paul."

"There'll be more."

"Yeah . . . well . . . take care of yourself, that's all—"

"You too, pardner."

I think I said, "I love you."

I think he said, "I love you, too."

But I can't be sure.

BOOK TWO

DRIVING out of the Lincoln Tunnel into Newark, New Jersey, in the fall of 1980—heavy traffic along Market Street—and the limousine passing RKO Proctor's Theatre (old Branford), the Davega's sporting goods store, Woolworth's, Bamberger's. Then a slow left turn onto Springfield Avenue past a white-pillared courthouse with LAW, JUSTICE, PEACE engraved in stone above the entrance. At Irving Turner Boulevard there's a housing project; on the other side an unpainted and decrepit pawnshop, a tavern, Pentecostal church, check-cashing store, a sorry empty lot with beer cans and bald tires strewn dismally . . . Newark people shambling by under a glary sky, and more rubble, more rust, more iron-grated storefronts, and blistered billboard signs advertising rock concerts which have long since been played. . . . Old stores, old buildings, old memories stirring as we cross the Garden State Parkway into Irvington. Stopping briefly to read inscription on plaque in Camptown Common: *In honor of World War II veterans and to commemorate the founding of Irvington in 1852* . . . Now going along Chancellor

7

Avenue and the limo slowing, swinging right and turning onto Union Avenue—396 Union—a brick apartment building four stories high, two entrances, patches of shrubbery in front, fire escapes from the second story up . . .

My childhood home. I stood there, turning thoughts back, quietly smoking a cigarette and thinking of this building I once lived in; of how it really was, and what it all meant. . . .

[2]

As a small boy I would sometimes sit in my grandfather's house in Brooklyn and listen to him tell stories of czarist Russia, of the evil deeds that were committed there against the Jews. That's why he and my grandmother fled their village in 1897, found their way to one of the large shipping ports in France, then sailed to America without knowing what America really was.

At Ellis Island, Grandpa Morris Levitch presented a letter of introduction to someone from the Hebrew Immigration Society. A while later an old friend showed up and brought the young couple to New York's Lower East Side, where they rented a cold-water flat in a sunless tenement building. It was here that Hannah Levitch gave birth to two children. Their names were Daniel and Gertrude. The boy was born in 1902. He's my father.

It's easy for me to picture the Lower East Side of that period. I've seen it a thousand times through the eyes of others and in books, photographs, documentary films— words and pictures that showed the way people lived in their sagging jumble of brick and frame structures, with the constant swirl of awnings, the fire escapes and wash lines. Peddlers lugging everything from wrapped fish to copper hardware on their backs, pushcarts jammed against each other, hordes of people pounding the streets and gutters, streets overflowing with noise. The hated sweatshops where the greenhorns stooped over worktables piled with dresses and coats, the lights so dim, the air so stale it's a wonder they knew what they were doing. This was my grandfather's world for five years. Then he and his family set across the East River. They located a nice apartment at 73 Grafton Street in the Brownsville section of Brooklyn. It had a bathtub and hot water, a big stove, big windows, and they could actually see birds fly over distant rooftops. To them, it was amazing.

But the important thing was to work. So Grandpa opened a neighborhood wine cellar. There, he served the same handful of customers day after day until, at last, his youth faded to tired old age.

That's how I remember him. Old. And working in the cellar. A cute little man with whimsical eyes, snowy white beard flecked with dust, his gnarled hands squeezing purple and light green grapes from the winepress into wooden barrels, then pouring the fermented juices into gallon jugs after the rabbi approved it kosher. And I remember him sitting on a battered chair, waving at me as I came down the cellar stairs, his fingers fluttering like butterfly wings.

His routine seldom changed. Nothing spectacular ever happened. An event to him would be to stand by the window in the wintertime and watch a quart of milk become seventeen inches tall as the cream popped out frozen.

I was five. Mom had dressed me up real spiffy in a blue corduroy outfit, with patent leather shoes. We rode the subway to Brooklyn. Grandpa and Grandma Levitch were waiting for us in front of the butcher shop, a few doors down from their apartment house. It was Sabbath. The green shade in the butcher's window had been drawn. But the nasty old cat with all the scars on his head sat between the shade and the windowpane, its yellow eyes wide, fixed, staring like a mystic. I kept looking at it, trying to appear nonchalant while Mom showed me off. The usual oohs and aahs; then something compelled Grandma to say, "Listen, Rachel—your son will not only be just an actor, but a *great* actor."

Grandpa instantly glanced heavenward and muttered, *"Kayn-eyn-horeh,"* a Yiddish phrase meaning, "No evil eye." Typical of him. If the slightest bit of good luck seemed ready to land on top of his head, God forbid he should brag about it.

I can't be sure how he felt about my father in those early days. Or, for that matter, how my father felt about him. Who's to say? I often wonder, what does any child know of his parents? What do I know of mine? I've been given a half-century to find out, and there are still large pieces missing from the puzzle. Is it because some strange, ludicrous truth deep inside had long ago ripped away our courage to speak love, or hate, when it was clearly necessary to do so? I know what love and hate mean when they are shown honestly. The other way can kill. There were instances when they nearly killed me.

Anyway, I'm certain that at an early age my father realized what it would be like if he were ultimately to take over Grandpa's business. He saw nothing but defeat in that. He wanted a *real* job, wanted to be more than a wine maker. But what?

He graduated from Public School 156. He didn't go to high school. Instead, he worked full-time and part-time for some local merchants on Pitkin Avenue. Sometimes he helped his father. And in his spare hours there would be things to do in the streets, like playing ball or joining the rest of the kids on a corner, where they would swap stories and compare baseball stars and ogle at the girls, frittering away the afternoon until his mother called for him to come home.

One summer day, as he walked among the Brownsville

crowds, he saw Al Jolson's name up on the marquee of a vaudeville theatre. He went in and heard him sing "Mammy."

Jolie—his hero of heroes. There was magic in the way the man bounced and strutted on the stage in blackface, his voice booming, echoing and re-echoing around the hall with such force that it brought my father closer to joy than he had ever been before.

Now all he wanted to do was sing. He spent endless hours practicing in front of a mirror, imitating Jolson. He memorized the songs and special material of other vaudeville headliners. Then he made the rounds. Using the stage name Danny Lewis, he went to a score of auditions. The variety agents liked his voice. They were also impressed with his husky good looks—felt he could grab an audience—and promptly booked him to entertain at kiddie shows, weddings, beer gardens and social clubs. Five- and ten-dollar jobs, mostly.

He even showed up on vaccination lines. In those days the city hired entertainers to perform for the schoolchildren while they received smallpox shots. If more than three kids were on line, he would be there singing. The fact is, he'd go to almost any length to please the agents, particularly those who said that he sounded exactly like Jolson. But that only happened when he had a cold. So he assiduously checked the newspapers for inclement weather predictions. The moment a heavy rain or snowstorm came around, Dad would invariably be outdoors with his shirt open, happy as a clam. Yet with all his dedication, tenacity and desire, somehow the major vaudeville jobs eluded his grasp.

Well, there was no big rush. If nothing else, the applause sustained him. Besides, he had established quick friendships with struggling performers like himself—people who had neither the leisure nor the inclination to think about failure. Occasionally after a show they would go out for drinks and a few laughs, releasing their private frustrations in each other's company. In the flush of youthful exuberance, there'd be lots of backslapping and good wishes among them. Three young guys stood above the rest. He played a number of club dates with them at the Half Moon Hotel in Coney Island. An incredibly funny act, just getting started in the business. They called themselves the Ritz Brothers.

Great experiences! But however exciting it may have been, my father's modest career remained modest. Slowly but surely, his finances dried up. To make ends meet he got a daytime position, working as a song plugger for the Fred Fisher music-publishing firm on West Forty-sixth Street in Manhattan. That was in 1922, in the midst of a dance revolution, when millions black-bottomed and shimmied to the melodies of Tin Pan Alley. Sheet-music sales boomed, as did sales of phonograph machines, radios and popular instruments. And talented piano players were worth their weight in dollars to the big retail stores.

One of Dad's accounts was the S. S. Kresge five-and-dime on Market Street in Newark, New Jersey. A nineteen-year-old girl named Rachel Brodsky worked there. She wasn't a striking beauty, but attractive, with an animated face and well-rounded figure. She demonstrated songs on the piano, directly behind notions and picture frames. The shoppers would stroll back to her department, gather around and sing along while she played the hits of Jerome Kern, Vincent Youmans, Louis Hirsch, Cole Porter, Irving Berlin, George Gershwin, George M. Cohan and down the list. She played them all flawlessly—a technically perfect musician.

My father met her there on a spring morning.

After introducing himself, he placed a couple of Fred Fisher tunes on the piano stand and immediately launched into "They Go Wild, Simply Wild Over Me." Then he whistled a chorus on the edge of his business card.

Their romance wavered back and forth for almost two years, mainly because she couldn't make up her mind. Meanwhile, Dad persisted. He'd often call from Brooklyn and say that he happened to be in downtown Newark—would she meet him right away? If she said yes, he'd jump on the subway, and she'd meet him when the store closed. Then they would take long walks on Market Street. If he had enough money in his pocket he'd buy her a dinner, and then they'd go see a movie at the Branford Theatre. Whatever they did, it was done properly. But one afternoon he got carried away and impulsively kissed her in the street. She walloped him with her purse. In the confusion her necklace broke. The beads scattered all over the sidewalk.

He was still apologizing at the front door of her walk-up flat at 327 Bergen Street when Mom announced: "I now accept the fact that we should be engaged."

They were married in January of 1925.

[3]

Fourteen months later, on March 16, 1926, my father played the Empire Theatre in Newark. I was born the same day, between his matinee and evening shows, and given the name Joseph, after my maternal grandfather.

It was not a smooth entrance. My mother had been in labor four days and four nights, and was finally rushed from her mother's apartment on 16th Avenue in Newark to the Clinton Private Hospital on Johnson Street.

She remembers waking up to a pervading, acrid smell of ether. Bleary-eyed, dizzy, her consciousness struggling against the fumes which saturated her brain, she came to herself upon seeing a shaft of sunlight pass "brighter than burnished gold" through the hospital window straight down over her bed. She decided it had to be a miracle. Whatever it was, her reverie became even more wondrous when she saw me lying in her arms. "Oh, he's gorgeous," she cried with happiness and then, methodically feeling the flatness of her stomach, let out an enormous sigh that could be heard all over the maternity ward.

Dad arrived at the hospital minutes before my birth, still wearing his stage costume and greasepaint. Bursting into the waiting room, he was met by Mom's three sisters and both my grandmothers, who guided him to a chair, where he sat in virtual shock, hardly stirring a muscle until the delivery nurse brought in the news—which triggered an uproar of emotion. He sprang to his feet, picked up his mother-in-law, spun her round and round the room and developed a hernia that bothered him the rest of his life.

The next morning a staff doctor stood at my mother's bedside. She remembers the grim smile, the soft, languid voice. "I must tell you, Mrs. Levitch, the baby is sleeping too much. There are complications, certain patterns. . . . You can see for yourself."

Her hand clutched the blanket. "What's wrong?"

"Well, you've had a long, hard labor. The baby's head took a lot of pressure. Now, that would not necessarily cause a reduction of oxygen to the brain, but there is a possibility some damage has been done."

She fell into a stunned silence. Nothing made sense. Everything became scrambled and then tangled into one gigantic knot. Finally: "Please, please—what's wrong with my baby?"

"We don't know for sure. But we have a procedure. It's called a spinal tap."

She barely got out the words. "I must talk to my family. I mean, I won't do anything without—" She couldn't go on. The sobs choked her.

Again the soft voice. "Now, now, calm yourself. Nothing is definite. Just take your time. Think things out. . . ."

As it happened, the spinal tap was never performed. Grandma Sarah Brodsky made sure of it. Using plain common sense and intuition, she figured the problem was simply a case of too much ether. "It will wear off soon enough," she told those in charge.

And Grandma was right. At the end of March the entire family attended my *bris*. By then, the terrible fear had all but vanished. Everyone had a reason to celebrate once more.

These things I've heard since the earliest, remotest years of my childhood. I heard other things, too. At the age of three or four, my imaginings melted into fairy-tale dreams, then turned into something ominously vague and uncomfortable during my waking hours.

At five, they broke through like dreadful demons, evoking sensations of pain, of loneliness and despair. None was forgotten; all of them were impossible to escape.

So I remember.

My father was on the road and my mother was playing cards in someone's house. . . .

Outside, a freezing rain thrashes the windowpane. I'm half-dozing on a pile of coats, listening to the buzz of conversation. I hear one of my aunts say, mockingly, "Rachel, maybe they gave you the wrong baby."

She laughs, answers in a sarcastic manner, but I can't make out the words.

I turn to the wall. My face is burning up.

And cards are being shuffled, and everyone is laughing.

So it happens that this sort of thing can remain embedded in a child's mind no matter how much happiness accumulates or how long the years move on, even if the happiness outweighs the sorrows a thousand times over.

[4]

An autumn Sunday in the Brownsville section of Brooklyn, 1931.

My parents were on the road. I was staying with Grandpa and Grandma Levitch at their apartment on Grafton Street. Drawn from that time is the memory of Grandpa . . . covered by a prayer shawl, only his nose sticking through . . . heating coffee in a saucepan and drinking it with lots of milk from a glass . . . sitting on a bench in a little park off East New York Avenue, hands lightly folded, squinting into the afternoon sun with faint head shakings and mutterings, all but lost in himself. . . .

It's Sunday. He's given me a dime, and I'm going to see the first movie of my life. A lovely warm day. Most of the stores are open; an army of people pushes and shoves to get to the bargain counters. And the streets pulse with a thousand sounds. Trolley cars rattle by, sidewalk radios blare, junk bells clang; at the corner of Legion Street a man giving out leaflets is being yelled at by an angry crowd. A cop comes flying down the block with his nightstick raised. I keep walking, unable to understand the bewildering ways of older people.

In front of the Loew's Pitkin, a ten-cent ticket comes sliding into my hand, producing a glow that only small children get when the simplest pleasures become attainable.

I scamper through the lobby, down the red-carpeted aisle to an orchestra seat a couple of rows from the stage. The place is swarming with kids. We squirm and fuss and holler at one another. We eat smelly sandwiches, blow up the paper bags and explode them with our fists. Suddenly a loud *"Shush!"* from the grown-up section. The lights dim, the curtains part and organist Henrietta Cameron begins her musical introduction to *The Circus,* starring Charlie Chaplin.

He's a riot! He does all sorts of things with his face and

body. He stands like a mechanical doll, twists his can while walking the tightrope, dashes out of the lion's cage and up a pole—there's nobody funnier than Chaplin.

And I'm falling out of my seat laughing at a scene in which he's trapped among hundreds of distorted mirrors, showing him in hundreds of different poses. But even then, I sense the sad reality of my own life. I feel that I'd rather live in a world of make-believe, where I can be anyone I wish—soldier, sailor, doctor, lawyer—*anyone*. Sure . . . I can be a clown! I can do it. I know that.

[5]

I vaguely recall the Great Depression, when Roosevelt closed the banks, when stockbrokers jumped out of windows, when breadlines formed in the streets. With all that, we were lucky. My father kept working steadily, and Mom pitched in by playing cocktail piano around town once or twice a week. Her agent, Arthur Lyons, would book her for five dollars a night, plus tips. Sometimes, after she got home, I'd wake up and hear coins jingling into a glass jar on her bureau. When they stopped, I could generally tell what kind of night she had, good or bad.

Anyway, between Dad's earnings and the few dollars she was able to put aside for a rainy day, they got along. They were never in a serious financial bind.

Of course, in those days a prime cut of beef cost thirty-eight cents a pound, and chicken cost even less. So we had plenty of chicken on our table while I was growing up. It became an accepted and natural order of things to sit down to a supper of chicken soup, chicken-fat cracklings smothered in mashed potatoes and good old roast chicken—*geschmach!*

But I also remember a particularly bitter night when my father was traveling with the Hurst Burlesque unit and

I sat at the table by myself, waiting for Mom to return from a job somewhere in Irvington.

I sat. The hours passed. Then a stab of panic; each minute built to a wild anxiety that I couldn't conquer. The words hammered in my mind, thoughts that were too shameful to admit: They don't love me. They don't care. They never will.

I went out to find her, moving along Chancellor Avenue, past the stores, across deserted streets and ghostly parking lots; stopping for nothing, plodding on through the downpouring darkness for a mile, then another mile, and another. I ran—ran like the wind.

A garish brightness. The sound of music and raucous laughter in the near distance . . . or did it come from an alien planet? I drew closer. There was a milk box. I stood up on it and looked in over the green-painted window of the saloon. She was there, playing.

Now a foul-smelling rush of whiskey and beer, the tobacco smoke cutting into my lungs like a razor. She saw me. Her fingers stayed glued to the keyboard. Shock mushroomed on her cheeks. "Joey! What are you doing here?"

"I got scared."

"My God! Wait till I—don't you ever do this again!"

On the way home she wept. "How could you—why? Why?" Then her arms came around me. There was a momentary embrace, and a kiss. There was the sound of our heels going click-click-click down the street.

She loved me. They both loved me. What a wonderful feeling!

[6]

Another summer approached. And with it came the golden hours of childhood fun. However, for some in our neighborhood it was a season of cold desperation.

Here and there, on almost every block, people lived from hand to mouth. A few went on relief. Others were too proud to accept charity, so they loitered on street corners and read want ads and talked about having to move somewhere else because they couldn't pay the rent. There were those who fared even worse.

A murderous sun blisters the street. Yet I stay rooted in a crowd watching my friend Marty, who stands with his folks in front of his apartment building, their household possessions stacked around them: furniture, bedsprings, mattresses, suitcases, books, toys. Alongside the curbstone is Marty's rocking horse, a wooden one, with brown and white circles painted on its flanks. The only time I had played in his apartment, he let me ride that horse. I thought it was the nicest toy anyone could possibly have. How small and shabby it looks now.

There's nothing I can say or do. Nothing. I start to walk home. And feel a sameness in the air, a sameness of children at play; of men in sweaty clothes coming home from work; of women waiting for them on red-bricked stoops, in hallways, at half-raised windows everywhere in the neighborhood, the same as always. But time has flown over all of us in a twinkling of an eye. The present no longer exists; everything is past. I can't figure it out, no matter what.

Life is still a mystery.

Early summer morning. My parents are talking in the kitchen. Their voices blend as one voice and drift into my bedroom. I don't miss a word.

We're going to the mountains!

To the President Hotel in Swan Lake, where Mom will work as a rehearsal pianist and Dad will sing, do comedy, act as master of ceremonies and double at other hotels like Grossinger's and Young's Gap in Liberty and the Evans in

Loch Sheldrake. That should guarantee them about two thousand dollars for the ten-week season. Half the money will go back to the President Hotel for room and board. But the main thing is, we'll be together. And there'll be plenty to do in the fresh outdoors. I'll be climbing over rocks, swinging on tree branches, tumbling in the grass, hunting for treasure and swimming in the endless, bottomless lake all summer long!

I hear my name called, which gets me out of bed in a jiffy. I go to the kitchen, and my father points me to a chair.

"You hungry?" he asks.

"I'll boil an egg," Mom says. "Meanwhile, have some milk. Good for your bones—makes your teeth strong."

"How?"

"Calcium!" Dad says emphatically, spreading his mouth wide and tapping his teeth with a fingernail. "You want teeth like mine, drink milk." His teeth look pearly white, hard as iron. I drink quickly, smack my lips and with an outstretched arm hold up the glass for a refill.

Mom bends toward me with the milk pitcher poised. She whispers in my ear, "After breakfast we'll take a walk to Grandma Sarah's house. She has a present for you."

"Ooooh! A baseball cap!"

Her forehead wrinkles in surprise. "She tell you that?"

"Grandma tells me everything."

It swells out of me. Grandma is the love of my life. She believes in me, always tells me I'm great, that I can be as big as anybody in the world if I put my mind to it.

She knows I want to be a baseball star, just like Bill Terry of the New York Giants. And though Grandma really doesn't know a thing about the game, she sincerely roots for him because he's my favorite player. Sometimes, during the baseball season, while at her house listening to the game, hoping that Bill Terry would sock a couple of doubles—or better still a grand-slam home run—she'd ask out of the blue, *"Zug mir,* did Bill Terry win today?"

A screwy grin, then feigned annoyance. "Naaaw, Grandma, he's a first baseman. How can he win?"

So this one special time she looks up at the ceiling as though it contains every answer to every question ever posed. And finally she says, "You know what, Sonny? If Bill Terry was Jewish, I think maybe he would win . . . with God's help."

That's Grandma Sarah.

She bought me a baseball cap, out of respect for my ambition. The day my parents and I went to her house, she placed it on my head with tender care. Stitched into the visor were the initials BT. To me it was worth at least one hundred zillion dollars.

The memories of that summertime in 1932 come swarming in with lightning speed; there's no sense of duration or chronological order, only a certain visual consciousness of voices and sounds. It stirs around me now, and I recognize myself as I was then, at a time when my utopian dreams really began.

Hotel billboards on Route 17. One after the other they pop into view, each with a similar message: Beautiful Rooms . . . Swimming . . . Boating . . . Spectacular Entertainment . . . Free Dance Instruction . . . Dietary Laws Observed . . . Inquire Now!

I tug at my mother's sleeve. "Are we there?"

"In a little while. Look—look out the window!"

I push aside suits and dresses that are draped on wooden hangers hooked over our car window. I see lots of milk barns, fences, cows feeding in pastures, horses pulling plows, men and women in straw hats working their land. The land is bright; the air is sweet.

And further on—"Are we there?"

My father glances back as if a grasshopper is perched on his shoulder.

"Sit still," he says, pushing hard on the accelerator. We go faster and faster. The wind whistles through the window cracks, flopping my hair every which way. Villages and farms and gas stations blur dizzily by. Now and then a whoosh of trucks and the shudder of steel, the clumpety-clump of rubber on gravel, and suddenly a big hill to climb. We roar on up. At the top I look out and see a forest of pine sunk down in green darkness, the mountains all around. In another minute we're coasting along past high rock walls into blots of shade, slowing a little as the car twists round banked curves to the floor of the highway. A grind of gears. We speed up again. It's late afternoon; we're still headed north on 17, the city far, far behind us and our car moving straight as an arrow into the heart of the Catskills.

And before I know it, we are positively and most definitely there!

The President Hotel sat on a sloping lawn off the foot of a quiet road in the vacation town of Swan Lake, New York, a white-painted, rambling wooden building, flanked by shade trees and edged with bushes, flowers and vines. A paved walk curled to the front porch, which jutted forward under a slanted roof. Behind the hotel was a space for children to play: teeter-totters; swings; a shed containing rubber balls and bats, hoops and jai alai paddles, a rusted three-wheel bike with a bell that actually worked—that is, until I broke it. A thicket of woods bordered the property. Beyond was the shiny lake. I must have floated in it dozens of times, facedown, holding my breath and counting off the seconds. . . . "Joey! Enough already! You want to drown!"

When it rained I usually stayed on the porch, bored silly

listening to some of the adults as they rudely talked and laughed into each other's faces, or snored loudly in their chairs, or argued over cards, or exchanged family snapshots and bragged about this genius son and that darling daughter while others shuffled from one spot to the next complaining about their rooms, the food, the service—everything.

Inside the screened porch, as the warm rain splattered on the roof, I would sit and wonder if there was anything better to do than just doing *that*.

A cloudy morning, the wind gusting across the ball field. Dust swirling into everyone's eyes during a championship softball game being played between the President Hotel staff employees and guests. And pow!—my father connects at the plate, rifling a shot over the center fielder's head to the trees! A cry goes up—"Throw the ball! Throw the ball!" It comes bouncing in on two hops to the shortstop, who wheels and pegs it home. And here comes my father racing down the line, now stumbling and straightening, now leaning and plunging headfirst under the catcher's tag.

"Safe!" the umpire screams.

My father gets to his feet. His face is smeared with dirt, but he's grinning like a fox. There's a tumult of shouts. His teammates jubilantly start to carry him off the field. He spots me in a crowd along the first-base side.

We're together, walking back to the hotel.

"Some game," he beams.

"I saw you!"

"Did you see that slide?"

"Yeah—it was great!"

We walk ahead leisurely, saying nothing else. My only regret is that Bill Terry of the New York Giants couldn't be here to see him score the winning run.

And there was something about the late afternoons that had a special flavor of its own.

At four o'clock the hotel held show rehearsals in the casino. Naturally, my parents were deeply involved on a regular basis, which in turn allowed me to hang around as long as I wanted, providing that I didn't disturb anyone or anything. With that rule clearly understood and obeyed, I would plop down in a quiet corner and almost immediately find myself enveloped in some kind of curious rapture, watching the scheduled mountain acts as they unlimbered, vocalized, blocked sketch material, timed intricate dance routines, cued for comedy blackout music—watched them breathlessly as they sailed into the final run-throughs while I sat there in muddy sneakers and damp bathing trunks, wishing all the while that one day soon I would be performing on a stage just like them.

That summer a majority of singers included, as part of their act, the Depression's most poignant song: "Brother, Can You Spare a Dime?" My father was no exception. Under a stark spotlight, with one hand extended pleadingly, his jacket collar turned up to convey a woebegone feeling of hunger and misery, and his voice wavering at the proper moments, he was able to milk the lyrics dry and at the same time melt even the coldest of hearts.

And at one of those performances, the idea finally struck me.

After many entreaties on my part and a great deal of patience on hers, Mom arranged it. Together, we spent hour upon hour rehearsing. She played "Brother, Can You Spare a Dime?" over and over, and I stood at her side practicing, singing and projecting for all I was worth.

Then, on a weekend night in late August, when the hotel ran a benefit for the Firemen's Association, I appeared as the "surprise" talent. I came out carrying a couple of rolled newspapers under my arm. I wore patched knickers, suspenders, floppy shoes and my baseball cap, which she had twisted sideways over the ears.

My father whispered from the wings, "Joey, be careful . . . don't step into the footlights."

Mom hit a note, and I started to sing.

I remember her taking me back to my room, putting me in bed, then giving me a glass of milk.

She said, "You didn't forget. Not a word or a syllable."

"Did I do good?"

She nodded. "Good, good; keep going."

[7]

As the summer ended, inevitably there came again that time for separation. Always the same. We'd return from the mountains, and all I knew was that my parents would soon have to leave; on any day, at any given moment. When the phone rang I'd hold my breath, hoping it wouldn't be Dad's agent calling him away on another road trip. What I felt then, as much as anything, was the difference between me and the other kids, the need to know what a mother and a father surrounded by children were all about. So during those times of impending loss, I'd force my presence in somebody's house. Even on school-day mornings, I'd ring the bell and wake up one of my playmates—maybe Joey Schoenberg or Brian Weismann— just wanting to have breakfast with him. Not for the food, but only because I could be around a family.

One afternoon I walked home with Brian, to find my parents packing their bags. I looked on helplessly, trying not to show the forlorn realization of it, yet wondering what my friend was thinking, whether he understood or really knew how I felt. Standing like a statue on our front steps, I listened to Mom saying, "The road is no place for a child. Grandma Sarah is here. She'll take care of you until we get back. And besides, you have to stay in school. . . ."

I could scarcely lift my eyes.

"All right. The car is waiting. So give your father and me a great big kiss."

When they left, Brian said, "You wanta go to your grandma's house?"

"Yeah"—watching them leave, my heart breaking, but after a long moment—"c'mon, Brian, I'll race you!"

And I ran around the corner, where Grandma was waiting to make things a whole lot better.

Grandma's house—I can remember every piece of furniture in it. You go up five brick steps to a screened porch. I used to sit out there at night and light punks. The door to the house itself wouldn't swing totally open because the piano stood on the other side, an upright Steinway, gleaming black, with a framed and autographed picture of cowboy-movie-star Dick Foran resting on top. To the right was a brick fireplace, also Grandma's beautiful mahogany dining room table; behind it her china cabinet, where she kept all the fine dishes and silverware. In the living room a soft chair, the couch cater-cornered, a Victrola which played brown Brunswick records that were like cardboard, her Singer sewing machine . . . One night I stretched out on the floor and drew close while she stooped over the machine, bobbin wheel spinning, pedal moving up and down, and yards of thread passing backward and forward through the cloth. I was half-asleep, launching fantasies of bold escapes and magnificent conquests, all of them brought about in order to save Grandma from a fate worse than death . . . then roused myself to get her attention.

"Grandma . . ."

"Vos vilst dir, Sonny?"

"Grandma, are you proud of me?"

A pause. The color of her face and eyes deepened. And before the machine started again, she said, *"Mein kind,* I am proud of when you breathe."

Crossing the living room, you'd go through a swinging door that opened into the kitchen, a big kitchen, in the middle of which stood a tiled, metallic table with a small chip on the edge. If you gave it a little *schscrib* it was like chalking a blackboard. I'd sit here before the big important Sunday meals, with the smell of bread rising in the oven; then, fascinated, watch her at the breadboard, where for some inexplicable reason she would always cut the bread against her chest.

On warm evenings, supper done and the dishes put away, we'd sit on the porch, sunk down in wicker chairs, listening to a whole range of programs on her Majestic radio. It was all wood and cathedral-shaped, and the bright orange dial had to be coaxed along with a pencil because the tuning knob had broken off.

We heard Jack Pearl: "Wass you dere, Sharlie?"

And Joe Penner: "Wanna buy a duck?"

And "The Court of Human Relations": "Try to control yourself, madame. . . ."

And Major Bowes: "Around and around she goes . . ."

And where she stops nobody knows. We just kept listening.

Then came the sudden thrill, that giddy sense of floating on pure air . . . hearing Raymond Paige and his orchestra playing the "Blue Moon" theme under a hubbub of gaiety and the sudden interjection of female switchboard operator Duane Thompson plugging us into "Hollywood Hotel." An imaginative place built for enormous enchantments, all filled with adventure, mystery, hilarious comedy . . . savoring it, now remembering that time when I blurted out, "Grandma, you know what? I'm going to Hollywood to be a big movie star."

Whereupon she vigorously shook my hand and said, "Have a good trip."

The memory of making her laugh, of seeing the tears course down her cheeks from laughing so hard when I'd get off a mouthful of Yiddish phrases, like, "Grandma, *ich vill* listen to Gabriel Heatter from before the Eddie Cantor show *eppes ist komen arrein* in an hour, *du herst?*"

Then a memory of myself, wholly unseen, weeping silently behind her couch. She was saying, "Don't worry, Sonny. Mama and Papa soon will come home. It's all right. Be happy. . . ."

This in spite of her own personal problems. Later, I was to learn why. But at the age of five or six, I could observe only that all the bad moments happened when her second husband, Sam Rothberg, was present.

Her first husband, Joseph Brodsky, made her a widow four years before my birth. Therefore, other than a couple of fragmentary stories gleaned from recent family reunions, I know very little about him. What filters through, however, indicates that my maternal grandfather led a hard but honest life.

Like the Levitch clan, Joseph and Sarah Brodsky came from Russia. He was a tailor. He did piecework out of his apartment and in various tailor shops around Newark. Grandma also contributed, taking in dressmaking jobs through recommendation.

Grandpa Brodsky loved music. My mother said that in Russia his big hope was to be a concert pianist, but his parents couldn't afford the lessons, let alone the piano. That is why he bought the upright Steinway, sometime during my mother's early teens. When she got pretty good at it, he felt his life had been fulfilled. In any event, Grandpa

Brodsky continued to work, scrimp and provide until the day he died.

Then along came Sam Rothberg, a complete opposite in nature and temperament. We called him Uncle. He was in the fur business, skins, in New York, and he brought a daughter and three sons with him when he married my grandmother. A tall, burly man, mustached, narrow-eyed, strong with the verbiage; up from the cellar he would come with homemade booze—brewed it there himself—and then put away two–three water glasses of the stuff at dinner, just enough to go to sleep . . . every night.

"Kom essen!"

His command for all to sit and eat, no nonsense, no grabbing at second helpings without his permission, his eyes scanning us, and the booze right there next to his plate.

Sometimes, when he got testy or loud, Grandma would turn to me with a protective look, as if to say, "I can handle it." But other times, while playing outside, I'd hear him yelling at her—"Nah, nah! Never! You drop *dead* first!"—and I'd run back to the house to see if she was OK.

We were at the dinner table. The whole family; uncles, aunts, cousins, all having a nice conversation. Then it happened, out of nowhere. He smacked my grandmother. He didn't even bat an eyelash. And I saw that he was going to hit her again—"What! You tell *me* I shouldn't drink!"

My Uncle Bernie went after him, hit him a shot; and I jumped from the chair, screeching, "I'll kill you!"—Like a gnat on his back, my arms hooked around his neck, full weight hanging. I squeezed and squeezed, and if they hadn't pulled me off, I would have stayed on him until he stopped breathing.

I had nightmares from that horrifying experience. I dreamed of cutting his throat with Grandma's bread knife

. . . of doubling up a spool of thread, stringing it tight against his throat . . . dreamed of Uncle lying in a coffin with me standing over him, smiling. . . . "Grandma! Grandma!"—I'd go to her room in the middle of the night, whimpering, sweating through my pajamas.

"I know, Sonny, I know. . . ."

Grandma. She was five foot three, squat and stocky, iron-haired; had a beautiful mole on her cheek, wore orthopedic shoes, never went into the kitchen unless she had her apron on. A strong lady wearing flowered dresses. God knows, I trusted her with my life, under any circumstances. And out beyond all measured time that blows fiercer than ever over the fragile remnants of childhood memory, I can still hear her words, actually singing in my ear. . . . "Don't ever change."

[8]

Springtime in Irvington, the first blossoms on trees up and down Rutgers Street—that first cut of my initials into the bark of the scraggly pear tree in Grandma's backyard— marble shooting; stickball; sitting on stoops with Mickey Myron, Seymour Frankel, Siggy Siegel, Bobby Berzon, Stanley Biolas, Joe Chiat, Herbie Diamond, jeering, arguing, silly talk: *"Frankenstein will getchya yah yah yah. . . . Betchya there's people up there on the moon. . . . You're crazy you know that Stanley. . . . So's your ol' man. . . . Who's the best fighter in the whole world I'll tellya Barney Ross. . . . What about Max Baer huh. . . . Didja see Siggy's new shoes boy are they dumb. . . . Yours ain't so hot either Bobby ha ha ha. . . . Let's do somethin' what what what. . . .* Playing tag, Johnny on the pony, ring-a-lievo; and rolling madly in the grass and racing our soapbox carts down Hospital Hill—I'm ten years old and I know I'm going to Indianapolis one day and be a champion—the wheels fly off, my ass is dragging, the wood's splintering, tearing my pants—and there's Grandma, rooting me on!

As in a slow dissolve under that lasting impression there comes an autumn scene of raw weather, the rumble of thunder and leaves falling, smoke smells in the woods, crows flapping across slate-gray skies with kids sounding off on Union Avenue in the school yard at play, vapors rising from their mouths; when suddenly everyone turns to look straight up at a huge airship that momentarily covers the sky, forcing us to draw in our breath and gasp as it slowly glides away. . . . Then the rattle of bottles slam-banging from inside an Ideal Farms milk truck, Leon Charash's father driving along past the school making gestures at Leon who calls after him, "Hey, Pop, did you see that zeppelin! It's the Hindenburg!" And the father shouts back a derisive reply, "You mean a Nazi cloud, Leon! A black Nazi cloud!"

That hazy understanding of what he means, but it's all secondary, lost at the time in restless, unending pursuits of a new day waiting—roller-skate hockey, touch football, snow, my Flexible Flyer sled . . . and the gang seeing me take a run and belly flop on the sidewalk cement. The sled stops, naturally. The friction, such burning of blades! Zoom—I go flying like Marvel the Magnificent out of a cannon, hit the ground some ten feet away, painlessly, bounding up with an exhilarated grin as they howl and slap their thighs—"Do it again, Levitch! One more time!"

The same autumn, 1936, I spent part of my days at the ABC Synagogue—Avrom Buchom Cheldem. It was a combination temple, community center and Hebrew school located in a commercial brick building on Chancellor Av-

enue. I remember great crowds gathering on the High
Holidays, the soft glow of lights spreading a feeling of
warmth; Grandma Sarah and I sitting together in a section
reserved for women and children, men on the right; Rabbi
Friedman standing at the pulpit bending over the Torah,
his voice rising and falling through lips that hardly seemed
to move; the congregation joining in, old people shouldering long, faded ritual fringes, their bodies mechanically
rocking back and forth, their incantations filling every ear
—*Adenoi elohenu adenoi echod*—prayers without change;
but I had no way of knowing what it was all about.

Then came my first Hebrew lesson. A whole bunch of
kids in a drab room on the second floor, winking, giggling,
our minds wandering; and Rabbi Friedman teaching us to
read from the haftorah, pointing to the strange Hebrew
words while glancing around and emitting little coughs and
reprimands . . . There he was at my desk in his blue suit
with small, distinguished beard, speaking firmly in a precise
manner, even as he frowned and asked, "Now, Joseph, do
you understand?"

No, not in the least. I didn't know an *aleph* from a
beth. . . .

Night. I'm reading for Grandma in her kitchen, hesitat-
ing over the letters, faltering, "*Yodh* . . . *kaph*—er—" I
stammer, blush and can't go on.

"*Lamedh*—" she gently coaxes.

"*Lamedh* . . . *mem* . . . *nun—er—*"

She smiles and waits, and then I see her brush a fork
off the table.

"Oy," she says. "Forgive me, Sonny. The noise broke
your concentration."

The picture of her hand outstretched and resting lightly
on mine, now patting it . . . My tenderhearted grandma,
the most understanding soul you'll ever find in this vast and
foolish world.

[9]

The Union Avenue School, on a winter day in 1937. The kind of day that evoked a restless longing to be elsewhere, anywhere at all, but not among some thoughtless grown-ups who couldn't see into the heart of an eleven-year-old boy.

It's December, right before the holiday recess. A bright beautiful morning, snow on the ground, and I'm here in the music-appreciation class with my nose stuck in a book. The teacher raps her knuckles against the blackboard. "Attention, children. We will now use our mimeographed sheets to sing a few Christmas carols."

Not on my life. I can't. The words are already formed, flying out of my mouth so fast there's no time to stop— "Mrs. Harcourt, if you sing Hanukkah songs, I'll sing Christmas carols."

She gives me a scathing look, points her finger directly at me. "Either you do as you're told like everyone else, or you will leave the room immediately and report to the principal."

Why? What law did I break? To me, the law is Mom and Dad. Every year about this time they've said, "No Christmas tree in the house." Instead, they placed an eight-branched candelabrum on our living room windowsill to show off the miracle of Hanukkah, and for eight successive nights we lit the candles in dedication of Jewish salvation from oppression.

So I report to the principal. Her name is Sarah Betz, a steel-faced woman with coarse hair and a storm-trooper voice. She leans toward me, the edge of a ruler pressed into her cheek. "We do not tolerate uncivilized behavior in this school. Not for a single instant—do you hear me?"

"Yeah, well, I can't—"

She explodes. "But you will! I want you to apologize to Mrs. Harcourt! And don't put your tongue over your lips! Monkeys do that, not normal children."

I walk back to class feeling grotesque, pathetically ugly. But I won't apologize to Mrs. Harcourt. And most of all, I'm glad I behaved abnormally in front of Mrs. Betz. Otherwise, I would've cried.

Christmas Day. At the crack of dawn, riding out of Irvington with Mom and Dad. We're in the backseat of a Plymouth sedan, going to Detroit, where he'll perform in burlesque for a week. Another act is driving us. We speed along on an enormous highway in the glare of sunlight, then onward into a swirl of darkness past miles and miles of snow-covered towns. I listen to the small talk, the old cornball jokes, the old razzmatazz songs and patter of burlesque comedy. And against a blowing wind, unaware of time and movement, I snuggle between my parents for warmth. It's the only place I want to be.

And then Detroit, of which I can remember a cold, gray skyline, clouds of smoke puffing far across the river, boats moving slowly under morning fog; seeing this, drifting in and out of sleep, waking up, peering through the car window at a big van parked on a downtown street and at weatherbeaten trunks piled in an alley of the deserted National Theatre. "It ain't the Palace," says my father, "but who gives a hoot? We'll make things happen here—right, son?"

We look at each other. His arm reaches around me. Our faces touch and our lives suddenly come together; so great and terrific, so complete, so full of love that I feel it has always been this way.

That's how I feel as we walk into the lobby of the Barlum Hotel. My chest swells with pride when Dad signs the register. He's impeccably dressed. His charcoal-striped suit is still unwrinkled after the long, wearying trip. He looks swell, absolutely sensational. He looks like Jolson, Harry Richman and Ted Lewis all rolled up in one. But I can see the tiredness on his face, and on my mother's face, too.

"You go to bed," she says. "You have to get some sleep before Dad opens tonight."

We go to our room. Within twenty minutes my folks are under the covers, dead to the world. Meanwhile, I'm lying on a cot next to them, swimming in creation and imagination. I can't sleep. Not a wink.

No. There's nothing more to do but get dressed again, tiptoe to the door, close it gently behind me and walk down the hall.

Exploring. Absorbing everything. Observing the people coming and going in the lobby and getting off the elevator. It's fascinating. I ride up and down so many times the elevator operator finally drawls, "Look heah, y'all want to learn how this works?"

"Uh-huh. Can I try?"

It's one of those old-fashioned elevators, with a brass pointer above the sliding cage and a brass swing handle that whisks us to and from each floor. I work that handle just right, then stoop down, lie flat on the linoleum and see if we're exactly even with the landing. After a while my good friend settles on his little wooden stool, grinning at me as though I've performed a feat equal in importance to steering the *Queen Mary* through an Atlantic storm. How I love standing there in total control of the elevator, hour after hour into the late afternoon.

At night I listen to the sounds of burlesque. Low, sexy music. The vendors barking, "Only a quarter here—get your pictures. . . ." The whole theatre steams as the band hammers out a fanfare, followed by drumrolls and rim shots. The front-row hecklers whoop and holler like Indians, stamp their feet, send Bronx cheers and catcalls from the rear, everybody in the audience whistling and screaming and the chorus line sashaying around on the stage apron while Dad sings, "A Pretty Girl Is Like a Melody."

After that he does a sketch with the other baggy-pants comics, playing the part of a German dunce. He works comedy or straight, depending on the sketch, but either way he's tremendous. Then the middle production number. He comes onstage with a whip, wearing a loose-fitting circus-ringmaster outfit and a pair of boots three sizes too small. He's trying to walk from pain. He can't take three steps without appearing as if he's going to tilt straight back and fall on his ass. Now the girls slink out in animal skins, purring, teasing, arching their bodies and showing lots of flesh. The place is roaring, and Dad's cracking his whip, coaxing, "Up, up, get up, Mona! Thatta girl, Sally! On the pedestal! Easy, Jackie, easy. . . . Oh, yeah! Oh, wow! I can't take it anymore—"

Someone down front cackles, "I'll take it, I'll take it!"

Burlesque. It's all fire and light. And I'm gripped by a new excitement, a contagion of emotions so penetrating I can't express what I feel to anyone.

It happens as I watch one of the classic strip routines, in which the girl walks onstage dressed in a high-necked Victorian costume with the white silk gloves and pink parasol, smiling demurely at the audience from every conceivable angle before removing the gloves; then spinning, unloosening the top buttons of her blouse, twisting around, reaching for the hem of her skirt, turning sideways and— bam!—catching me gaping at her from the wings.

The effect, I somehow knew, was not entirely lost.

My father sat in front of the makeup table in his dressing room, staring at my mirrored reflection while he wiped the greasepaint off his face. When the last traces behind his ears were gone, he said, "You look flushed. What's the matter, you coming down with a cold or something?"

"Naw, I'm just excited and everything."

"OK. That's swell." Then a burst of enthusiasm. "Listen,

there's a delicatessen we can go to. They have the best pastrami in town. Terrific food, it'll clear your nostrils."

We walked toward an exit door leading to the lobby, where Mom was waiting. Whenever Dad worked burlesque, she would see the show from a house seat and then go to the lobby after each performance, thereby avoiding the raunchy backstage jokes and hard-luck stories that usually kept everyone hanging around until there was a good reason to leave. My father always left early when Mom traveled the circuit with him. She was a born diplomat. By meeting him in the lobby, it meant he could make his excuses without having to create a big fuss about it.

Anyway, before we got to the exit, I noticed the stripper easing a path through a ring of admirers, waving and throwing kisses as though she had just won the Academy Award for the best performance of the year. And suddenly, "Hi, Danny. That your kid?"

"That's him. Say hello to Marlene, son."

"H-h-h-hello."

"Don't be shy, sweetie. I won't bite you. My goodness, ain't he the cutest thing?"

She left me floating ten feet in the air.

So it happened that a night or two later she led me to her dressing room. We were alone. Whatever we did, I remember it took only a minute. After that she talked to me about her little boy. She hadn't seen him for a long time. She said he was staying with his father. Then she showed me his picture. When I left, her lips were trembling and her eyes looked awfully red.

At the Barlum Hotel, lying awake in my room long past midnight, shifting the pillow from one position to another, I wondered if she really liked me and knew it made no sense to have such thoughts. . . .

Burlesque people. So many of them were unspoiled and uninhibited. They acted spontaneously, saying what they had to say openly and honestly. I could relate to that and also derive a great deal of satisfaction in speaking their language, flavored with all sorts of tangy words and phrases. During the backstage breaks I would lean in and listen while they lighted cigarettes and chewed gum and gabbed about life on the road; about the Wheel season and the two-a-day grinds, and why Fiorello axed the burlies in New York, and why that walking towel bombed in Pittsburgh, and why a certain Fally Markus cheated this dumb act in Omaha—"Farkus-Shmarkus, it's better than laying off!" says a third-banana comic, laughing nervously, his creased and heavily pancaked face revealing misery and pleasure at the same time. A clown's face—the eternal symbol of show business.

What a world! Everybody backstage was willing to teach me what I wanted to know. The electrician, the sound man, the man on the board who worked the gelatins—they had an answer for everything, every time I asked them *Why?*

So I learned. Nothing escaped my attention. The smallest detail snapped into sharp focus, and the whole burlesque scene became a private vision in which I could see things that were unknown and unfelt before. Now I knew the location of lighting apparatus, the method of scene shifting, the function of flats and drops and battens, every piece of equipment in the theatre. And I could tell why the comedy bits and production numbers had worked perfectly, and why they were screwed up. I knew it immediately. But I never said anything to the performers. Only to Dad, who would turn to my mother and say something like, "Out of the mouths of babes . . ."

I thought I knew it all.

New Year's Day. A snowy morning, cold and blustery wind buffeting the train station in Windsor, Ontario, across the river from Detroit. A picture of Dad standing on the platform as Mom and I head out to Niagara Falls on a sightseeing trip before going home. And thoughts of him getting smaller and smaller as the train lurches forward and then scrapes along the tracks in a series of stops and starts, hissing steam with its whistle blasting, and rumbling and shaking and now clattering down the line towards the Falls about 220 miles away . . . White-faced, white-covered father of mine—now gone in the snow.

[10]

Back to school.

I was still coming down from my great adventures around show people, so everything connected with school or some late-afternoon fun in the streets seemed to be frivolous, even boring at times. The same old teachers and books, same rules and regulations and spitballs sailing past my ear, the same kids laughing, and I knew who they were but didn't care. I would look dreamily out the classroom window, thinking of my parents playing at theatres in towns I had never heard of.

During the long, dreary winter and spring months, an occasional phone call or penny postcard would arrive, letting me know they'd been traveling on dusty trains, checking into two-dollar hotels, eating in greasy diners—*Closing Sunday, opening Monday*—*Take care, be good, love to everyone*—and me getting the news while staying with Grandma Sarah or different relatives back in New York and New Jersey.

As a consequence I was absent from school for approximately three months. Now it was June, final day in the fifth-grade home-room class, and our teacher going up and down the aisles handing out report cards. I heard all those happy sounds, thirty or more students buzzing excitedly about being promoted and yelling the names of teachers they would have in the fall. I sat there, looking on hopelessly.

"Stay in line, children. . . ."

They filed out of the room, marching down the hall to the sixth grade. Some went by peering at me with quizzical, broken smiles, as if to say, "What happened to you? You left back, Joey?"

Yes. And I thought I was a dummy, a misfit, the sorriest kid alive. I never felt more alone than just then.

Leon Charash with thin, smooth face, hair dark, straight, a cowlick over his brow, eyes wide and serious, sits next to me on the front steps of his house on Webster Street. It is late afternoon, the sky bursting with sunshine, and from all around the noise of skate wheels and whistles and youthful cries resounding in the heat; Leon nods his head and says in that well-bred manner of his, "My father is getting a new milk truck next week."

"Why?"

"Well—his boss ordered it."

"Do all Ideal milkmen get them?"

"No. Only those who have special routes."

"Oh."

"Anyway, they're going to make him a manager, so I guess he won't be driving a truck very long—he told me last night."

"Yeah, well, my father's gonna play the Palace, and that's no lie."

"Who said it was?" He leans on the step, fidgeting with a bicycle clip. "Do you know what I'm going to be when I grow up?"

"What?"

"A doctor. What do you think of that?"

"It's OK. But I'd rather be in show business and make people laugh."

"Ha ha," testily, as he gets up saying, "I'm going to ride my bike. Too bad you don't have one, so we could ride together."

He pushes off and goes wheeling down the block without looking back.

I walk home, cutting through alleys shadowed by wood-framed houses, and stumble onto concrete pavement, sidewalks shimmering with heat, the sun reflecting off chromium grilles, all the cars glinting and shining fiercely in my eyes. Finally turning into Union Avenue, I see my mother coming along, carrying two armloads of groceries.

"Take a package," she says.

We go upstairs, and while putting things away in the refrigerator, she mentions almost casually, "Mr. Geker is looking to hire a boy in his grocery store."

"So?"

"So maybe you could work there. Mornings . . . sweeping the floor and delivery . . ."

"Aw, I don't wanta—"

"You're capable. You'll make some spending money."

I go off to think about it, in my room, lying on the bed gloomily scanning and appraising everything. Grimy linoleum. Faded wallpaper. A thousand shapes forming on the ceiling. The red light of afternoon . . . I look around with a wondering weariness, my thoughts drifting and slowly stealing away—boyhood with all its moods and contradictions.

Geker's was a typical old-fashioned neighborhood grocery store. You could fish a pickle out of a barrel for a penny, and scoop coffee beans from burlap sacks and have Geker run them through his fancy red grinder, the smell unbelievable! On his counter there were huge wedges of cheese with little samples (not to be touched by children), and wicker baskets filled with farm-fresh eggs and all sorts of rolls still warm from the morning delivery. And pistachio nuts, Indian nuts, Brazil nuts, cashews and sunflower seeds, stored in metal bins inside the window . . . That heavy brass Toledo scale that weighed everything from potatoes to tomatoes—but you always had to watch Geker's fingers.

"You got a bike?" he asked.

"No."

"Well, there's a lot of deliveries"—scratching his head—"can you handle a baby buggy?"

The next morning I was pushing it around, the front wheels wobbling, the back wheels squeaking like mad, and me going doggedly from one customer's door to the next, nodding and blushing whenever I saw my friends in the street, everyone looking on with incredulous grins: "Heyyy, Joey! When didja become a mother?"

I made three dollars a week, delivering Geker's groceries and sweeping out his store; and after learning the ropes I began to entertain his customers. Boy, did I cut up. Maybe to get even with life, or just for the fun of it, or whatever; but the fact is I did some real screwy things.

One afternoon a woman walked in and ordered six onion rolls. Geker pulled them out of the bread basket. She never checked. Fifteen minutes after she left, the phone rang.

I heard Geker say: "Yes . . . what? I don't understand. . . . That's impossible. . . . ! Listen, lady, I don't make it a habit to bite into my rolls before selling them to customers. . . . Yeah, well, if there are teeth marks in them, they ain't mine!"

I confessed, and Geker fired me.

Then I worked for a couple of weeks in Gersten's drugstore; then at the Roxy soda fountain where I didn't exactly overwhelm the boss—Irv Hubshmitt—who caught me serving a banana split with the peel still on it. That job lasted an hour.

And there was one other place. Hymie Fishbein's vegetable store. Fat Hymie with his sweaty neck and frazzled nerves. He kept me on the run for nine weeks, carrying heavy packages up Hospital Hill; a long, miserable climb, mosquitoes swarming out of the weeds, following me everywhere. And always the same mangy black dog nipping at my heels.

Meanwhile, in the back of my mind there raged this great determination to hang on to every dime I had earned in order to buy a bike at Wallach's Service Station. It was in the window. It cost twenty-seven dollars, a blue bike with a bell and a horn on the handlebars.

So that summer I worked seven weeks to buy it. Then each morning, no matter where Fat Hymie's packages had to be delivered, first I would ride by Grandma Sarah's house, blow the horn, ring the bell and wait till she came out, waving from her porch, looking so awfully pleased to see me on my bike.

Now I was set to join the gang of kids who already owned bikes. And how we rode them! We'd go anywhere from Chancellor Avenue down past Camptown Park and up through Newark's busiest thoroughfares, racing hard, sun and wind in our faces, sticking close and sharing the gladness, the sheer exuberance of imagining ourselves as true road and sky heroes like Barney Oldfield and Eddie Rickenbacker, because it was all so easy, somehow all so real. And what better thing than finally to come to a stop, quietly assemble at the very lip of the Hudson River and gaze across at Manhattan Island—sprawling, tall and terrific.

One night Herbie Diamond and I pedaled way out to Newark Airport just to see the Los Angeles flight come in. It was one of those new high-performance commercial DC-3 airplanes; silver-winged, blinking its lights and now roaring overhead, almost touching the airport tower.

"Let's get there—hurry!" yelled Herbie through the tumult.

"Wow! A monster!" I hollered back, pumping steadily toward the American Airlines terminal.

A little later, the two of us joined a big crowd behind roped lines at the arrival gate, to stand there gawking while spotlights swept over the plane. They rolled out a red carpet, flashbulbs started to pop and in the excitement I felt my heart jump as Claudette Colbert and Fred MacMurray stepped down the ramp, smiling as if they knew the whole world was looking at them. I had gooseflesh three-quarters of an inch thick.

In the autumn of 1938, I produced, directed and played in a show that the Union Avenue School held at the Rex Theatre, Irvington's biggest and most popular movie house.

It was for the Red Cross . . . a matinee amateur performance between the double feature, forty or fifty kids in the cast: Lillian Messinger as Baby Snooks; Joyce Santoro, Dorothy Arbeitman and Lillian Barber singing "The Three Little Fishes"; Leon Charash playing straight man to me in a laundered burlesque sketch; etc. And that kidding moment backstage when I told Lillian Messinger that if she didn't let me have a quick feel, she was out of the show. Scorn and indignation, then a flash of her beautiful smile before walking away . . .

Comes dusk, near the woods right across from school, little Leon runs up with a nasty look and grabs me by the collar—"What did you say to Lillian Messinger?"

Instead of answering, I land a punch that draws a trickle of blood from his nose.

"Ow—you broke it—"

I give him a handkerchief. "Tilt your head back. It's nothin'. Anyway, you shouldna grabbed my new shirt."

"Ow—when will it stop bleeding?"

I take a look. "It's stopped already."

I'm getting pleasure in all this, just like some kind of big nose specialist, and by now Leon seems as though he's ready to be friends with me for life.

Funny the way things turned out. In 1950, Leon Charash got his MD at Cornell University Medical College, went on to serve as captain in the U.S. Air Force, then established himself as a leading practitioner in the field of pediatric neurology. And today he is chairman of the medical advisory board for the Muscular Dystrophy Association.

I was twelve. I couldn't make any headway with girls. I was the oddball, the seventeenth kid in line at the party, putting the lights out for spin-the-bottle or sticking a lampshade on my head for laughs. The court jester. Never had a date. That is, until June Feldman finally said yes.

Oy! June Feldman . . . she had 400,000 curls. She used to get up at quarter to two in the morning to make school at eight, just to comb her curls. If they had cut her hair, there would've been enough to weave a throw rug for all of Indonesia—and she still wouldn't have been bald. I was crazy about her.

So one afternoon I got up my courage and asked for a date, sitting there on my bike in front of Hymie Fishbein's store with June going past, flipping her curls and saying, "All right, we can go to New York and see Tommy Dorsey at the Paramount."

"Sure," I said. "And we can hold hands."

"Boy, aren't you a hot one? Phooey. I don't know about that. Let's just go see Tommy Dorsey."

Another blow to the heart.

The next day I walk into her house all combed and handsome, wearing a thick button-down sweater, a sleeveless underneath, white shoes, clip-on bow tie and corduroy pants. Remember those days when Mama sewed in the press? Well, I've got such bulbs on each side of the press the only way my pants will stay neat is by wearing bicycle clips—if you know what I'm talking about. In other words, I looked like a Western Union putty-putz.

Meanwhile, June is dressed to the teeth but already crestfallen, frowning as she sees the bicycle clips. "I thought we were going to the Paramount."

"Yeah—" I bend down to remove the clips. You'd think I had joined an Indian tribe from my red face.

Two hours later we're upstairs in the balcony of the theatre, the Tommy Dorsey orchestra onstage, and vocalist Jack Leonard singing "Marie" with liquid intensity, while Dorsey pushes notes from his trombone in soft, long phrases, a gorgeous sound. I'm looking at June, yearning for her, but sitting miserably rigid, afraid to make a move. My groin is killing me. I can hardly keep from letting out howls of pain because during the Gary Cooper film preceding the stage show I tried to kiss her, and she said, "You have to wait."

I waited a minute, then tried again.

"Not now, Joey."

"Aw, stop foolin'—when?"

"Maybe when we're older."

"Older? What's that got to do with lips? Lips don't have a calendar. What are you saving it for—the worms?"

So there I am, suffering.

And that was it. My first case of blue balls. I couldn't understand how I took off height when we got outside. I walked in a crouch going down Broadway toward the subway two steps ahead of her, the whole sad date ending and the pain still smoldering in my bones.

Hello, June Feldman, wherever you are.

[11]

Winter of that same year my father worked at a small resort hotel in Lakewood, New Jersey. It was called the Arthur, and was owned by Charles and Lillian Brown.

Dad had spent the previous winter there doubling as master of ceremonies and entertainer. Now, sometime in early December, he called home telling Mom she should round up a drummer and saxophone player and get ready to start playing at the Arthur for the next three months. Also, he said I could come along and attend school in Lakewood until February. . . . "Wouldn't that be nice?"

Was it ever. Even at this very moment my recollection of that time spent at the Browns' hotel is sharp and given over to dreamlike scenes. . . . A little ballroom, little gold chairs, the musicians sitting placidly in one corner and the guests clustered around while Dad sings and Mom plays the piano . . . Outside, a winter wonderland; the night filled with stars, sleigh bells, laughter from near and far . . . Mornings down at the pond, all the kids skating, their faces rosy, bursting with smiles . . . It's all fun; everything is icy bright, yet warm and inviting. . . . All these things and more—

Charles Brown, an athletic-looking man, dark and handsome, gregarious, charm pouring out of him; he'd always have some joke or funny story to tell at the drop of a hat but could just as easily get very sentimental if he saw me brooding. In a second he would somehow know; his arm would go around my shoulder, and that was all I needed to feel good again.

And his wife Lillian—precise manners, almost regal, a stunning woman with strawberry-blond hair. She loved the hotel that bound her and Charlie together. They were partners, oftentimes hardfisted business people who worked long hours without complaint, treating everyone right. A rare combination they were—they treated me as one of their own. And from the first day on I never called them anything other than Uncle Charlie and Aunt Lil.

As for their daughter Lonnie—though only fourteen years old, she was mature, perceptive; someone you could easily relate to, knowing she'd keep your deepest secrets and listen to your problems, big or small, without losing sight of them. She soon became a real sister—so to speak—as well as my closest friend.

One morning we clomped the whole distance over snow-banks to Gottlieb's drugstore in downtown Lakewood. Lots of people, hordes of them tracking in and out as we sat waiting at the counter, watching Mr. Gottlieb pump the syrup and plop big scoops of ice cream into our frothy glasses, then swirl the whipped cream to a peak before topping it off with a juicy red cherry—

"OK, kids," he said, "this oughtta hold you." A wink. "Don't tell nobody, but we've got the best sodas anywhere in New Jersey."

"Sure looks that way," I said. Turning to Lonnie, "Did you know I was a soda jerk once?"

"No—where?"

"At the Roxy drugstore in Irvington. I guess I wasn't too hot. I used to flip the ice cream up in the air and try to catch it in the cone. Sometimes I missed—hah!"

"Oh, no!"

"Yeah . . . I didn't like the job anyway."

"Well—"

We sipped our sodas, momentarily quiet, just glancing at each other. I felt awkward, as though there was nothing else to do except finish my drink and go back to the hotel with her.

"You're a funny one," she said with sudden gravity.

I asked her what she meant.

"The way your moods change. I think you *know* what I mean."

I nodded and swallowed. "It's really nothin'. I get a little worried sometimes. Even here. I mean, it's great—but that's the trouble. When I'm having a good time, I always feel some stupid thing will happen to make it bad."

"Like what?"

"Well, like I remember things that happened, that's all."

"No, it's not all. Otherwise you wouldn't have mentioned it."

"Ah"—shrugging and growing silent, then turning slowly on my stool. Thinking. Remembering the nights of restless sleep, of coming awake in the darkness, waiting through a long stillness for the voices of my mother and father to filter into my room. Listening and hearing nothing, only the stillness as it kept spreading, covering everything, filling me with dread.

Lonnie looked at me. "Are you all right?"

I wanted to say, no, I feel terrible. But I grinned and said, "Yes."

Moments later we were outside, walking back to the hotel, our hands stuck miserably in pockets. Then I heard her say quietly, "What's wrong, Jerry?"

"Well, if you really want to know"—suddenly leaning over to scoop up a handful of snow—"it's just this. I'm by myself a lot." And after savagely flinging it away, I blurted, "That's how it is. Because my parents aren't home much. They keep moving me around from one place to another. A week here, a month there—sometimes with my Aunt Betty, or my Aunt Jean, my grandma in Brooklyn—I get tired of it. I get lonely."

"Jerry. Listen to me. I'm sure your parents don't mean to—"

"Sure, sure. They tell me the same thing. They don't mean to do it. They have to . . . there's no other way. But

even if it's true, every time we're together they don't talk to
me enough. I think—it's like this. You see your parents;
you talk to them and you feel they understand you, but they
don't. So all you see is a wall. A *big* wall. And that's what
I've been thinking about."

I waited nervously for her to reply, but she stared ahead.
Then: "You know what I once did?"

Again no response.

"OK. I'll tell you. When I was a little kid—about five
years old—when they were away somewhere, I got so mad
I threw my cat down the stairs. Killed it. You can get bad
dreams from that, you know."

Startled, she dropped a few paces behind me for a while,
saying nothing. Then I heard her call, "Wait up!" And
alongside—"Oh, Jerry—I wish I could help."

We walked on in the snow, which sparkled beneath wide
gaps of blue sky, reminding me of past winter mornings
when I lay snuggled in bed at Grandma Sarah's house, the
wind whistling through the trees and hedges outside, and her
kitchen filled with the aroma of hot rolls, eggs, steaming
coffee, a special delight of one sort or another already
baking in the oven. . . .

And now, as Lonnie and I approached the hotel, I
stopped for a moment, grasped her arms and looked
straight into her eyes, saying, "Listen, you helped a lot. So
don't worry. There's nothing more to worry about, honest."

She smiled and started up the steps. I watched her, trying
very hard to believe everything I had so earnestly professed.

That winter I entered the public school in Lakewood,
attending from eight-thirty in the morning to three in the
afternoon. My folks, meanwhile, at the Arthur were working sixteen hours a day rehearsing and doing shows in the
casino; or making scheduled lobby appearances, where they
served up a bunch of old-time songs that would get the
sideliners off their fannies to participate in musical chairs,
wild hand-clapping folk dances and other festivities that

were the rage when Lakewood shone as a high-grade resort town. I spent a marvelous winter there, if only to peek through those casino doors each time Dad came onstage. Just to watch him was to know where I was headed myself someday.

And soon.

There were two waiters who took care of the dining room, Norman Smithline and Joe Unger. Happy-go-lucky types. They made forty dollars a month, room and board, and a dollar a chair for tips. And once a week, after waiting on tables, they'd run downstairs to change, then go on to help my father put on skits in the amateur-night show.

At the time I was working as a tea boy. You won't find many of them around anymore, but back then it was an expected part of the general routine. I would circle the hotel lobby, offering tea and cookies to the guests after each evening performance. An easy and ignoble task, yet if it didn't seem like much, it did form an idea that made things more interesting for me.

Smitty and Joe Unger sparked it. The three of us had gone to a movie in town, a snappy Western starring Ken Maynard and his horse, Tarzan. Forget the dialogue; what really had us excited were the spectacular jumps, the leaps from cliffs into swirling waters, the belching guns, ambushes, stampedes, rustlers biting the dust and devilish comedy interludes thrown in for good measure.

Leaving the theatre, Smitty pulled an imaginary gun on Joe Unger, starting a bit of make-believe histrionics which soon had us galloping like maniacs through the downtown streets and panting the last few hundred yards to sink dead-assed on the hotel porch.

Smitty: (Wheezing heavily) By golly, I think we oughta try this again.
Unger: You're plumb right, fella.
Me: (With great anxiety) How about the lobby? I'll

play Black Bart! It'll break up the old tea-and-cookie routine.

And in from the porch we went.

Later, during the Christmas season, our improvised playlets became a regular thing, anticipated as much as the casino show itself. One night we'd put on a Western, another night a takeoff on the Marx Brothers—across the floor, up and down the stairs, over the couches, the whole dumb charade ending almost in the guests' laps. And came New Year's Eve, there we were again, flashing into the lobby to perform the famous international adagio dance; Smitty dressed as the Apache, Unger as his rival and me playing a señorita, with a rose.

It was one of those nights—

We go off to Mom's music, amid roaring laughter and hurrahs. I spot Dad in the crowd excitement and yell, "How'm I doing?"

"OK, son!"—shouting back. "Why ask—you don't hear boos, do you?"

Shifting his eyes to avoid mine, he suddenly bounds over to the piano, waves the crowd noise down, announcing "How 'bout those kids, huh? You give 'em an inch and they'll take a mile—"

"Aw, Pop," I say to myself and start upstairs, one plodding step at a time.

Then I'm in bed, listening to the piano and sweet horn sounds below, and I can see all my days ahead . . . somehow in some peculiar way they're perfect, with money and success and popularity piling up endlessly before an admiring world. . . .

And I'm thinking, "Forever and ever, Pop, you'll see . . ."

A February morning in 1939, the lobby choked with guests, whole groups on couches and chairs reading the

Sunday papers, their kids engrossed with the funnies; others peering through frosty windows at all the snow outside, fresh snow just waiting so children could jump in and dash around. The right kind of morning for Lonnie and me.

She had a room on the lobby floor, down a corridor past the front desk. When I got there, I could hear soft music being played. No mistaking the sound: Tommy Dorsey's band, with Edythe Wright singing, "You're a Sweetheart." Kinda corny, but nice.

I knocked on the door. Lonnie was smiling as she opened it. "Hi, Jerry. Come in. I've been practicing."

"Yeah? Practicing what?"

"My records."

"Oh . . . that's good." I couldn't figure what she meant.

"Sit here. I want you to listen—" There was a chair facing her desk. I pushed it back and sat down, surveying a small dresser with matching mirror against the opposite wall, a wind-up Victrola and stuffed teddy bear placed on the floor next to the dresser; on the left was her bed, strewn with phonograph records.

She gave me a significant look. "Just listen and watch— I'm serious; I want your opinion, so please don't laugh."

She picked up the teddy bear, then went to the Victrola, wound it carefully, tapped some invisible dust off the needle and placed it on the spinning disk.

Leaning forward to rest an elbow on my knee, watching intently, I saw her turn and sway lightly about, gazing down at the little toy animal as the record spun. Like in a Sunday afternoon movie—

It begins with the syncopated blare of Tommy Dorsey's trumpet section, and quickly old TD takes a chorus on his trombone, the camera dollying in for a side-angled close-up, holding for a slow fade to the vocalist, who now comes floating onstage, singing:

> You're a sweetheart
> If there ever was one,
> If there ever was one,
> It's you . . .

Lonnie Brown singing over Edythe Wright's voice, her cheek against the teddy bear—

> Life without you
> Was an incomplete dream,
> You are every sweet dream
> Come true . . .

And so on—

It wasn't overwhelming; at best she rated three stars for trying extra hard. . . . "Well, what do you think?" she asked, pursing her lips while I thought some more about her performance, and while something else perked excitedly in my head.

"Gee, I like it."

"Really?"

"Sure, I told you—really, you sing good. Almost like Edythe Wright. Except, well . . ."

She nodded silently, her face beginning to blush. At last, "I'm not that good, am I?" she asked in a strained little voice.

"Lonnie, what I mean"— and this I said gripping her hand—"why sing almost like her when you can *be* her!"

"Me? Don't be silly."

She seemed dumbfounded, but at the same time intrigued with my answer. And gleefully I kept building the fantasy, as though I had lived it a hundred years. "It's simple as pie, Lonnie. You could do Edythe Wright and Helen O'Connell and, uh . . . Betty Hutton, Kitty Kallen, Jo Stafford—I tell you, there's no end to it! The whole trick is to *make believe* you're singing—see?"

"How?"

"How? Jeez, lemme show you!"

Soon I had her perched on the chair watching me with perfect gravity as I began playing the same record; meanwhile clutching the teddy bear to my heart, completely preoccupied, the bit wholly imagined and feeling totally alone in the pleasure of my own making—

Just to see myself spinning crazily away from the Victrola the moment that TD's solo leads into the vocal spot, then silently mouthing the first note exactly in time—

You're

Pear-shaped it was, or absurd, but anyway—

> A sweetheart,
> If there ever was one,
> If there ever was one
> It's
> YOU . . .

While staring pop-eyed at the teddy bear, then jumping out of the trance with a happy gleam to fling it up at the ceiling . . . Now on my knees, I mouth a lament over little Teddy, who's lying there on the floor—

> Life without you
> Was an incomplete dream,
> You are every sweet dream
> Come true . . .

And at the finish Lonnie's off her chair in a screaming fit.

So it went, one song leading to another as the day faded, and we forgot all about our planned sleigh ride along Lakewood's main drag. No need for any of that, only the need of a funny imagination and the right kind of records so we could rehearse them over and over again.

A Saturday night show, the casino crowd stirring around, hollering for the big event. Comedian Red Buttons, a "favorite son" of Lakewood's Brunswick Hotel (he was doubling there as a bellhop), had not yet arrived to do his stuff.

"Where the hell is Red?" Charlie Brown was asking Dad, all the while watching a ballroom dance team stretch their already insufferable act.

Dad shrugged. "Who knows? Maybe he got hung up carrying satchels. . . ."

"I'll call his hotel," said Charlie. "Meanwhile, get ready to sing in case he doesn't show."

And five minutes later, in an amazing rush off Dad's frantic call for a novelty interlude, Lonnie and I had the old Victrola out, and before you knew it we were working on the bill.

She did the Edythe Wright number. Then it was my turn to strut and shake à la Jimmy Durante. (Just a minute! Everybody wants to git inta de act!) Finally we cut loose with the famed Jeannette MacDonald–Nelson Eddy "Indian Love Call," finishing to cheers.

Yep, Red Buttons had arrived!

We played maybe half a dozen shows that winter. It wasn't enough, so I'd step right into the grinder and badger my father's agent, Harry Cutler, trying to raise his interest so he could get us booked at any one of the many small hotels in town. But he'd merely blink those dark melancholy eyes of his and say, "Not now, there's plenty time later," and I finally told Lonnie, "Maybe we shouldn't rehearse. What for?" And she said, "Guess you're right. Who wants to bother with a couple of kids?" It brings a laugh when I think of it now; yet it's kinda sad, too, if you've ever dreamed.

[12]

March was the month for going home. There in Irvington again, at Grandma Sarah's house, I would begin to wait with a renewed feeling of hope. Which lasted only a short while.

"Sonny," she said quietly, "you'll study hard with Rabbi Friedman. This Saturday he will ask you to read the *maftir*. Such a blessing," she cried. "First your bar mitzvah, and soon graduation from public school. This is what your grandma wants to see. . . ." Her eyes were filled with tears. She rubbed them and with an exasperated gesture ran a finger across her nose, sniffing. "Ach, look at me, a cry-baby I am. . . ."

"You hurting somewhere, Grandma?" Worrying myself into a nervous laugh, then reaching out to put my hand over hers.

A sigh. "No, no, Sonny. I'm all right. Hah—after all these years, *now* I should be hurting?" Here she slipped her hand away and brushed my cheek, winking her tears back. "I should never feel better. And Saturday, God willing, I'll feel better yet. Oh, I can just see you—"

"Sit close so I won't be scared, Grandma."

"OK, OK, good. I'll sit, we'll be happy—everybody should be happy!" Fingers weaving about her face, as though drawing a picture of herself that I'd always remember, for my own good.

We grinned shy grins at one another.

"You want to eat?" she suddenly asked.

"Naw, I'm full from supper."

"All right, I'll make tea." She pushed back from the kitchen table, looked down and said, "Wait . . . my slippers."

"Here," I said, leaning behind my chair to get them. Now

she sat again, lifting her dress to step into the slippers. There was a large purplish lump above her ankle.

"What is that?"

"What?" And she touched it gingerly. "Ah, it's nothing. Pay no attention—"

"How did you get it?" I persisted.

"Such questions from my grandson. Didn't I tell you?"

"No."

She moved toward the stove, deliberately, and stood over it now to put the kettle on, looking gray and old in the yellow radiance of the overhead light.

"So what happened?" I asked.

"I don't know. A fall, maybe. It's nothing. A little fall, meaning nothing."

"There's no such thing as nothing, Grandma."

She thought about it, then half-turned and smiled. "I believe you. It's *something* not to worry about. So we'll have a cup of tea, then you'll study for the *maftir* and Grandma won't worry about a thing."

And I laughed, and after a while we had tea.

Saturday morning.

Drizzly weather, the *shul* enfolded in an eerie silence as we come in. I'm wearing a blue suit and carrying a velvet pouch containing my silk prayer shawl, also a pair of phylacteries, one for the hand and one for the head—yet I'm only vaguely aware of these religious symbols. My parents aren't here, though they had telephoned from Lakewood, wished me *mazeltov* and said nothing would keep them from attending my bar mitzvah. Well, Lakewood to Irvington by car takes an hour, an hour and a half at most, but their call came early in the morning, and it's now almost eleven o'clock.

Grandma finds a front seat. In a dark taffeta dress she sits alone, while across the aisle four elderly men wrapped in faded shawls bend forward with their holy books, mur-

muring through unseen lips. I'm sweating. The knotted tie at my throat is choking me, stifling the breath out of me as Rabbi Friedman motions the cantor, who nods and slowly opens the Ark, then removes the Torah. A ceremony in itself, forming a processional to the raised platform, where I stand aside waiting the rabbi's instructions. He faces the congregation and chants: *"Shema Yisrael"* (Hear O Israel, the Lord is our God, the Lord is One). I glance around the nearly empty hall to the closed door in back, praying that my parents and all my aunts and uncles will come rushing in. My heart is pounding with anxiety. Everything is collapsing. I try to understand the ways of God. . . .

Outside, it was getting warmer. The drizzle had stopped. And as I walked from the *shul* with my grandmother to her house on Rutgers Street, I saw a flock of birds that suddenly crossed the sky and wheeled down like tiny bits of paper to hide in trees or on roofs. I watched and wanted to hide, too.

She said, "It happens. The world is full of disappointments. But you'll get over it, Sonny. They meant well. So when they come later, you'll tell them how nice it was, how beautifully you read from the *haftorah*—yes?"

"No." My lips tightened. "It doesn't matter. Anyway, I don't care." I fumbled in my pants pocket and drew out a handkerchief. "I mean it, Grandma"—gulping in a sob— "that's that! I just don't care anymore."

"Sonny, child. The time flies fast, and before you turn around you'll remember . . . I tell you true, you'll remember that your mama and papa love you."

"Oh, sure . . . yeah—you wanna bet?"

"What is that—bet? Who bets with love? And today of all days, when I have the good fortune to walk beside my dearest grandson—"

I gave her my handkerchief. She blew loudly into it and looked up, laughing and crying at the same time.

That woman. Her whole life spent working and caring

for others. At first I couldn't speak, then said simply, "I
know," knowing only that she mattered to me more than I
could ever tell her.

A few minutes later we stood by her front door. She
paused. "Oh, I'm embarrassed."

"You lost your keys?"

"No, no, I left something inside. . . ."

"What?"

"Just something. We'll go in. I'll give it to you."

I followed her. She shuffled into the dining room and
opened a drawer in the china cabinet. There, a small, gift-
wrapped box, the paper tied with a gold ribbon, and as she
held it her face glowed against the cabinet pane. My heart
almost broke.

"Grandma!"

"For today," she said. "And for a hundred and twenty
years may it bring you success."

I lifted the chain, the attached Star of David with the
number thirteen welded to the back—all in eighteen-carat
gold!

My arms went around her. Then: "Grandma . . ."

"Yes?"

"It's so beautiful. But tell me—why thirteen?"

"Aach! You don't know how old you are?"

It makes you cry.

There was a party. A whole gang of relatives at her house
wandering around with plates of honey cake, seeking each
other out and posing together; aunts and uncles asking after
nieces and nephews; grand gestures, serious talks, jokes;
so many people passing through the tiny rooms while Uncle
lounged at the dinner table, drinking whiskey with grim
pleasure. And there was Mom listening to Grandma's
account of my bar mitzvah, Dad standing behind them,
relaxed, grinning . . . about what, I didn't know.

But a long time ago it was, and the rest just wriggles away.

To think of another time, some weeks later, when my grandmother got very sick, the leg swollen, ugly and ulcerating badly. On a Wednesday morning the ambulance came. Two white-garbed attendants went upstairs with a stretcher to her bedroom, then brought her down. She looked at me wearily, her lips forming words, but not speaking.

Friday night—from her kitchen window I could see the Irvington General Hospital. A red light was on above the emergency entrance: *Surgery in progress.*

They were operating on her gangrenous leg. I kept staring at the light, thinking of the days when we would be walking with my hand enfolded in hers, laughing as we walked, talking about school, about my friends, about suppertime meals and all the nice things she would sew for me next fall. I swallowed hard, trying to still the feeling of helpless grief which started to wind itself around my heart. I prayed.

And moments later the red light went out. I picked up the phone book and located the hospital number.

"Can you tell me how Sarah Brodsky is, please?"

The voice said, "She has expired."

"Does that mean she's getting better?"

"No . . . I'm sorry. She died."

[13]

After graduation from the Union Avenue School, I went to live with my Aunt Jean in Brooklyn, then took a job ushering at the New York Paramount. Later on that summer I also worked at the Strand, the Loew's State, the Criterion and just about every theatre on Broadway.

Furthermore, I saw a lot of Broadway Sam, who operated his Piccadilly Theatre Ticket office alongside the Paramount. It was a scrubby little office, always busy. Each day you'd find the place crammed with all sorts of people: bookmakers, truck drivers, female secretaries, garment center salesmen, retired couples from Palm Beach, newly-weds with that fresh open look of Iowa; they'd come in wanting to obtain tickets for a musical, maybe a ball game, an opera, the circus or some other attraction playing around town. I killed many an hour there, mostly waiting until he stuck a freebie in my hand.

I had first met him in Lakewood, not long after Mom brought me to the Arthur Hotel. There was an introductory glimpse one evening as he came swaggering through the lobby, looking tall as a tree, with a velvet-lined cashmere coat slung across his shoulders and a big-brimmed hat cocked perfectly on his head.

I asked my mother, "You know him?"

"Naturally. Everyone in show business knows Broadway Sam."

So right off I followed him around like a puppy dog, hanging on his every word because there was a great aura about him, this marvelous ability to take the simplest story and turn it into an epic. He'd transfix anyone, just mentioning the many celebrated actors and athletes with whom he was closely acquainted. I can still hear him saying, "Now, Joe DiMaggio calls and tells me that he has all these buddies in from San Francisco to see the Series; OK, wonderful, but meanwhile Bing Crosby is stopping at the Plaza and wants a block of tickets, so I'm trying to figure how to make Bert Lahr understand . . ." And so on, until it seemed as if Broadway Sam had every legendary character in New York clamoring for his attention.

Well, the last day at Arthur's, saying good-bye and all that, he suddenly reached into his jacket and came up with a theatre ticket.

"This is for you, kid."

Wow—I had an orchestra seat to the Rodgers and Hart musical *Higher and Higher*.

Then, a moment before leaving, he said, "Anything I can throw your way—give a holler."

I hollered the next summer and, through Broadway Sam's connections, got my job at the Paramount. The one and only sheerly magnificent Paramount Theatre, a festooned temple which served all the gods of Swing: Benny Goodman, Harry James, Gene Krupa, Glenn Miller, Jimmy Dorsey—and me, roaming the aisles searching for lost articles with my Eveready flashlight, not to mention directing people to the john. When the manager wasn't looking, you'd find me in the back eating jujubes and copping smokes. Then sometimes I'd be stationed out front, under the marquee, barking announcements—"Immediate seating in the upper balcony! Stay in line there!"—while wearing this forty-pound coat meant for a giant. When I walked, it seemed as if I had skates on. You never saw my feet.

Bob Shapiro managed the theatre. At the end of two weeks, I asked him for two things. A shorter coat and a raise in pay. He was miffed. He said, "Levitch, get the hell out of my office!"

The next afternoon I cornered some ushers in the employees' locker room and launched into an impassioned speech. "We don't have to tolerate Shapiro. We're human beings exactly like him, so I think we oughta call a strike and demand extra money. And uniforms that fit! And another thing . . ."

A tap on my shoulder. It was Shapiro. His last words to me were, "Levitch, turn in your dickey!"

Then came the Criterion, the Astor, the Capitol and so forth. One way or the other, I was fired from them, too.

In the fall I entered Irvington High School. From the beginning they loaded on studies that kept me going morning, noon and night, reading Shakespeare's *Hamlet* without clearness of understanding, ditto the rules of algebra and the formulas of chemistry. The whole thing amounted to a complete waste of energy, as far as I was concerned. I even tried out for football, if only to relieve the classroom pressures.

Saturday practice, a cool breeze whipping across the field, players and coaches everywhere, and I'm standing among a group of freshman hopefuls, trying to make it as a wide receiver.

And now I'm crouched, leaning forward, aching to run out for a pass.

The senior quarterback chants: "On one, on two, hup, hup—"

I take off, fly down the field and make a sensational catch, tumble backwards, roll on the grass and jump up grinning.

The head coach rubs his hands with happiness. As I go by, I hear him say to his backfield assistant, "The kid's small and skinny, but he runs like an antelope."

On the next go-round, I make a quick cut to the sideline, grab the ball by my fingertips, drag it into my stomach and shoot past the goalpost for an imaginary six-point score.

"Attaboy, Levitch," says the coach. "Be here tomorrow. We'll put you into pads and see what you can do against the defensive backs."

So the next day I suit up and practice with the regular receivers, showing moves that remind the coach of Jim Lee Howell, the great New York Giant end. When the whistle blows, signaling the first play from scrimmage, I trot over to my position seeing visions of myself at the Polo Grounds, racing untouched toward the end zone . . . thousands cheering, on their feet screaming, my father among them. . . .

"On one, on two, hup, hup—"

A nifty zigzag, which fakes the defensive end into a sprawling miss. I scoot between two linebackers, keep going and look for the ball to drop from the clouds. And wham!— the safety hits me like a truck, as painful a shot as I've ever taken in my life.

His hand reaches down. "You feel all right?"

The guy's puffing with pride, all teeth as he lifts me from the turf, saying, "I think you should try something else before you get killed."

I hobble to the bench, knowing it's my last day of football at Irvington High. Still, I managed to have a good time that autumn, mainly because I got involved as a sideline performer, the only boy in an otherwise beautiful squad of cheerleaders.

At the home opener I wore my official orange sweater, turned somersaults and wound up at halftime on enemy ground, where an hysterical mob of opposing cheerleaders began chasing me, first to our own side, then straight out the front gate and into the Irvington traffic.

The crowd loved it. I was the village idiot, and all village idiots are popular.

Stop me if I'm wrong.

The following spring the best game of all came around, as it does every spring, with a thousand splendors cutting across the April sky, producing a thousand phenomenal sounds never really forgotten by any of us who had once stood on a high school baseball diamond in full-growing youth. There, thumping, a six-dollar Davega Lou Gehrig model glove, spitting into it and bending low and hollering, *"To me, baby, over here, over here";* then waiting for the flash of your pitcher's mighty right arm, the swish of the bat, the ball to come crackling out on a line . . . Yes, for that one great, exhilarating moment everything is locked in, floating in infinite time and remembered forever.

I won my baseball letter and wore it proudly on my varsity sweater, which came fresh from the Poppy Knitting Company. During the hottest days of summer, even if the temperature rose to 107 in the shade, I would wear it. If everyone else had to go around in shirt-sleeves, swell—I strutted the Irvington streeets with Vaseline in my hair, showing off my Poppy sweater.

"Hey, Levitch, waddaya say, waddaya hear?"

It's Herbie Diamond, doing his Jimmy Cagney impression in front of the Roxy drugstore, early in June of 1941, a morning of shock and grim despair as I'm soon to feel right after answering, "Well, your Cagney stinks."

He shuffles up and unfolds the *Daily News.*

"Oh, my God—"

NEW YORK, June 2— (AP)—Lou Gehrig, great first baseman of the New York Yankees for 14 years, died tonight after 2 years' illness of a rare disease that everyone except himself believed incurable.

The "Iron Horse" of baseball, who would have been 38 years old June 19, passed away at his home in the presence of his wife after a critical span of only three weeks.

The disease, which erased Gehrig from the lineup of the mighty Yankees on May 2, 1939, was diagnosed as "amyothropic lateral sclerosis," a hardening of the spinal cord which causes muscles to shrivel.

He wasted away sharply in the final weeks and was reported 95 pounds underweight and barely able to speak shortly before he died.

"Go figure," says Herbie.

To which I don't reply, because I'm concentrating on Gehrig's photo, on his creviced face with upturned grin and wistful eyes looking off. I can't tell Herbie how I feel, but inside something grinds away, something that perceives and knows the horror.

I say meekly, "Yeah . . . go figure."

"Would you believe—he shrunk to nothin'. See?" he says, pointing to the unpronounceable words describing Gehrig's disease. "What the hell is that?"

"I don't know."

Meaning I want to lose the shattering thought of the "Iron Horse" dying at thirty-eight.

"Where you goin', Levitch?"

"Home."

But as I round the corner, here come my folks riding in this old Chevie coupe with sketch comic Lou Black honking on the horn, bellowing, "Onward to Loch Sheldrake!" and Dad calling out the window, "Hey, son, you had us worried!"

The car idles at curbside. I walk over.

"You've been gone almost an hour," says Mom. "Couldn't you wait? We have to go. There's lox and cream cheese on the table. And I left a key to Aunt Rose's house, and also five dollars—which you'll spend wisely, don't forget."

"Yes, Mom."

Lou Black honks again. "Let's not dillydally, folks. We've gotta buck the traffic, you know."

And they all wave: "So long! Take care!"

"Bye."

I watch the car speed away, fumes spewing from underneath, the sickly smoke gagging me and causing my eyes to water. Then I start walking home.

Later that month, right before summer vacation, I got word from Mom. Not the usual scribblings over the back of a penny postcard, but a carefully written letter on onionskin stationery, saying that since Charlie and Lillian Brown were now co-owners of the Ambassador Hotel, and because Dad had talked their ears off about my baseball and cheerleading exploits, they had decided to hire me as an athletic director, teaching the guests calisthenics, organizing softball games and the like. I'd get room and board and ten dollars a week. . . . *So please let Mr. Brown know. Meanwhile, Dad and Lou Black are breaking in new material for their mountain act, and it sure is funny. . . . If only the big-city nightclub buyers could see them . . . Dad's been working a lot with comedians Tillie and Jimmy Girard. . . . The audiences have been great. . . . It's the same old hectic pace. . . .* She guessed things would go along pretty well straight through Labor Day. *We think of you always. We miss you terribly. We love you more than anything in the world.*

And—

P.S. As you know, it can get chilly here at night, so bring along your corduroy jacket.

Freshman year over. Now on a Saturday afternoon I was weaving and ducking past the Newark shoppers and prancing finally into Davega's sporting goods store, where I bought a pair of Keds sneakers, socks, sunglasses and an impressive-looking brass whistle. Then I beat it home to start packing my suitcase. Next morning I was on the bus headed for Loch Sheldrake.

When I arrived some three hours later, it was to see a

much bigger place than the one Charlie and Lillian Brown had run in Lakewood. The Ambassador featured all the amenities, including a 400-seat ballroom as classy as you'd find anywhere in the mountains. Over the next ten weeks I'd always walk knowing a great comic was working the stage—comics like Smiling Bill Taylor, Larry Alpert, Larry Best, Eddie Schaeffer, Mickey Freeman, Gene Baylos, Jackie Phillips, Lennie Kent, all of whom unfailingly drove the audiences wild with glee.

Here, also, my pop, Lou Black, Tillie and Jimmy Girard, perennial "Borscht Belt" performers in a wide-open world that scarcely knew where the Borscht Belt was, let alone what it meant.

Ask Danny Kaye, Red Buttons, Jan Murray, Alan King, Buddy Hackett, Jerry Lewis—they'll tell you. When it comes right down to it, all climbed from their humble mountain beginnings with three things that separated them from the pack: an instinct for mass appeal, creativity and incredible luck.

Anyway, that first day at the Ambassador I was given a personal tour by Lillian Brown, then during the afternoon sat in a deck chair at poolside next to my folks as they talked about all the acts around. At one point Lou Black joined us to crack a joke or two, egging Dad into a simple question which triggered a two-way shpritz between them. Nothing unusual. They'd been giving it to each other for years. Only now, to me, it was a brand-new thing. The gags sped back and forth like tracer bullets. A quick-roaring, full-fledged explosion! Within seconds they had me hurtling into the pool just to stop laughing.

It's one of life's riddles why certain incidents stick in the mind, while still others blow away before you can blink an eye. That moment stuck. And when I began shaping the act with Dean, it was there, clear as a bell: the thought of Lou bouncing off Dad and doing the comedy, then instantly changing to straight man the moment Dad took over the funny lines. Bing-bang, that was their magic, the same kind that Martin and Lewis had, even if it happened in somewhat different ways.

However, there was no magic in what I did as an athletic director at the Ambassador Hotel. Immediately after breakfast I'd give calisthenics lessons to women. They'd come out in bathing outfits and sandals, mince around on the lawn looking at everybody else with embarrassed grins, then snap to attention as I blew the whistle.

"Awright, ladies, we're gonna do some knee bends to loosen up. So follow me and keep the rhythm flowing. Ready now, on the count—"

Down they'd go. Bones cracking. A couple of *oy veys* and tremendous grimaces.

"Wonderful. Let's try it again."

Down and up, down and up, until I had them all lubricated like Model T Fords.

The job was a cinch.

Besides, I met Phyllis Kuritzky, a teen-aged girl who came from an upper-class Newark neighborhood where her parents owned a bakery. What a beauty Phyllis was! A harmony of sweetness and light sitting there every morning on a bench, watching her mother do knee bends. And I kept looking at Phyllis. Yet all during her stay, whenever we'd meet, I would remember June Feldman and our little scene in the balcony of the Paramount Theatre. So I held myself in, worrying over what I'd say that might sound outlandish, stupid, or worse. At fifteen, though I was beginning to realize what it could be like to love a girl and be loved back, I still didn't know how to make it happen, any more than I could understand why there was so much love stored inside me and no way to get it out.

So I hung around Phyllis, always in heat but always in check, and always within earshot of her parents, who re-

garded my interest as nothing more than an ordinary display of friendship.

Now the second week. A fresh batch of arrivals. And
there in the crowd is this muscular Amazon, standing a full
foot over the others, waiting with challenging leers for the
lesson to begin.

After the preliminary warm-ups, I decide to spring my
own version of a stomach-tightening exercise on everyone.

"OK, gang, let's form a circle here. C'mon, get the lead
out!" I step to my worktable, where sits an old crank-up
phonograph machine and a ten-pound medicine ball, which
I lift and carry back to the group in a through-the-swinging-
door Jack Norton stagger, saying, "Now, the idea is to
pass this around counterclockwise—in time to the music.
You got it?"

They nod. I transfer the ball to one of the ladies, then
start spinning John Philip Sousa's "Stars and Stripes Forever."

And the ball is thumping from belly to belly with me in
the middle of everything, arms churning like a weather-
vane in a tornado, when suddenly it comes spinning off the
hands of the Amazon—whomp!—into my ribs.

Some sense of humor. I drop to one knee, gasping.

At the Monticello Hospital they took X rays. Nothing
serious, only bruised ribs and pride. A few hours later in
Charlie Brown's office I resigned as athletic director,
figuring at the rate I was going, eventually he would've
fired me anyhow. But all was not lost.

"We have an opening for a busboy," he said. "Can you
start this Saturday morning? That is, if you're up to it?"

"Oh, sure."

"Then be in the kitchen at six."

"Thank you, Uncle Charlie. I'll be there."

Neat idea, because for one thing the tips would come
pretty good; and secondly, I pictured spending it on gor-

geous Phyllis Kuritzky—anyplace in the world with her alone.

Mom was trying to rouse me out of bed. "Come on, Jerry, move your *tuchas*. It's twenty past five."

I snuggled down into the pillow and pulled the covers over my head. A short silence, then her voice called more persistently, "What is this? Look at you—hurry, get up already."

"Yeah, Ma . . . give me another minute, will ya?"

"I'll give you a minute—" She yanked the covers off. I raised myself on my elbow, saw the spangled dress she was still wearing from the night before.

"Where's Dad?" I mumbled.

"In the lobby, talking to Lou Black."

"What about?"

"What else? Show business."

I swung my feet to the floor, stretched and let out a big yawn.

She said, "We'll be at the Majestic Hotel tonight. Maybe you can get a ride and come over to see us."

"I guess so."

She went to the window, then said quietly and wearily, "Your father and Lou will be doing a showcase for the Morris office. That's why they're talking. You shouldn't ask from the hours of talk, not to mention all the rehearsals. A person's gotta be made of iron to keep up with them."

"So go to bed, Ma. You don't want to get sick."

"Don't worry, just get dressed. And brush your teeth."

She took off her earrings and placed them on the dresser. "Joey . . ."

"What?"

"You'll make Dad very happy if you come to the show. He's been working so hard, trying and trying. All he needs is a break . . . a help. . . . Maybe you'll bring him some luck, huh?"

The words echoed in my throat. "Oh, Ma, you always do that to me. It sounds as if I'm responsible."

"What do you mean?"

"I mean you know that Dad's going to do fine. For God's sake, he and Lou have been teaming up for years. They don't need me or anyone else to bring them luck. All they need is a good agent with enough brains to get them into the right places."

A little later the door opened and my father came in. His tuxedo was as wilted as his face. "Good morning, son. How come you're up so early?"

"I have to go to work. I'm a busboy, remember?"

"Well," he said, shaking his head in sudden wonder. "Yes, waddya know, I forgot you start today."

I put on my jacket, looking stonily at the floor. But as I left, I smiled at him and said, "Good luck on the show tonight."

At a long table in back of the dining room sat the waiters. They were eating breakfast. Some I knew real well, like Norm Smithline, Joe Unger, Sid Hoenig, Murray Brown— the old gang from Lakewood. After a few minutes, mostly listening to a lot of carefree instructions on the ancient and sacred art of being a busboy, I finally got around to asking Smitty, who had charge of the meal stations, "Can I be assigned to the Kuritzky table?"

"Sure. Why not? I suppose you'll make out pretty good there."

I happily finished my breakfast, then went to work polishing the silverware.

And that night at the Majestic Hotel I saw Lewis and Black throw everything in the book at an ecstatic audience. It was all there: Dad's brilliant song-and-dance routines; Lou's hilarious comedy violin solo; the two of them combining in a knockabout sketch, rolling from joke

to joke that worked the crowd into hysterics, then going off
with cheers and bravos ringing everywhere.

The only problem, nobody from the Morris office
showed.

[14]

It was a grueling time, rising every morning at dawn, then
hurrying down to the Ambassador kitchen to find twenty
busboys and waiters already there. You could hear them
jabbering:

"Boy, am I sleepy."

"Watch the doors!"

"Outta my way, simp."

"Up your nose—"

"Hot stuff coming through—"

"Hey, who wants table thirty-three?"

"Oh, for the life of idle play—"

"Sure, sure . . ."

"Boy, am I tired."

All this, and one break between lunch and dinner.

Meanwhile, Phyllis Kuritzky had returned to Newark,
leaving me with a quick kiss on the cheek. What else? Her
parents had been circling about like hawks, protecting the
nest. To top it off, Mr. Kuritzky nodded a curt good-bye,
hesitated a moment, then plunked a heavy hand on my
shoulder. "Work hard, kid, it's a tough world out there."

One Friday evening . . . Sabbath, and our hotel rabbi
delivering the traditional blessings, his sonorous voice
wafting across the dining room; hundreds listening, hushed,
reverential, when out of some kind of unconscious fog I
came waltzing through the kitchen door, bumped against
a waiter on the other side and dropped a tray full of dishes.

I wailed, "Oh, God, I didn't mean it!"

It was a wipeout. Even the rabbi laughed.

At which point it seemed like an ideal thing to start clowning my way through every meal. The clown. The one guy who could make people laugh in spite of themselves, giving pleasure by creating an illusion of wild absurdity. It was all I wanted to do in the first place. So you can imagine the stunts I pulled during those busboy days at the Ambassador. Suffice to say, the more absurd the more they liked it.

July. A big home-field softball game against the Evans Hotel kitchen squad. Lots of strategy: surprise bunts, intentional walks, delayed steals; the stuff major-league managers would have applauded. Then it started to rain. Mud up to our ankles, the base paths disappearing altogether under pools of glup. Still, the game went on. In an overtime inning I hung a fat pitch into left field, sped around first and skidded, leaving the ground as if a rug had been pulled out. The second baseman put the tag on. I trotted off, snarling.

We were beaten by the Evans nine on a freak home run, the damned ball getting lost in the mud by our klutzy center fielder. If that wasn't bad enough, my right arm had swollen and hurt like hell from the fall I'd taken. Norm Smithline gave it a swift look. "Might be broken," he said, an appraisal that was later confirmed at Monticello Hospital (a familiar place by now) when the doctor discovered a hairline fracture of the right radius.

Such are the breaks that can turn life completely around. Or, as they say, in pain there is gain.

I was at the Majestic Hotel, catching my folks in a show that also featured Sammy Birch, who did a record act. Until then, amazingly, I thought nobody other than Lonnie Brown and myself had done pantomime in that form. I thought we'd invented it, never dreaming there had been dozens of record acts working in this country and Europe since the early thirties. Anyway, it was terrific watching Sammy perform, and after a stimulating chat with him backstage, I left the Majestic knowing exactly what I wanted to do in show business.

"Ma, can you spare thirty dollars?"

"Oh, my! That's a lot of money. What for?"

"To get a phonograph machine."

She clapped her forehead. "I should've known. You liked Sammy Birch, huh?"

"Yep. The thing is, Ma, I have almost enough money saved, but with me not working—"

"The money will come. Your arm has almost healed. In a week you'll be back in the dining room. . . ."

"I know that. Meanwhile, I could use the time practicing with the machine."

"Very nice. Wonderful. To be a new Sammy Birch, I suppose. And then what? To eat your heart out if nobody hires you? Besides, what about school?"

"School is in September."

"That's no answer. I want a son who's got an education. Look around you. Look at all the uneducated morons fighting and struggling to stay alive."

I sit on her bed and turn my face away. "Ma, you know I'm gonna go to school. Why the lecture?"

A moment later she replies, "All right. I'll talk to your father. Maybe he'll have the thirty dollars so you can get your cockamamy phonograph." She comes over, crooks a finger under my chin and says, "Have you heard the new Danny Kaye record? It's funnier than the last one."

The Ambassador game room had a great jukebox. I'd drop a nickel in the slot and mime Danny Kaye or Frank

Sinatra, Al Jolson, Jimmy Durante, Cab Calloway or some other favorite, and as long as I believed it, I was them.

In the room we also had a Ping-Pong table, pinball machines, a bunch of old 1930 movie posters on the walls. And I'd stand in front of the massive jukebox. A melancholy ballad floated out—*All or nothing at all there is no in-between* . . . My hands were clasped, shoulders hunched forward, bravely. . . . The room was full of kids from Brooklyn and the Bronx, boys in peg pants, girls in saddle oxfords. . . . I heard the sudden groans, the cries of delight, "Oh-h-h-h-h, Frank-eeee!"

The bellhop—a balding, sad-eyed fellow named Irving Kaye—hung behind the crowd. The previous winter he had worked the Arthur, carting luggage back and forth and looking about as though anticipating immediate misery. Yet if my parents wanted someone to keep an eye on me, they went to Irving, knowing he could be trusted to steer me in the right direction.

Now he was watching me finish the Sinatra ballad, leaning against one of the pinball machines, a cigar ever present in his mouth, twirling it with intense earnestness while his huge brown eyes twinkled behind horn-rimmed glasses.

I said, "Well, how did you like it?"

"It'll do."

"You mean you didn't like it."

"I said it'll do—but later you'll get better."

"I hope you're right, Irving."

"Yeah . . . me, too."

Then suddenly, Charlie Brown's voice calling: "Irving! Go get a satchel!"

He hurried to the lobby. I saw him stooping over two large suitcases, almost forgotten in the midst of noisy farewells and bear-hugging embraces; a checkout crowd getting ready for the long drive back to New York City. And just then, as Irving went into his Groucho Marx crouch through the front door, he glanced around and winked, like he knew all this trouble and woe would soon end, not only for him but for both of us.

A day or so later I went into the town of Liberty and bought the phonograph machine, along with a whole stack of records. What a mix: Cyril Smith and "The Sow Song" (snorting, whistling sounds of the farm and barnyard); "Figaro" and "The Barber of Seville" by opera singer Igor Gorin; Danny Kaye's "Deena" . . . *Is there anyone feena in the state of Caroleena, if there is and you know her, just show her* . . . Also, there were songs by Jerry Colonna, Louis Prima, Louis Armstrong, Kate Smith, Deanna Durbin and so on.

I was in business, spending most of my waking hours working to a mirror; and when I needed a speed change, a hesitation or the effect of a crack in the record, Lonnie Brown was more than willing to help me with the mechanics. I did all those devices, always finding ways to do different things. Finally, the act was set. I tried it out at the Cozy Corner, a dumpy little restaurant about two minutes down the road from the Ambassador—lots of hamburgers and garlic bread.

The place was filled when I came in with Lonnie and Irving. There were waiters and waitresses, dishwashers, camp counselors, swimming instructors, summer-job kids like myself sitting at tables covered with beer pitchers, and everybody singing and yelling and celebrating, some calling through cupped fingers, "Hey, Jerry!"

In a tiny space cleared for the performance, directly under a glaring light bulb, I lip-synced "Figaro," wearing a strawberry fright wig and a tattered coat. Bent out of sight, Lonnie handled the record while I worked myself into a frenzy doing crazy things with my hands, eyes, lips, tongue; in fact, every part of my body that could move, moved all at once.

It was almost midnight when I finished. The owner gave me a crisp five-dollar bill. I held it up to the light, snapped it a couple of times, then put it in my pocket.

Outside, the August night, the air cool and calm, starlight bouncing off the lake, a sound of crickets and the night echoes, too, with faint calls and cries coming from inside the Cozy Corner.

We moved toward Irving's old flivver. Lonnie squeezed my hand. "I'm so glad for you, Jerry."

I squeezed back. "Jeez, Lonnie, it wasn't that bad, after all."

[15]

The arm healed. And in the remaining time before I returned to school, there were no boring moments. By day a busboy, at night running to this or that hotel—the Waldermere, the Nemerson, the Laurel Park, Flagler's, Young's Gap and how many others I don't remember. I went on as "Joey Levitch and His Hollywood Friends."

Between both jobs, often with Irving slumped inscrutably in a corner of my room, I'd rehearse the records, allowing the energy to flow nonstop. The room smelled like a clogged toilet. In addition to my smoldering cigarette butts, there was the foul odor of Irving's nickel cigars seeping into everything. Sometimes when I opened the window to get rid of the smoke, it looked as if we had an honest-to-God fire started in there.

"Irving!" I yelled one day. "Your cigar is killing me! How do you expect me to rehearse?"

He lofted a heavy smoke ring, watched it spread to the ceiling. "Easy," he shrugged. "Give up cigarettes. I can't stand them."

Through such acid tests some friendships are sealed for life.

The day I got back to Irvington, I called Phyllis Kuritzky—immediately pouring on the charm.

"Bonjour, ma petite. C'est moi, Joe-ee!"

"Oh, really? Oh, how are you?"

"Listen, you wanta go out?"

"Well . . . when?"

"Tonight. I'll take you to a movie."

Muffled sounds on her end of the line, then her father's voice booming, "Not him! You mean the crazy busboy?"

I almost curled up and died right there in the Roxy drugstore phone booth.

"All right," she finally said. "There's a swell picture at the Branford. I can meet you around seven. In the lobby, OK?"

"Très magnifique! I'll see you!"

So we went out and soon got to know each other real well. I don't mean we did anything to be ashamed of—we didn't—but we had lots of fun trying. Anyhow, I gave her a ring. It was no gem. It turned her whole body green; she looked like a mermaid. Worse yet, her parents turned green when they saw her wearing it, which is why Phyllis and I called it quits in the winter of 1942. Besides, a bunch of other pressures were crowding in around that time, mainly the heat I kept getting from my own parents because of school difficulties.

But first a word here about my early years in grade school, when I knew I was different, that if I couldn't handle the prejudice, I'd never make it through.

In the mid-thirties there were hundreds of people in Irvington who supported Fritz Kuhn and his German-American Bund. He ran a "sports" camp some thirty miles away in Andover, filling it with rabble-rousing Nazi adherents. One Sunday morning they paraded down Chancellor Avenue. I stood at curbside, gaping at a tangle of Stars and Stripes and the swastika, the gray-shirted bundists in Sam Browne belts trooping by with drums beating and trumpets blaring. At last I started to walk away, faster and faster, past the stores and faces along the parade route, and finally racing at breakneck speed to pull free of the sound.

But in school it was a different scene when one boy or another showed his true colors and wanted to kick my Jewish ass.

Like Arnold Hutter. I always knew from his eyes that a fight was coming on. They'd shift from his pals to me. A smirk, then the vicious remark: "A Jew is nothing but a nigger turned inside out."

One day we went at it, swinging roundhouse blows on a flight of iron stairs while changing classes.

When I got home, Grandma Sarah wiped my bloody nose and said, "Sonny, you can't fight the world."

I said, "Grandma, I wasn't fighting the world. I was beating the crap out of Arnold Hutter."

Now, an October morning of my sophomore year in the Irvington High chemistry lab . . . Everybody bending seriously over microscopes with Bunsen burners and groupings of tubes containing phosphorus, sulfur, mercury, carbon, ammonium nitrate and whatever else happened to be sitting around on tables all plugged for the assigned experiments.

I was trying to show Joey Schoenberg how to make dynamite.

"Stop worrying," I said. "The information is right out of the *Wonderland of Knowledge*—so what can go wrong?"

"Nothin', I guess. I'm watchin', ain't I?"

"Yeah, yeah. Now, I'm gonna hold this tube over the burner."

"What's in it?"

"Oh, just a little ammonium nitrate and some other stuff . . ."

What followed you might say was no earthquake, though

it sure sounded like one in the lab, and for all I know clear down through the Lincoln Tunnel and out the other side. I could've done "Mammy" with all the black showing on my face. So I couldn't blame our principal, Mr. Herder, for shaking his head and giving me savage looks when I was hauled into his office by the chemistry teacher.

"You want to see me, Mr. Herder?"

"I see you, Levitch. And do you have any idea what I see?"

"No, sir."

"I see a wise guy. Are you a wise guy?"

"No, sir."

"But you want to be a wise guy, is that it?"

"No. I was just doing this experiment, that's all."

He planted his knuckles on the desk, leaned forward and began: "Why is it that only the Jews—"

I hit him flush on the mouth. He reeled back, dumb-founded. Without another look, I walked to the door, feeling neither hatred nor pity for him. It was more like a sense of waste.

That same afternoon Mr. Herder had me expelled and ticketed to Irvington Vocational High School. And then the horror crept up; I wanted to get away from everything and never come back. Instead, I called my parents, who were working in Lakewood. Dad answered the phone. I told him exactly what happened.

"Oh, no," he groaned. "Wait, I'll put your mother on."

I repeated the whole experience. And she said, "Do you know that vocational school is one step from the reformatory?"

"Aw, it's not that bad. At least I'll learn a trade there."

"Give me a f'r instance. You're gonna be a safecracker?"

"Of course not."

"Jerry, I only meant—" Her voice broke. I heard her stifled sob.

"Ma . . . stop it, willya?"

My father got on the line again. "Listen, don't let it get you down. We're just sore because of Herder. The man is sick, pathetic, a miserable little worm, but what are you going to do? There's a million more walking around. Forget him. He's not worth your spit."

Objectively speaking, I guess Dad had something there. But going down the steps of Irvington High, everything seemed inaccessible and lost. I took one last backward glance at the building, then heard myself saying, "What next?"

Well, the reality was, vocational school turned out to be a snap. The teachers were fair and the kids friendly. Even the toughest students had an honor code. If you didn't bother them, they didn't bother you.

I chose electrical maintenance and repair for my major. Also, we had a shop class in which they taught us how to calculate logarithms on a slide rule. I got pretty adept at it, but one day I said to the teacher, "I'll never need math. When I get out of here, I'm going into show business."

"It's your choice," was his only comment.

So the years flew by. And now it's 1961, and I'm sitting in my studio office preparing *The Nutty Professor* with a half-dozen staff people around watching me use a quarter-inch scale on some sketches, approving and disapproving each one and saying, "I need six feet here . . . four feet there . . ." when who walks in but my old school teacher from Irvington Vocational High School. Not a peep out of him. He stands there, arms folded, grinning from ear to ear; and when the staff finally leaves, the first thing he says is, "Go ahead. Tell me you don't need math in this business."

Funny, when I think of it now, it's easy to see that at sixteen, like most kids, I was going through a phase, feeling I knew more than the teachers. The difference, though, between me and the lucky ones is that I couldn't cut it. On my sixteenth birthday I put school behind me and rode the subway into Manhattan. There, in a score of Broadway office buildings, sat all kinds of agents eager to greet young talent who might at any moment spring through the door with a new act, a great gimmick, a certain unmistakable flair—march right in completely unannounced and cocky as hell, shouting, "Here I am, make me a star!"

There I went, filled with an immense hunger and thirst, propagating this big spiel about my brilliant record act in front of a dozen and more agents. The experience turned out to be an awful letdown. The agents listened, pursed their lips, smiled, then took my eight-by-ten glossy, thanked me for stopping by and, in effect, told me: *Sorry maybe sometime in the future meanwhile gimme a ring when you're showcasing somewhere in town and best regards to the folks and see you around boychik . . . anytime.*

What a way to spend my sixteenth birthday!

The next morning I began making the rounds again, a bit more wary than before, yet still aching as much as ever for the best possible life on earth—the life of an entertainer.

As it happened, at six o'clock that evening I was sure of nothing. No agent. No little helper. Not a single person anywhere willing to take a shot boosting my practically untried career.

Mournfully, I leaned against a subway newsstand at the corner of Forty-second and Seventh, hands stuffed in pockets, my head hanging and swimming with vague ideas on how to plan the next more. Then surprisingly a voice rang out—"Hey, Jerry!"

I looked straight into the glowing ash of Irving Kaye's cigar.

He said, "What are you doing here?"

"Trying to find an agent."

"How come? I mean, aren't you supposed to be in school?"

"Naw, I quit. It's a long story."

"So you'll tell me. C'mon, I'll treat you to a hot dog at Grant's. We'll talk there."

Grant's was a few steps away. Eight rows of vinyl-topped counters, spicy delicatessen food, big pots of mustard and foaming birch beer straight from the tap. We gorged ourselves and in the meantime caught up with each other's *mishegoss*. He had spent the winter bellhopping in Lakewood, was now in town for a couple of days to see his daughter, then would go back and help close the Arthur at season's end. Mom and Dad had never said anything to him about my quitting school.

"Because they still don't know," I said. "When they come home I'll tell them. First, I have to find an agent and get booked. Otherwise . . ."

"Hold it. I know somebody."

"Who?"

"A guy who packages shows for the Loew's presentation houses. I'll take you to him tomorrow."

The audition was held at a rehearsal studio off Broadway. That little piece of business got me a string of jobs playing the Loew's circuit in Hackensack, Patterson, Passaic, Jersey City and Newark, a six-week run at twenty dollars a night. So I had enough work to keep me going, to be independent.

It was a time, also, when I switched my name to Jerry Lewis, taking the last name because I wanted to continue the tradition set by my father, and dropping Joseph for Jerry because (vanity of vanities) I didn't want to be confused with comedian Joe E. Lewis or heavyweight champion Joe Louis.

When my parents came home, I explained everything, that is, as much as I could explain anything I ever thought and felt about us, together or apart. After I finished, my mother broke into a raspy laugh. "So we'll all go on and make the most of it." Now, looking at my father, she added brightly, "We went through the same thing ourselves, isn't that right, Danny?"

He stared down at his shoe tops for a moment, then gave me a sideways glance. "Yeah, it's a great life if you don't weaken."

It took a couple of harrowing weeks on the circuit, but I finally had the act running smoothly. Regular as clockwork, too, Lonnie Brown would come in wherever I played. After the show we'd usually wind up sitting in some ice cream parlor, she with a proud shy smile and me sneaking looks at her sensitive beautiful eyes; I'd see a girl who'd one day get married and raise a family and be damned good at it, and on this particular night as we talked, so nice and fine, I could tell her, "Come on, say something about me. What kind of kid am I?"

"A good kid."

"That's good. What else?"

"Well . . . cute. And maybe a little silly."

"Is that all?"

"No. I also think you're vulnerable."

"Vuna-ba-bull? I gotta look it up. What is that—soft?"

"Not exactly. More like easily hurt."

As with old buildings, a lot of memories have collapsed in my time, but not that unforgettable moment with Lonnie.

[16]

I was playing the Ritz Theatre on Staten Island, just minding my own business, really, when into the dressing room walks this cadaverous little man with a face so waxy it looked as if he had spent his entire life under the moon.

"The name's Abby Greshler," he said.

I suppressed an urge to ask, "When did you die?"

Well, soon enough I would find out that Greshler was a high-powered independent agent, a go-getter in every sense of the word—indeed, the first one there while the getting was good, as I also discovered later on, to my dismay. But then, as we chatted, I had no inkling of that. He fascinated me.

The following morning my father took me to Greshler's office at 1250 Sixth Avenue, where I signed an agreement appointing him as my manager. Before the ink dried, he raised a knifelike finger and said, "I can put you into the Palace Theatre in Buffalo. How's that for a start?"

It was my first engagement on the road. While I was preparing for the trip, Irving showed up with a pair of socks and a toothbrush sticking out of his pocket. "Your mother insisted," he said.

On the train to Buffalo I felt excited, already imagining the opening night performance, the audience roaring, "More! More!"

It seemed that only a few minutes had passed when I awoke to hear a foghorn voice calling out the Buffalo stop. I glanced at my watch. It was past midnight. "How far did Greshler say the theatre was from our hotel?" I asked Irving.

"Walking distance."

"Great. Let's go take a look at it."

An hour later we stood in front of the seediest, most decrepit burlesque house I'd ever come across in my life. Half the light bulbs on the marquee were busted, and underneath was an unmistakable smell of urine.

I stared at Irving, sick. "Maybe there's another Palace. . . ."

He slowly shook his head. "I didn't tell you, but I've been here before. If you think this is bad, wait'll you see what it looks like inside."

Opening night. I went onstage almost comatose with fear. For there sat eight or nine perverts in an otherwise empty theatre, all of them moving rolled-up newspapers across their crotches and screaming, "Get the fuck off! Bring on the girls!"

I cut the act and got off.

So now I'm in the dressing room, packing my suitcase, ready to leave Buffalo and show business forever. Irving doesn't interfere. He stands against the makeup table, glumly watching.

Suddenly a baggy-pants comic shuffles in. I keep packing, hardly noticing him. A full minute goes by, and finally he says, "Are you Danny Lewis's son?"

"Yeah."

"No, you're not. You're a fraud. Danny Lewis's son would never walk away from a show."

"Who are you?"

"I'm Max Coleman."

I stop what I'm doing to look at his face. Remember the National Theatre in Detroit, the jawing and bantering backstage, and that third banana, the guy with the sad clown face, saying, "It's better than laying off. . . ."

"Hey . . . sure. Well, I was just—" And go on, much stronger, "Who says I'm walking?"

The old comic hooks his thumbs under his suspenders, then slides them down so they rest under the edge of his pants. At last a measured look, a slow-rising smile, and he says, "You got a show to do in two hours. When the time comes, get your ass on the stage. This is what you have to learn. It's what our business is all about."

I went on. And Max Coleman stationed the chorus girls in the wings. He got the laughs started. It was beautiful.

I pulled it off.

I made it.

vington: Union Avenue School on the far right. Grandma Sarah's house is the second one in from the street.

ighth grade graduation, 1940. I'm in the front row, far left; Leon Charash is also in the front, sixth from the right.

Dad (on the right) and Charlie Brown in the Catskill Mountains in the 1930s

Dad

Getting my start in the mountains

The record act

Irving Kaye and me, July, 1948

Sonny King, who introduced me to Dean

A handsome man and a monkey

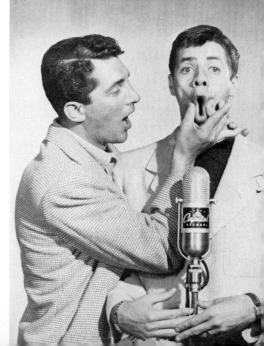

Dean and I hit the big time: the Copa, 1948.
The saxophonist is band leader Dick Stabile.

The Chesterfield Show

Getting hung up on fame

With Dean, Diana Lynn, and Don DeFore in a publicity shot for my first film, My Friend Irma

Irma *opens in New York*

In Ed Sullivan's dressing room
(PHOTO BY BILL CRESPINEL)

The premiere of At War with the Army

*Always a plane to somewhere:
Dean and me with my parents*

A scene from
That's My Boy, *1951*

Dedication of the Dean Mar
—Jerry Lewis Playhouse at
Brown's Hotel

BOOK THREE

I WAS sixteen and drawing as much as $150 a week playing Loew's presentation houses in towns like Baltimore, Philadelphia and Boston, traveling the circuit with Irving Kaye, now my official road manager and trusted friend. How rewarding to be around him; he moved in a world free of care and trouble. He had only to concern himself with train and bus schedules, baggage, the phonograph machine, the needle and me. No jealousy, no guile, no whining or complaining. Not Irving. He had the patience of a saint. He needed it.

For example, we were on a Penn Central Railroad shaker going to Philadelphia, which was no bargain, riding the tracks in the middle of the night surrounded by hordes of servicemen, loud coughing, things falling down from the racks and dust. Irving sat next to me, oblivious to the noise and confusion, already in dreamland some twenty minutes out of Newark Station.

Anyway, he smoked El Producto cigars, two for a quarter. He had one stuck in his jacket pocket. It would have to last him till the Philadelphia stores opened in the morning.

When the train slowed for the Trenton stop, I made my move. Then I tapped his shoulder. "Irving, wake up! Hurry. Get the bags."

"Wha-what? Where are we?"

"We're coming into Philadelphia. Grab the stuff and run. I have to use the john for a minute. I'll meet you on the platform."

He clambered off the train in a daze.

I ducked in my seat and waited. And sure enough, when the train started to roll out of Trenton, there was Irving standing on the platform with his head swiveling from side to side and his eyes searching, searching.

He spotted me giving him a high sign through the train window, one hand waving *ta-ta* and the other holding up his El Producto cigar.

Four hours went by. Then a soft knock on the door of our hotel room in Philadelphia.

I threw the Great Gildersleeve into my voice. "Ye-e-e-sss?"

"It's me. Open up."

I opened the door. He walked in, quietly put the bags down and said, "I gotta have a smoke."

A night at the Bradford Hotel in Boston.

Once again I'm horsing around with Irving, full of mischievous intent. Gripping a soggy washcloth, I begin wiping the old leather chair he's sitting in. A little rub here, a squeeze there, and pretty soon rivulets of water leak down the back and over the arms of the chair. Irving nods a long-faced sigh, then says, "Have you finished with the monkey business?"

"I'm trying to get rid of the germs."

"Well, I think a bunch of them are under your bed. Why don't you try there?"

Now, complete inspiration, a sensational idea struggling to get out. I slam my palm—whap!—and say, "I want to tell you something. It just came to me—you listening?"

"Certainly," he says, a shade of anxiety stealing into his eyes.

"OK, I'm thinking of doing a record. A guy and a girl—the nuttiest duet you ever heard."

"Jerry, I appreciate the offer, but I'm not—"

"Hey, I'm serious. I'm talking about a sure thing. Now, picture this. I'm wearing a costume, see, with one-half made up like a real Northwest Mountie uniform. . . ." I take a deep breath and a choking hold on my belly. "That's Nelson Eddy. And the other half—"

"Don't tell me. Jeannette MacDonald in a fluffy red dress."

"The color should be pink. I'll have it cut low so my dimples hang out." A glance down. "Well, what do you think? Could be a little bigger, huh?"

He stands and goes to the door. "Jerry, my boy, I just remembered that I have an appointment with the barber. Meanwhile, keep working on it. I'll be back in an hour."

He's blocked off. I flit around him like a bird, singing, *"When I'm calling you . . . boo hoo hoo . . . boo hoo hoo,"* and skimming to a top register which suddenly fades to an embarrassed grin when I see him turning purple in front of me. "OK, I quit. What's wrong?"

"It's a very funny bit," he says.

"Then why aren't you laughing?"

He returns to his chair and sinks into it, this lovely little man who has shown me nothing but kindness ever since those first days at Aunt Lil's and Uncle Charlie's place in Lakewood. He says while looking at his fingertips, "Jerry, do you know how many kids out there are doing a record act? It's no secret. There must be hundreds—look in

Variety." He hesitates. "If I'm going too far, tell me and I'll shut up."

"Naw, go on. You're my pal. I know you want to help. But don't worry about the competition. Someday I'm gonna reach the top, make a lot of money—like Berle, like Chaplin. I won't settle for less."

He says, "There's only one Berle, one Chaplin, one Jolson, one Barrymore. . . ." He tilts his face up a bit and gazes somewhere into space. "The first actor I ever admired was Barrymore. I wanted to be like him."

"With your accent?"

"Maybe it sounds stupid, but deep down I thought of myself as a Jewish Barrymore. Anyway, that was my dream."

"So what went wrong?"

"So I hung out on Broadway, bumming around and bull-shitting with all sorts of starry-eyed guys no better off than me. It was a waste of time. Then one day I met a social director who got me a job in the mountains. I made ten dollars a week as a bellhop and a couple of bucks more doing Jewish humor . . . but you know all that. The thing is, I stopped kidding myself long ago about being a serious actor. I concentrated on comedy. And to me nobody was a better comic than Milton Berle. When he played the New York houses I used to sneak backstage and watch him. It could have been a club date at the Waldorf, or two weeks of vaudeville in Hoboken, he always had them screaming. No greater comedian ever. He's an original."

"He sure is."

"And you want to know something else?"

"What?"

"I stole every joke he did." He shakes his head and wearily lowers himself in the chair. "So where did it get me? I'm shlepping bags for a living. . . . Jerry, you want to wind up a winner in this business, stop imitating. Forget the lip-sync stuff. Change your act."

His little speech is over, but it strikes a nerve. I'm angry, and I say in an intolerant manner, "I'm only sixteen years old, Irving, but I know what I got. I have talent, and sooner or later I'm gonna be a star, no matter what you or anyone else thinks."

"Who said you didn't have talent? Would I be here with you if I thought you weren't someone special?"

There's a long pause, and he says plainly enough, though his voice barely rises above a whisper, "Jerry, find yourself soon. Not twenty-two years from now . . . or maybe never, like me."

I answer with a vague, grimacing nod, then go over to the dresser and, without considering the consequences, remove a sheet of hotel stationery from the middle top drawer and write out the following at the desk, by the lamp: *When I make a thousand dollars a week or more, I will give Irving Kaye, my kind benefactor, 10 percent of my gross earnings. Jerry Lewis.*

"Here," I say, "this is what I want. Read it."

He studies the thing solemnly, then scratches his head with a bemused expression. "Don't you know this is no good? You're under age. It'll never hold up in court."

I watch him shred the paper and airily drop the pieces into a wastebasket. "Don't get me wrong," he says. "I'm satisfied with the way things are going right now."

A most wondrous Monday morning in Boston, the sun bright but the weather cool and pleasant as we come running up to the Greyhound station, Irving carrying the bags and me lugging the Victrola to the bus leaving for New York.

And off we went, plopped comfortably in a rear seat as the bus emerged from the Park Square barn, turned up

Charles Street, moved steadily through town and then onto Route 20 heading south out of Brookline. The road unfolded. Everything was fine. I didn't have a care in the world.

Then Hartford . . . gray and dull insurance towers, white frame houses and churches, isolated apartment buildings, roadside inns, suburban sprawl . . . the sun blazing down, forcing me to turn from the window.

Irving was reading his *Variety*. I looked at him for a minute or so. Now a big yawn and a slight edge to my voice. "Anything interesting in there?"

"Not yet," he said, still reading.

"Well, forget it. The fact is, I don't give a shit."

He slowly lowered the paper. "What got into you all of a sudden?"

No answer. I leaned my head back on the cushion, feeling irritable and tired.

In brooding silence I thought of my closing show in Boston the night before . . . taking bow after bow, the Loew's balcony crowd cheering without letup, the MC doing his best to quiet them down—"Honest to goodness, folks, he's run out of records." Then some unexpected visitors in my dressing room. People with flat New England accents, a plump, high-bosomed woman bustling around me, chirping, "I never heard anyone sing 'Figaro' so mahvlously. You ought to be in opera, my deah." The remark stung like hell. I moved away, mumbling to myself. And I didn't utter a single word to Irving during our walk back to the hotel room.

I remembered standing inside the doorway after he switched on the light. What a dump. Four walls and a few sticks of sagging furniture. No better or worse than all the other rooms we had stayed in from job to job. But the ugliness suddenly disgusted me. I felt trapped. . . .

The Connecticut hills rolled by. Great puff clouds above,

the sun peeking in and out, and now a dark shadow falling across the highway, racing alongside the bus. I watched it, let my eyes swim in the nothingness. . . .

And out of a long-lost dream I could hear the sound of train wheels clicking over the rails, the low moaning sound of a whistle trailing off . . . and then the clacking, screeching, bumping sound of train wheels rising in my ears again. Noise. The noise getting louder, my senses growing sharper, and sharper still . . .

I wake up and gaze sleepily at my parents. They sit opposite me on the train. Vapor steams from their mouths. I see them shivering in their heavy winter coats.

We get off in Albany, where my Uncle Bernie and Aunt Betty live. They meet us at the station. There are hugs and kisses, and then I hear my mother say to Aunt Betty, "I'll be going on to Schenectady with Danny after he closes here. Can you take care of Jerry for a week?" And Aunt Betty says they have plenty of room, of course they would.

We walk along the platform. I begin to whimper, "Take me home . . . I want to go home. . . ."

We walk down the steps to my uncle's car. Outside, the fog lies on the street like a blanket. Yellow snow melts underneath. I slip in the snow, fall into a muddy puddle. My father grabs my hand, makes a motion to slap me, then stops. He laughs, but his face isn't smiling.

Mom brings me to his dressing room. He's bent over a chair, leaning on one leg and polishing his shoes. I go up to him. He says, "Are you having a good time? Are you glad you came?" And then a crash of music, saxophones and trumpets wailing in from the stage through the walls . . . and faint applause and commotion. He says, "We'll talk later. Be a good boy."

My mother folds her coat, places it on his makeup table. I lie down. She unloosens the bulbs overhead. In the half-

*darkness I watch her follow my father out and slowly close
the door. . . .*

Our bus came to a stop at the West Thirty-fourth Street
terminal in Manhattan. I got up on rubbery legs, then
nudged Irving awake. We gathered our belongings, stumbled off the bus and walked out on the Eighth Avenue side.
The street was steaming hot. I set the record player down
and looked for a cab. None in sight. So we began walking
uptown to our hotel on West Forty-second Street. All the
while Irving was telling me his little jokes. I felt like yelling
at him to shut him up, but my mouth wouldn't work. It
was as if a wad of cotton had been stuck in the back of my
throat.

[2]

I played the Central Theatre in Passaic, New Jersey, the
following week.

Louis Prima and his band had been booked in to headline. His specialties were Italian songs, tunes like "Pleeze
No Squeeza da Banana" and "Josephine, Pleeze No Leena
on the Bell." But he had also written many fine jazz numbers, including "Sing, Sing, Sing," a Benny Goodman
standout that launched Goodman's drummer, Gene Krupa,
to stardom.

Prima's female vocalist was Lily Ann Carol, a twenty-
year-old brunette who got her start in show business by
winning an amateur contest at the Fox Theatre in Brooklyn. A few months later she joined the Prima band.

When we met at the Central Theatre, something nice
happened. We had loads of laughs. She especially got a kick
out of me mouthing such gems as "I'm crazy for you" from
the wings while she sang onstage. So she'd come off sticking

her tongue out, saying that I was one of the funniest kids she had ever known.

Her family name was Greco. She lived with her parents and four brothers on Pulaski Street in the Williamsburg section of Brooklyn. Her father worked at the Navy Yard as a day laborer. A friendly man, but somewhat formal with me. I guess he venerated his daughter. When she was in town I would turn up at her house, having to face him and his four sons. Chips off the old block. They'd all greet me with hesitant smiles while I waited for Lily Ann to get ready. And she'd come downstairs to the parlor looking radiant, setting them at ease and making me feel important.

There were some important moments. Something felt and seen and imagined, whether I held her hand or kissed her on the couch or simply talked to her on the phone. I thought I loved her. All I know is that it felt good to be around her.

One night she called me from Philadelphia. She was playing the Earle Theatre on the first leg of an extended tour with the Prima band. The prospect of not seeing her for a long while really had me down. But I managed to hide my disappointment. I told her with as much cheerfulness as I could muster up, "Just drop me a line when you can, so that I'll know how you're getting along."

This was about eleven o'clock in the evening.

An hour later I caught the last train out of Penn Station and at two A.M. was deposited by cab in front of the Benjamin Franklin Hotel in Philadelphia. I dashed through the almost deserted lobby and took an elevator up to her floor.

I rapped on the door five or six times. No response. I banged louder and yelled, "Lily Ann, are you in there?" A faint noise, someone being disturbed and shaken out of a sound sleep.

She was clad in a pink chenille bathrobe. She had a startled look on her face.

I stammered a greeting. "How are you? . . . Look, I happened to be in the neighborhood. . . ." I felt awkward, suddenly absurd and inept, and, most of all, as stupid as the words I had just uttered. "You see, the thing is . . . really . . . I need somebody to talk to."

"Well—now that you're here, you may as well come in."

"Fabulous!" And with that I clapped my hands over her shoulders and gently steered her into the room.

She yawned. "It's been a long day. I have to get up early for rehearsal. I hope this is important."

I grinned back at her. "Nothing special. Like I said, I needed somebody to talk to." I kissed her lightly on the neck, whispering, "Did you ever hear my imitation of Louis Prima?"

"Oh, Jerry," playfully pushing me away.

"Wait a minute. You're gonna love it—"

And before she could say another thing I was doing impressions of Louis Prima and whatever else in his act came to mind, including her big record hit, "I Got It Bad and That Ain't Good"—using the wall as a drum, beating out the rhythm with two pencils.

The phone rang. She picked it up and listened, then spoke a few mumbled words into the mouthpiece. She placed the receiver down. "That was the front desk. The people next door have complained. We better behave ourselves."

"Sure, sure. I'm sorry. I don't want to get you into trouble. I mean, I had no right to embarrass you." The air went out of me. I sat down lumpishly on the bed.

She gave me a searching look. "It's not *that* serious. You haven't committed a crime. And I'm not embarrassed, honest."

I lifted my head. "Lily Ann, all that stuff I told you on the phone last night—it's a joke."

"A joke?"

"In a way. Seeing as how I feel, what I really want—can you understand that?"

"No, not completely."

I shrugged. When I turned to her again she had a tight smile around her mouth. "Is it about you and me?"

"Yeah. I like you a lot, and I missed you—plenty."

She was silent.

"The thing is, we've been going together for a few months, and I figure, well, maybe we can be even closer." I entwined an index and middle finger, held them over my heart. "Like this . . . like a family."

"Oh . . ."

"Because we're right for each other. I feel that, Lily Ann. Don't you?"

"I'm not sure. I don't know . . ." She walked to the edge of the bed and stared at me gravely. "You're so young."

"I'm old enough. I'll be seventeen soon."

She sighed. "What do you want me to say? I'm very fond of you. I guess I always will be. But I have to think of my career. It's more important to me—it's all I really want right now."

I hung on desperately. "Listen, I wouldn't interfere. Only, you gotta realize I'm working hard, too. And I've saved money. Someday I'll be rolling in it. The trouble is, what good will it do if no one is there to share it with me?"

"I'll tell you something," she said, taking my hand. "You're going to be a big star. I know it. And whatever happens, we'll always be friends."

I blinked. "Yeah. If you say so, Lily Ann."

A few minutes later we were outside in the hall, both peering sadly at the elevator light. And when the elevator came I stepped inside, held it for a moment and managed a lopsided grin. "I'm gonna run all the way to the train. You know why?"

"Why?" she said softly.

"So I can get older much faster."

[3]

In the summer of 1943 my parents moved to the Holland Hotel near Times Square. Cheap rates, just another place to flop for a while, so bye and bye I checked in with Irving, the two of us sharing a room down the hall from them.

After some very dull weeks of city life, came October and I landed a job at Dave Wolper's Hurricane nightclub. It was a cavernous room full of that subtropical, shrouded atmosphere: purple walls, stuffed birds, rubber palm trees; the whole jungle trip with people digging the big cabaret stars and supporting acts.

For me it was a lucky break, my first appearance on Broadway; and a couple of days after I opened, the newspapers began to take notice. Columnists Leonard Lyons and Lee Mortimer gave me good write ups; there were strong trade reviews; and word-of-mouth spreadings also helped to fatten the attendance. Wolper was impressed. He decided to hold me over. As it turned out, I stayed until the following spring.

During the run Duke Ellington and his band came in to headline. What an organization! Brilliant, scorching, incredibly talented, the quintessence of pure cool jazz at its very best. Each night Duke would have the customers roaring to "Take the 'A' Train" and falling into misty-eyed reflection when "Sentimental Journey" swept over the room. The Duke mesmerized them. He was a wizard, conjuring up from his vast musical storehouse all the great buzzing excitement of wartime New York, and the loneliness, too.

Sure, I lived it, sometimes downstairs in Jack Dempsey's Restaurant, where I'd have a solitary meal between shows and then stop by and say hello to the ex-champ at his regular corner table near the window facing old Broadway. He sat there quietly, content, neat and well dressed, presenting his profile to the crowds on the street; the parading scene that always slowed to gape and point for a moment, and then tap the pane with a feeling of, "Wow, it's really him!" And Dempsey would nod back in a completely unselfconscious gesture of sincerity, giving an added touch of class to the Great White Way.

There, the air rang with the sounds of taxis and trucks and squealing trolley wheels. On Broadway, lost in the bright halo of electric lights, I would pass the huge Camel sign with its fabulous smoke rings blowing clear across Times Square; and everywhere the neons, the movie houses, the hot dog stands, the dance halls, the music bars jammed solid with young guys in uniform. And then, in the hum and murmur of Broadway, I would hear the paper vendors, gruff, growling, Brooklyn-accented voices calling out: *"Extry here . . . Extry! Get your* Mirror *. . . Get your* Daily Nooz!"

Headlines of retreats and advances; of unfamiliar places like Cologne and Bougainville and Anzio and Madang; the well-known names of Rommel, Eisenhower, Tojo and Montgomery. All those places and people over there—

While over here the draft boards were looking under the bushes to keep the ranks filled.

They wanted me two days after I reached my eighteenth birthday.

I showed up at Grand Central Palace in a blue suit and a skinny orange tie, ready to meet my fate along with hundreds of other eligible teenagers. In the massive induction center you could see a city block of faces: sad and cocky, confused, and some terror-stricken by the whole process.

My turn came.

The doctor said, "Cough."

He jabbed an iron finger under my crotch, probing and pressing so hard I wondered how many potential recruits he had put out of commission during the exam.

A Claude Rains type. The sort of character who seemed haunted by sinister thoughts, illusions that could drive him right out of his bird. Like the wife having an affair with a colleague of his, or maybe the seltzer man, or the mailman, or all three—in his house at this very moment.

"Cough!"

There were five doctors, one after another. And finally a decision from the top man.

"Son, you evidently have a problem."

"What is it, sir?"

"You have a slight heart murmur and a punctured eardrum."

"Gee whiz, I didn't know that."

I had no idea. My last physical had taken place at the Union Avenue School. A quickie in the gym; they had given me a clean bill of health.

So I said to the top man, "How bad is it?"

"Nothing to worry about, son. All you have to do is get plenty of sleep and stay away from the water."

"Does that mean I can't enter the service?"

"Oh, you can enter the service—the service entrance, that is. But the war will have to go on without you."

It was a horrible kick in the behind to see myself rejected from military duty, to end up with a 4-F card hidden deep in my wallet. I guess that shamed me most of all, just knowing it was there.

Anyway, there was no getting away from it. Not by a long shot. Not with the war going on and sad GI songs filling the airwaves; and no one really knowing what kind of world we were to have when victory came. As each day passed, I found myself reading more and more about the war, devouring newspaper accounts by Ernie Pyle and other crack correspondents who were covering the action in blacked-out England, the South Pacific and North Africa.

I wanted to get into the action, too. So, early 1944, I hitched up with a Camp Shows company of the United Service Organizations (USO), anxious to be shipped out from New York to the wilds of New Guinea or some such godawful place where our boys were huddled in foxholes . . . listening to strange jungle sounds, cries in the night, the rustling of leaves and the unseen enemy calling: "Yank, Yank . . . Babe Ruth stink!"

It was a six-week tour. Not actually what I expected, being that it was limited to a whole bunch of military bases and hospitals in the United States. And the company didn't have any big Hollywood names, only five small-potato troupers: an accordion player; a magician; a busty blonde singer; and myself as The Great Impersonator, ably assisted by Dr. Krank (none other than Irving Kaye).

Our first stop was at St. Albans Naval Hospital in New York City. There we played to a couple of hundred sailors, half of whom sat in wheelchairs, the lights shining down on their gaunt faces. I felt panicky for an instant. Then everything went great. A continuous roar, howls and whistles for the big blonde, and when Irving started popping pills into my mouth to change me from one record personality to another, it was marvelous just to hear those poor guys clapping and laughing so hard. The finish—Spike Jones and "Der Fuehrer's Face." It brought the house down. What cheers—like the war was over and I had personally won it for them.

After the performance one of the sailors wheeled himself up to me. A young kid, seemed hardly more than eighteen, with a pure gaze and bright smile, the kind you'd see in toothpaste ads. The only thing wrong, both his legs were missing.

I'll never forget. There was a pencil in his right hand and a hospital menu in his left hand. He held them out tentatively, as if, if he held them long enough, I'd be able to know what he was thinking.

I said, "You want me to sign that?"

"Yes," he answered. "It's for my girl. I can write to her now and tell her I'm doing OK."

"Hey, I'm glad—listen, man, all you guys made me feel OK, too."

I wrote down a few words to his girl and signed my name.

Going back to Manhattan on the USO bus. The big city of the world right there at my feet. A peaceful afternoon in America . . . I opened my wallet, then took the 4-F card from its hiding place and slipped it into the plastic case in front.

No longer ashamed, but grateful for all I had.

[4]

Detroit—stage entrance of the Downtown Theatre on an August day, 1944. A big truck pulls up. The back doors open, and puffy-eyed musicians tumble out in brown suits that look like accordions from being slept in. It's the Ted Fio Rito orchestra coming off the road. They congregate on the sidewalk to stretch, light cigarettes and shake off the rigors of an all-night stand.

Well, I observed this cute little chick walking toward the stage entrance, carrying a blue makeup kit. She wore a tight-fitting jacket and Joan Crawford shoes, and as she went by me I could see the turn of her ankle—out of sight!

The reaction was instant and overwhelming. I called, "Hey, girlie, you should have dinner with me tonight."

Her head whipped around. "Are you for real?" she hissed and kept walking.

Undismayed, I followed her down through the plumbing that led to the dressing rooms. Then a crowd of musicians swarmed by, and she vanished in the rush.

For a while I gazed into space, building glowing pictures of what I would do and say to win her over. And now, unconsciously leaning against a boiler pipe, I began to smell something burning. My jacket—my one and only suit!

I was not lucky.

The stage manager told her who I was when we gathered at rehearsal about an hour later. She came over and apologized. "I thought you were just looking to pick up girls," she said in a sweet tone. So the ice was broken.

Anyway, the road-company version of the "Arlene Francis Blind Date" national radio show led off the bill. I was the intermission act, somebody up front of the curtain to stall the audience while the Ted Fio Rito orchestra set up.

We did the first show. I noticed her standing in the wings, watching alertly as I did my stuff, nervous as hell, playing more to her than to the crowd. At one point, in the middle of Danny Kaye's "Deena," I turned full to her and went completely out of sync. It was as though all the clocks in the world had run down and all time had stopped. I froze. I think if I could've untracked myself, I would've flown straight into her arms.

As I came off, Irving said, "What happened? Your timing was terrible. You stood up there like a green kid."

"It's nervousness, that's all." I brushed past him and went immediately to her dressing room. Above the old, dilapidated makeup stand, in wonderful privacy, I wrote in lipstick on the mirror:

HAVE DINNER WITH ME TONIGHT
PLEASE——I'M FOR REAL

It was an Italian restaurant called Papa Joe's. Her hands were folded and resting on the clean white tablecloth.

I said, "You don't look like a Patti Palmer to me. That's your stage name, isn't it?"

She smiled without answering. Her face was full of expression, as serene as a child's, yet holding all the secrets of womanhood. I bent forward, flushed with excitement. "I know you're not a Palmer. You're Italian, aren't you? Come on, what's your real name?"

"Esther."

"Ah-hah! Esther what?"

"Esther Calonico."

I placed my hand over hers. "Glad to know you, Esther Colanico. I'm Joe. Joseph Levitch."

"Well," she said impressively, "I'm glad to know you, too, Joe."

"Good. I mean, that's really swell. When I first saw you, and you walked away—well, it was like my heart fell out."

She blushed slightly and was about to reply when a waiter brought over the wine list. He turned to her. "What will the lady have?"

"Oh, I think—" Her eyes met mine. "Would you like some wine, Joe?"

A sudden realization that I had seven dollars and change in my pocket. "Uh, I don't drink. But you go ahead, Esther. Drink up, have anything you want."

She turned to the waiter. "A glass of chianti, please."

He nodded and said, "Are you ready to order the dinner? We have antipasto, minestrone, chicken cacciatore, veal parmigiana, stuffed zucchini, stuffed clams, mussels . . ."

As he droned on, I added numbers in my head. Three dollars and fifty cents for the parmigiana, three dollars for

the chicken cacciatore and two dollars for the other din-
ners.

"I'll have the veal parmigiana," she said brightly.

"Very nice," said the waiter. "And you, sir?"

"I'm not hungry. I'll just have coffee."

The waiter marched off. So we talked about the show. I
told a few jokes and made her laugh. I felt happy, more
than I had been in a long time. I wanted to know everything about her.

She said her father had come from Italy when he was
about twenty. He drifted out to a little town in Wyoming,
coal-mining town called Cambria. He worked in the mine.
He drank a lot. He beat her mother. And she remembered
her mother throwing a butcher knife at him once. The
knife stuck in the door. Her mother pulled it out and put it
against her chest, saying she would kill herself if he ever
touched her and the kids again.

"Mom walked my brother and me through the snow to a
neighbor's house. We stayed there overnight. The next day
we moved to Detroit, and she got a job in the Chrysler
plant. Soon after that, Dad was back with us. A reconcilia-
tion. But it didn't last long. The fighting started all over
again. So he took my brother and me to St. Charles, Michigan. He boarded us on a farm. Moody people, who also
had children. We were the strangers."

"It must have been awful."

"Yes, it was. There were some evenings when they gave
us the smallest portions of food and sent us to bed earlier
than the rest. My brother and I would lie there, listening
to the loud talking and parties, and other things going on
outside our door."

She pressed her lips together. In a moment she continued. "My mother remarried. Then she and my stepfather
came to the farm and brought us back to Detroit. We were
torn, 'cause by then the farm seemed better than what we

had at home. Anyway, the whole thing wound up in court.
My brother clung to my father. And later the judge separated us that way. I was put into the custody of my
mother."

"Was it any easier with your stepfather?"

"No . . . he beat my mother, too. More agony, more
bruises and black eyes."

She turned slowly in her chair and said, almost to herself,
"I used to sit under a lovely tree near the farm. I'd look up
into the branches, and I'd see myself flying off somewhere
. . . away from all those people who always seemed to be
so gloomy, so imperfect."

"Yeah, I guess I was going through the same thing, in a
way. . . ."

She ran a finger along the edge of her wineglass, looked
straight into my eyes with a fragile smile. "Gosh, I never
talked so much as tonight."

"I don't mind. I love to hear you talk, Esther."

There was a pang of something inside that felt ridicu-
lously like love, and a streak of silence before I could re-
cover.

The waiter came over with a check. I peeled off five
singles and told him to keep the change.

He nodded a grim smile as I ushered Patti out of the
restaurant.

Going to her house, sitting in the cab, waiting for each
other to make the first move. Finally: "Can I give you a
kiss, Esther?"

"If you want to."

"What do you think?"

"Well, if you want, it'll be all right."

She puckered up her lips and closed her eyes. I clumsily
shoved my arm around her shoulder and crushed down on
her mouth. She twisted away.

"What are you rushing? I can't breathe."

I fumbled with my tie.

"Are you like this with all the girls?"

"Aww, what a load of stuff. You can't believe that."

"Hmm . . . I'll bet." Now a lowering of her voice. "I do like you, Jerry. You're really sweet."

Our hands touched, then joined. We rode along, looking this way and that, not daring to look each other in the eyes.

The cab pulled up in front of her house. One swift kiss, and zap—she was gone.

I slumped back as limp as a rag. I thought: Esther Calonico, I love you. I *really* mean it. I meant it with all my heart and soul.

But later that night in the silence of my hotel room, there were still other thoughts. The desire to call Mom and tell her how glad I was to have found someone like Patti; then thinking of her sure reaction, the heavy pause, the hard questions: "Colanico? An Italian name, isn't it? What— she's six years older than you? Jerry, are you out of your mind?"

So I thought: Why call? She'd never understand.

The next few days were beautiful. Patti and I saw Detroit as though standing on a mountaintop, seeing the whole earth around us and knowing with certainty that it held everything we could ever wish for. The romantic image of rocking chairs and flowers by the porch, moonlight, sweet music, endless hours together . . .

We dreamed.

Meanwhile, our engagement at the Downtown Theatre was winding to a close. The band and Patti would be going on to New Bedford, Massachusetts. I had to get back to New York for a string of one-nighters.

Ted Fio Rito had a reason to breathe easier. Every time he saw me taking Patti out someplace, he'd have this look of annoyance on his face; and one night backstage he let loose, giving her a big serious talk, loud enough so that I could overhear the words—"Forget him, will you? He's an idiot"—and she stood there listening to this with her eyes all wet.

I clenched my fists and approached him. "Who are you calling an idiot?"

He peered at me through half-closed lids. "Did I invite you into the conversation?"

"No, but I see where it's going. You better lay off her. Don't try to—"

"Cool it, kid! Get out of my way!" He stormed off, cursing under his breath.

I couldn't believe it.

"What the hell's wrong with him, anyway?" I snapped at Patti.

"I don't know. I guess he's worried."

"Oh, yeah, some worried. He hates my guts."

"It's not that. Not you, Jerry. I can't explain, but—well, he gets overprotective. And then he starts acting like he's my father."

"Isn't that wonderful!"

I wheeled around and went straight upstairs to his room, ready to knock him flat on his ass.

He was waiting, holding a match to a cigarette, the light flickering coldly in his eyes. "Now what?" he asked.

"You tell me," I said, staring back at him.

He nodded. "All right, you might as well know that when it comes to my people, I have pretty strong feelings for them. And Patti is a special case."

According to Fio Rito, it was plain and simple. When Betty Grable and Betty Hutton were with his band, he had taken them to Hollywood and helped to make them stars. Now he wanted the same thing for Patti. And since the band was due out in California to film some shorts, he was planning to coach her—how to walk and dress and present an image for the cameras. No sweat, he said, because Patti had the voice, the looks and everything else to be a real success in pictures.

"So what's the problem, Ted?"

A brief smile. He seemed amused. "As far as I'm concerned, there isn't any."

I didn't move, just stood there wondering what kind of phony game he was playing now.

The wall phone began to ring. He grabbed it. "Yeah? . . . Uh huh . . . definitely . . . I'll be down in a minute." And hung up the phone, mumbling about a missing trumpet part. "I gotta go, kid. Some other time, Ok?"

He clasped my arm and walked me through the door, paused for a moment and said, "Look, I don't have a thing against you. It's only that Patti doesn't need a romance at this point in her career. And if you ask me"—starting down the steps—"I don't think you need one, either."

"Well, screw you, Fio Rito!" I yelled at his disappearing back. Then a sudden urge. I had to see Patti. Fast.

The house seamstress sat at a table in her dressing room, working over a costume. She looked up, as if affronted by the interruption.

"You know where Patti Palmer is?"

"No."

"Well, can I wait for her?"

A sideways glance. "This room is strictly for ladies."

"I know. But please—she should be here any second."

The seamstress bit off a thread and reluctantly waved me to a chair.

A few minutes later, still no Patti. I guessed she had ducked out to get a sandwich. Or maybe she had been cornered by Fio Rito. Another one of his lectures, maybe, or a threat to fire her if she kept seeing me. I wouldn't put it past him.

I touched the seamstress's arm. "I better leave."

In the theater manager's office just before show time, I typed a note:

To my one and only—
If you marry me I'll give you the following—a dia-
mond tiara (I spelled it teeairra), *a house with a white*
picket fence, two cars in the garage, lots of kids . . .

I listed ten things. And if it were fashionable for a
woman to have worn a dirigible, I would have written down
a dirigible. I would have tried to get her anything in the
world.

She and I, strolling in the park near her house after midnight, exchanging whispers; then finding a bench next to a
lamppost and sitting there, her head resting on my shoulder.
    "What I said in the note is true."
    "You didn't have to promise me anything."
    "What promise? It'll happen."
    She bowed her head. "Do your parents know?"
    "Not yet. Why?"
    "I just wondered."
    "There's time, Esther. I'll tell them when I get back to
New York."
    And the guilt was smothered by her kisses.
    Then, out of the corner of my eye, I saw a shadowy
figure staggering toward us, an old man, wearing a grimy
raincoat tied with a rope, beat-up shoes, stocking cap
pulled over his forehead, the most pitiful bum I ever laid
eyes on. And under the lamplight he stopped, lifted the
cap off his head, bowed grotesquely and said in a thick
whiskey voice, "Ah, love, what a grand thing it is."
    We turned away from him, hoping he'd leave.
    "I won't bother you, but could you spare fifty cents for
a little snort . . . just a weak little drink, mind you. . . ."
    He reeled back a few feet, then half-straightened himself
with hands on his knees, squinting at us through bloodshot
eyes.

I took a dollar from my wallet. "Here. Have an extra drink on me."

"Well, thass very kind of you, sir."

We watched, amazed, as he wormed deeply into the pocket of his raincoat, struggling as though something big and dangerous had caught the tips of his fingers. And it came out, looking somewhat like a ring.

"Give this to your girl," he said.

I was embarrassed enough to take it.

Now a wave of his cap, and he slowly moved off toward the park entrance, almost theatrically, neither tragic nor comic, but fading mysteriously into the shadows as if on a stage with the curtain descending.

I looked at the ring. A bent piece of nothing.

"You love me, Esther?"

"You know I do."

"Then hold out your finger."

I had to settle for her pinkie. The darn thing barely made it over the first knuckle. But once on, it suddenly looked shiny new and beautiful.

Next day we said good-bye at the train station, holding each other tearfully.

She said, "You *will* write to me, won't you?"

"Twice a day. But I'm not much good at spelling."

A little smile and a long tender kiss. "Good-bye, Jerry."

"Bye, honey."

I let her go. She climbed aboard the train. Then, head down, I walked into the waiting room of the station and bought a ticket for New York.

[5]

I hadn't seen Patti for a week. In that time I could not believe I was capable of writing her so many letters, which,
in truth, were vast stumbling efforts to shape my thoughts
on paper, with dozens of schoolboyish incantations like—
*I'm going to be your Prince Valiant and scale the heights
as they have never been scaled before . . . and my mighty
shouts of love for you will fill the skies, reach out to the
furthest planets in the furthest gallixies of human compre-
hension . . .* That's how one of my letters went, page after
page.

Nothing, however, was more inspiring than a letter she
sent which had two penciled lines scrawled across the sheet
of hotel stationery: *See you when we play the Roseland
Ballroom in New York.   Love,   Esther.*

That Friday afternoon we met in a back booth at Hanson's drugstore on Broadway. For a long time I stared at
her over the top of my raised coffee cup, feeling that I
would find my strength and comfort in her, that I would
love her to the day I died. . . .

She said in a chiding voice, "You're making me forget
what I want to say—there's so much to tell you."

"Go ahead. It's only two o'clock. We got all day."

Above the chatter of customers and loud music pouring
from a jukebox, she talked and I listened, completely surprised by the recent turn of events in her life.

What happened was that she and Ted Fio Rito had a
blowup in New Bedford. It was over me. He had raged and
argued and finally threatened to fire her if she had anything more to do with "that Jew."

I gulped and said nothing.

"Anyway, Jerry, it got so sticky that I quit the band. I'll
play this last job at the Roseland Ballroom, then join the
Jimmy Dorsey orchestra in Pittsburgh."

"What a gas! But how—"

"I heard he was looking for someone to replace Kitty Kallen, so I sent him my picture and a record. And he hired me."

"Boy, that's really something."

"Well, there you are—looking at Jimmy Dorsey's new vocalist."

"Yeah . . . I'm proud."

She was silent for a moment and then, with a hesitant smile, said at last, "Jerry, are you Jewish?"

I shrugged my shoulders indifferently. "Why, does it matter?"

"No, of course not. It's just that I didn't know."

More silence. Then, trying to throw off the heavy mood that had fallen on me, I said as cheerfully as I could, "Well, I guess it's because you never asked."

"It never crossed my mind."

"But would it have made a difference if I had told you in Detroit?"

"No. I mean—I love you no matter what you are."

"So when are we getting married?"

"I don't know. I didn't tell my mother yet. Did you tell your parents?"

"About what?"

"About us wanting to get married, silly."

I avoided her eyes. "Naw, I think it'll be better if I don't."

"Why?"

"Because it would only complicate things."

"But why?"

"Lots of reasons. We got problems. Mainly, they see things one way and I see them another."

She gave me a twisted smile, then looked down. "You mean they wouldn't accept me. . . ."

"They wouldn't be happy—let's leave it at that."

"Oh."

I leaned across the table, caught her arm and kissed her

cheek. "Don't worry, honey. Everything will work out, honest, it will."

Her eyes looked steadily into mine. She knew, was aware now, of the deep gulf that existed between me and my folks, and somehow understood it would be best not to question the reason—that it was beyond her power to change what couldn't be changed by her. I saw this and sat back with a heavy smile.

"Jerry?"

"Mm."

"Do you want to go for a walk?"

"OK . . . where?"

"Just around."

"Good, I'll show you the sights."

"I bet you can."

I smiled more easily. "Say, have you ever been to the top of the Empire State Building?"

"No."

"Neither have I. Let's go."

And there, on the tower—peering through telescopes—amazing views, gasps, sharp puffs of wind as we look down at the city, the streets all grown together in endless grids of brick and stone; we look, pointing and laughing and feeling glad, our eyes wide with hope, looking to a future that will fix everything.

She went to Pittsburgh; I stayed in New York, getting a job at the Glass Hat, a decorous bistro located in the Belmont Plaza Hotel on Lexington Avenue. Busy nights and lonely days, times when I found it almost impossible to concentrate on the act, when I would walk back to my room at the Holland Hotel praying that I wouldn't have to face my parents and see the ice forming in Mom's eyes over my silence, eyes that would say, "A mother always knows."

Patti kept in touch by phone and mail. In one of her letters she said, "I'm doing well and getting more confident each day because Jimmy Dorsey is a wonderful boss. Everybody in the band seems so real and friendly, it's like I've known them a whole lifetime. . . ." She also wrote about Dorsey's musical arranger, Sonny Burke, a "dear man" who had set her songs in the right key and stood in the wings with her that first night in Pittsburgh "before I went out to sing 'I Walk Alone' (ha!)." And then she sent along the band's road schedule through the following spring, attaching a note which said, "From here to the Capitol Theatre in New York! I can't wait to spend every possible moment with you. I love you. All I want is your love, and if I have that, it's enough. Always and always. Esther."

My madonna, my Lady . . .

Finally, I got a telephone message at the Glass Hat. She was in town, staying at the Piccadilly Hotel. I rushed over, all dressed and ready to take her out. I can see it again— calling her from the Piccadilly lobby and getting no answer, then being told at the desk she was at the Capitol Theatre. And how well I remember coming within an inch of being hit by a cab while cutting across the Broadway traffic in a mad dash toward the stage entrance. There to be stopped until the guard could send word to Patti that someone by the name of Jerry Lewis was waiting for her.

Now, in a doorway, standing and talking to comedian Henny Youngman, she suddenly spots me, throws her arms around my neck, whispers, "It's been so long. I only want to be with you and get married."

And Youngman behind us, grinning, tucking a fiddle under his chin and playing, Dum dum de dum—Here comes the bride—this going on right out in the hall with the musicians ambling over and good old Peg Leg Bates tap-dancing his way up to us, followed by Jimmy Dorsey himself, everyone nodding smiles like they knew the bells would soon be ringing for Patti and me. Which I considered a beautiful but nerve-racking experience, since a few of the guys knew my parents—the last people in the world I wanted to see just then. So if everything seemed great and romantic, nonetheless, I was getting closer and closer to the wall, no matter how I felt about anything.

Early morning at the Holland Hotel, an October day in 1944 when I woke Irving saying I was going to meet Patti at Grand Central Station, ride all the way to Greenwich, Connecticut, with her and find a justice of the peace to marry us.

"Justice of the peace?" he stammered, still not quite awake, and he wagged his head like a sheep dog crawling out of the water. "You mean you're eloping?"

"Yes. I'm leaving now," holding up my overnight bag so he could see that I meant it.

"Well . . . go ahead. I guess you know best."

"Yeah, but—don't say anything to Mom and Pop."

"All right," he said, showing tense concern. "When are you coming back?"

"Tomorrow."

An awkward hug. Then, very quietly, I walked to the door, snapped it open and peered into the hall. It was dark and silent. I tiptoed out, went softly past my parents' room, down the stairs, trembling. If at that instant either of them had hollered down at me, without question I would've died on the spot.

A small house in Connecticut. Rustic. Pine-paneled study. The magistrate wearing an old woolen sweater over a pair of baggy tweeds. An old clock chiming the hour in the middle of our ceremony . . . He intones, "I now pronounce you man and wife."

It was done.

And after that we had lunch together in a quiet restaurant near the railroad station. But the thought of returning to New York and spending the night there now seemed unexciting; in fact, overwhelmingly dull and depressing. I ground out my cigarette in the ashtray and said to Patti, "It's ridiculous, so stupid. I should've remembered—"

"What?"

"We can have a great honeymoon at my Uncle Charlie's place."

"Uncle Charlie?"

"Well, he's not my uncle, but I call him that. Anyway, he and Aunt Lil own this hotel in Lakewood. We can go there."

She smiled uncertainly. "If you want, Jerry."

"Sure. I'll give them a call. They'll love you."

At about four o'clock that afternoon we were in Lakewood. Uncle Charlie was waiting for us on the hotel steps, showing a grin right up to his ears. A moment later Aunt Lillian appeared. *"Mazeltov!"* she cried, then turned to Patti, gently cupped her face while looking at me. "Oh! She's so cute! What a doll!" And Patti, suddenly touched and moved, embraced her in wordless affection.

So in some extraordinary way of which this world is made, there we were, feeling special, prized and, above all else, loved without reservation.

But in our room that night, rain lashing against the hotel and Patti lying next to me, silent, asleep,—once again the discomforting thoughts came back. Again I heard a monotonous drip of water from the kitchen faucet, the sound of car engines turning at the end of the street into Union Avenue, muffled laughter, a key slowly turning in the door. . . . I lay there in the warmth of Patti's arms, still doubting myself, feeling the same unmistakable fears ghosting about, and heard myself saying, "I'm married now. . . ."

I was young and married and happy. So why should I feel guilty for that?

Irving was looking at his watch as I came out of the cab in front of the Holland Hotel. "Quarter after seven," he muttered. "You better hurry or you'll be late for the first show."

I pushed a dollar toward the driver and swung around, deliberately ignoring Irving. He opened his mouth as if to say more, then closed it, shaking his head, and trailed behind me into the lobby.

I glared at him. "Is that a way to greet a friend? I just got hitched. Where's the congratulations?"

He looked flustered. "So . . . congratulations."

"What's the matter? Do you feel all right?"

"No. I feel terrible. I'm suffering from stomach cramps and heartburn."

"Come on, Irv. I'm in no mood for jokes. What's happening?"

His gaze dropped. "You mean with your parents? I haven't told them a thing. Besides, I wasn't *that* sure you would go through with it."

I laughed metallically. "Here's the ring on my finger. And tomorrow Patti and I are looking for an apartment."

There was a silence.

"Well, say something."

"OK. Your parents are upstairs."

"Oh, shit."

"Yeah . . . I'll wait for you here."

I tossed him a weak smile. "If I'm not down in fifteen minutes, call the coroner."

My father was sitting on the bed, bowed over, scanning the back of his hands. "Anything else, son?"

"Well," taking a deep breath. "We went to Greenwich and had a justice of the peace marry us."

Mom at that instant shot up from her chair. "You didn't! You didn't! How dare you!"

"It's my life," I answered stubbornly. "I love her, Ma. She's a wonderful girl."

"I don't want to hear! I've had enough of this—you're making me sick!"

A family situation.

The three of us filled with such inconsolable pain, all in the name of love.

"What did I raise you for?" she cried bitterly. "To run off with a Catholic? Shame on you!"

"Ma, for God's sake—"

"A shame, a shame . . . if your grandmother was alive, she'd drop dead."

I shivered, closed my eyes. "It's no use talking to you. I'm leaving."

Then Dad suddenly stood, waving his hand violently, yelling, "Who needs you anyhow! Go! Get the hell out of here!"

In the elevator, now alone, descending slowly to the lobby, walled in and crying as though something inside me had finally torn. The tears rolled down my face. Well, let them, let it all out. It's worth it . . . and the day will never come when I'll have any regrets.

Irving by the elevator, looking like, "Oh—" with darting, helpless eyes.

I laughed and brushed away the last tear. "Come on, let's do a show—"

[6]

Jimmy Dorsey's band was about to take off for the hinterlands—north and south and across the Midwest all the way to California. At the last minute Patti and I found a top-floor apartment on Lehigh Avenue in Newark. Two-and-a-half rooms in a middle-class neighborhood, sixty-five dollars a month with gleaming hardwood floors and an eat-in kitchen. So we moved our suitcases in, and that night by candlelight, with the radio turned on to soft music, we treated ourselves to a great fried-chicken dinner, then a good night's sleep before Patti went on the road.

And here, keeping busy during the weeks that followed, I tinkered around, arranging and disarranging the furniture, put up some shelves, hung pictures, dusted and cleaned and even wallpapered the bathroom—one of the worst jobs of paperhanging in history, but I couldn't afford a professional. I was broke as can be, still wearing the same blue suit with the shine in the pants and the burned spot on the jacket from the time Patti first met me in Detroit.

To make matters worse, while she was traveling with Dorsey, my jobs had fallen off to practically none. So before all the success, it was like this: going to Hanson's looking to buy coffee and a Thomas's English muffin. That's what my days brought . . . drinking coffee, scribbling stock jokes on napkins, sitting and hoping for work and bumping into a lot of other acts with the identical thing in mind. Now, if you had a car, that was something else entirely. Which reminds me of the fabled story: the Catskill agent listening to an aspiring comic who stands in his office, mumbling, apologetic, clutching his eight-by-ten glossies, his made-up bio; and in the middle of his phumphering, the agent looks at him cold and hard, and says: "Do you have a car?"

"Yes, sir. Listen, sir, I do some great things in my act."

"Is that so? Well, tell me, how many people does the car hold?"

"It's a sedan. Seats six comfortably. Now, about my act, the opening is sensational. I come out carrying a raincoat over my shoulder—"

"Does your car have a radio?"

"The best. Anyway, I do a terrific imitation of Sinatra."

"Hmmm . . . how much luggage does your car hold?"

"Plenty. Now, listen, about the act . . ."

And the agent says: "Send me pictures of your car."

I didn't have a car (I lied). And then, when I was supposed to drive three other performers to the mountains, I called the agent and said there was an accident; the car ran into a ditch, busted the radiator, or whatever. So I went by bus and got ten dollars for the job. But what's surprising, really, is the staggering amount of people who were willing to work the mountains for that kind of dough.

Meanwhile, Patti was doing well, earning $125 a week with the band. More times than not, she'd forward a large portion of her paycheck home to keep me above water. On top of that, when the hops took her anywhere close to New York, she'd send me the train fare.

I'm thinking of a winter day in New Haven—she had come down from Boston to meet me at the railroad depot. A lyrical time . . .

There was a radiant glow to her cheeks, a sparkle in her eyes as she got off the train. And after a long kiss she said coyly, "I have something nice to tell you . . . you'll never guess."

Unbelievably happy, it is enough just to see her. "OK, why don't we walk and find a place to sit? You can tell me then."

We strolled the New Haven streets, window-shopping and dreaming of all the new things we wanted for our apartment, then crossed the Yale University campus—ivy—gray stone buildings—winding paths—finally to sit on the library steps in the sun, rubbing our hands to warm them, saying how hungry we were. . . .

She bent her head on my shoulder. "I went to the doctor yesterday. And you know what he said?"

"Nope." But half-guessing and looking at her with all the calm and control of a jack-in-the-box.

"We're going to have a baby."

"You sure?"

"Sure, I'm sure."

I let out a whoop that could be heard throughout the campus. "Yaa-hoo! We're gonna be a family!" And to the rest of the world: "Did you hear that! I'm a father!" I had her in my arms, kissing her and lifting her up and beaming at everybody in sight.

Late afternoon, snow dust swirling around the railroad station, smoke mushrooming from the Boston train and people rushing furiously to get aboard. She steps up, turns to give me a last lingering look. I stand there subdued, hardly knowing what to do. So I reach out and gently brush my hand across the front of her coat, talking to my baby, "Hey, in there, you're gonna be the first Jewish Pope, you know dat, don't you?"

Over the next few months I couldn't find a steady gig anywhere, though I managed to hang on, playing the mountains, playing weekend club dates in Brooklyn, the Bronx and Long Island, earning as little as thirty dollars a job, or even less. So out of pure desperation I began to hoard small change in a drawer. Pennies, mostly. The quarters I carried. That was heavy cash.

Meanwhile, a continued stand-off between me and my parents. We just didn't speak to each other, though I did hear through relatives that they were stoically persevering in a grim sort of way. "Like how?" I would ask. "They're prepared never to see you again," would come the answer, shortly followed by a confidential suggestion, "Of course, Jerry, if Patti were to become Jewish . . ."

Which made the whole thing hopeless for a while.

In the sixth month of her pregnancy, Patti left the Jimmy Dorsey band and came home. It was April, one of those drizzly afternoons when I picked her up at the bus terminal in Newark. There she stood, surrounded by suitcases and sticking out endearingly.

That night in our bedroom we talked and talked. She asked me all kinds of questions about my act. Then, staring into my eyes with real concern, she said, "You haven't mentioned anything about your parents."

"There's nothing to tell. . . ." Flustered and ripped with thoughts that I didn't want to impose on her.

"Oh, Jerry, I know it's hard, but you must realize . . . it worries me terribly. There must be some way to make it better."

"I tried. They won't bend."

"It's the same old story, isn't it?"

"Yes."

"Well, then, maybe we can find a way. I mean . . . now with the baby coming, I thought I might see a rabbi."

I said nothing. We lay there in the darkness, silently, listening to the rain on the rooftops. And after a few minutes I fell into a deep and troubled sleep.

We went to visit Grandpa Levitch in Brooklyn, presenting our problem as though delivered at the feet of a great sage. Yes, Grandpa and his little white beard—a man of faith—spending his last years among the old dreamers of Brownsville, where the collective wisdom of Jewish law passed from mouth to mouth on street corners and park benches day after day; old men at home with the precepts of talmudic reasoning, debating like ancient prophets and philosophers what was proper and improper, what was allowed or forbidden in daily Jewish life . . .

"So, Patti, you must satisfy certain conditions before a rabbi can perform the marriage. . . ." Grandpa tugged at his beard, then sank gently into a chair, elbows resting on the arms, musing, strumming his lips as if he had not realized we were in the room.

I coughed. "What does she have to do, Grandpa?"

He sighed and took Patti's hand, shaking his head sadly. "In the old country there were many problems, but *this* kind we didn't altogether expect. Ahh—what's past is past. It's a new world, and I should be glad I'm here to see it. . . ."

I coughed again. "Grandpa—"

"Yes, Sonny, all right. What I'm saying is that the first thing she must do is read some books. The rabbi will give her, I'm sure." Now looking up at Patti. "You have to study, know about the holidays, the prayers, prayers for everything . . ."

"I'll learn," she said.

He nodded, leaned forward and asked softly, "Have you got a mama and papa?"

"Well . . . my mother lives in Detroit."

"Have you told her?"

"No. But I will. She'll understand, Mr. Levitch."

He stroked his beard. "What Mr. Levitch? Grandpa! You call me that, it'll bring me joy."

What meant more to me, however, was that my mother and father got the message real fast. A couple of days later they showed up at our front door, willing to forgive and forget. It was an interesting party of sorts. We sat around talking to each other quite easily; in fact, had some honest laughs and at one point exchanged toasts of undying fidelity with the wine they'd brought along. So at least the hatchet was buried, and when they left I felt a great deal of love for them, maybe more than I ever did before.

As for Patti, somehow it seemed to me that she had been trying just a little too hard to be warm and gracious in their presence, yet I wasn't about to start probing into the whys and wherefores; no indeed, not after all that had happened.

It was time. She needed a maternity dress, something she could wear for the wedding, a religious ceremony at the

Belmont Plaza, with only my family and a few friends attending.

One Saturday we went into New York and shopped along Fifth Avenue until, sharp-eyed and excitedly, I saw this cute little dark blue item in the window of Lane Bryant's dress shop. A price tag dangled from the sleeve, thirty-four dollars.

In my arm I carried a paper bag filled with nickels and dimes. "If you like the dress, sweetheart, there's enough here to pay for it."

She laughed. "OK. Let's go in."

And now, as she emerged from the fitting room with a chubby-faced saleslady fussing at her side while throwing the superlatives my way, I could tell that Patti was dazed by the transformation.

"What do you think, Jerry?"

"You look gorgeous!"

"It's too big!"

"It's supposed to be big! You have to understand about babies, Patti"—pressing her tummy—*"this* will get bigger!"

We bought the dress. The saleslady patiently added up the change for a half-hour before we were able to get out of there.

On a Sunday in April, we walked down the aisle and stood together under the *chuppah* (bridal canopy), where the moment arrived to hand her a ring and say: "Behold, thou art consecrated to me by this ring according to the faith of Moses and Israel—"

The rabbi added, "And the laws of the State of New York."

An unbeatable trinity.

For the final act, a wineglass wrapped in white cloth was laid at my feet.

The rabbi (whispering): "Break the glass, Jerry."

I stomp on it, grind it, beat it, give it everything I have. Nothing. Not even a tinkle.

My father (stepping forward eagerly): "Here, lemme show you—"

Crack, bam—he pounds the glass to smithereens.

Three months later, our funds almost nil and Patti due to give birth any minute, I grabbed a nightclub job in Baltimore. One hundred dollars a week.

So one night when I'm playing there, wouldn't you know that Patti went into the hospital? My mother called, and right after the last show I hopped a train for New York, all coiled up tighter than an overwound clock. And sometime late that afternoon I had my nose pressed against the nursery room in disbelieving astonishment, going, "Bu-bu goo-goo," and, "Hey, that's my boy—"

Yep. Gary Lewis, born July 31, 1945.

Lest I forget, among my souvenirs is a five-day hospital bill, which came to $120. It's stamped: Paid in Full. But I don't have the foggiest idea how I managed to bail Patti and Gary out.

BOOK FOUR

T<small>HE</small> year turned. I was almost twenty, seeing a little more of life, getting a bit smarter, but not smart enough to realize that there were other things happening outside the boundaries of show business.

It was also a period in which I felt more anxiety, more uncertainty, a keener sense of restlessness than ever before. How I would go about changing the act, what was to be the first step, where I should begin and by what method I could make the sudden leap into big-time earnings—to these questions I had no real answers, only the uneasy feeling that all my inflated dreams would evaporate in the reality of anticipation and want.

February came. I had another booking at the Glass Hat, $110 a week. After expenses and bills, it would allow for a brief, inexpensive vacation. So a few days prior to the engagement, Patti and I temporarily locked up our Newark apartment and with baby Gary arrived at the Belmont Plaza Hotel, checking into a small but pleasant room facing Lexington Avenue.

Patti knew how to cut corners. She shopped daily at a

local grocery store, buying cold cuts, salads, fresh fruit, milk and baby food. We feasted on it in our room. When we went out to eat, it was to the Automat with its chicken pot pies for forty cents, or to Hector's Cafeteria on Broadway, where they served a full-course meal for a buck and a half. I also remember drooling over the ice cream sodas at Tofenetti's in Times Square and savoring the hot pretzels in Central Park. At the zoo there would be a nickel bag of peanuts to share with the animals—and me nonchalantly tossing them into the lion cage, then unleashing all sorts of raucous sounds until, at last, with a loll of his head, old Leo disgorges a chunk of meat from his fangs and splits the air with an incredible roar! A near panic! People spin on their heels, and there I am, eyes hooked on my infant son. He's cheerily going, "Da-da, Da-da." And I'm saying to Patti, "Did you hear that—he can talk!"

Then a special evening in our room. I was standing at the window, getting a view of the tall buildings and swanky shops, the cabs speeding by, the lights sparkling as far as the eye could see.

As I watched, Patti called softly from the bed, "Hey, old man, come over here and talk to me."

"Yes, ma'am."

I sat down and glanced at the baby. He was cradled next to her, lazily slurping his bottle. I said, "You think we've got room for another kid?"

She grinned. "I hope—that's what we both want, huh, Jerry?"

"Yeah. It's what we both promised, remember?"

"I remember."

"We'll have thirteen. That's my lucky number."

"You're crazy!" she squealed.

"Naw, just stubborn. So you can count on having a dozen more, 'cause our house is gonna have lots of bedrooms. We'll get there, Patti. I know it. I just *know* everything will turn good this year."

"Jerry, Jerry. All I want is for you to be happy. The way
you were on our first date . . . the way you are this very
minute." Her mouth curled into a wistful smile. "We'll be
fine. Don't worry."

It was about two in the morning. She had fallen asleep.
I pulled the blankets up, then switched out the light; and
an ache came back into my limbs. I knew that everything
on earth that I wanted would be absolutely nothing without
her.

The billing was propped on an easel in the lobby of the
Belmont Plaza. Beneath the picture, a strip of fancy letter-
ing: Jerry Lewis—*sotto voce*. Here I was, knocking my
brains out doing a record act, and they were calling me a
sotto voce!

I tucked a hand under my chin like Rodin's *Thinker*.
Already I could hear some of my Jewish friends saying,
"What's with the Italian billing?"

Somebody cried, "Hey, Jer. Good luck on your opening
night."

It was one of the bellmen. I nodded a thanks and absent-
mindedly watched him cart off a load of baggage to the
elevator. The doors opened. A group of elderly women got
out, followed by a tall fella in a camel's hair coat, his
shoulders so wide he looked like a Green Bay Packer line-
backer. He had coal black hair waved over his forehead,
blue-tinted eyes; the sole blemish of his otherwise faultless
face was a telltale sign of recent surgery coming down at the
bridge of his nose. The complete picture exploded in full-
bodied technicolor when I caught sight of his shoes. Pimp
shoes! Red patent leather tops gleaming under the lobby
lights. And even as I stared at this unknown, sensationally
handsome person, I found myself waddling at a safe distance behind him to the front entrance. There, he exchanged a word or two with Ernie, the doorman, then
headed across the street.

I grabbed Ernie's arm. "Who was that?"

"You don't know each other?"

"Nope."

"That's Dean Martin."

I lit a cigarette. "He looks very important."

Ernie smiled. "Could be. He sings on WNEW."

"No kidding—what program?"

His palms pointed to the sky. "Beats me. All I know is that he does some kind of sustaining radio show."

"Hmm."

In another minute I was walking crosstown to Sixth Avenue, all the while thinking: That's some singer. He doesn't even have a sponsor.

Abby Greshler leaned across his desk and stared at me as if I were an ingrate.

"Do you know how long it took me to come up with the right billing? What do you think, it was easy?"

I gave him a limp shrug.

He continued, "For your information, it feels right. It's chic, classy as hell. Trust me; all you have to do is let the words roll off your tongue a few times—"

He enunciated, kissed his fingertips, rotated his eyes, the whole continental bit. "Aaaah . . . sotto voce! I love it! It's gonna open a lot of doors—put us right on the map."

"Now, don't get hysterical, Abby, but I gotta tell you something—"

"What?"

"Well, you see, I never studied Italian. I'm not sure I know what it means."

He slowly rose from his chair and smiled owlishly. "You amaze me. Sometimes you can be a walking 'Information, Please' . . . but there are gaps, kid. Huge gaps!" He sighed. "Allow me to explain. Sotto voce means a low tone, or an aside. . . . The connotation here is that you use somebody else's voice—you understand?" A look of victory stretched at the corners of his mouth.

I mumbled self-consciously, "Yeah . . . I guess it ain't so bad."

"All right," he said. "Now, will you please just do the entertaining and leave the managing to me?"

"Sure, Abby. You're the boss."

I gripped his hand gratefully. He walked me to the door.

In the hall I silently repeated the words, "Sotto voce . . . sotto voce," trying to live with it but feeling without a doubt that it didn't fit me at all.

At the Glass Hat that night the crowd noise built as I ground out another opening show. A near standing ovation. It sounded terrific, yet the fact remained that I was still working for crumbs near the bottom of my profession, and the top seemed a million miles over my head.

The next morning Patti returned to Newark with the baby.

I was alone again.

Sonny King was a singer and a pal of mine. I'd known him since the Sunday night talent shows at Leon and Eddie's, where we'd stick around at the bar all night waiting for a chance to get up and do a big ten minutes before the joint closed at dawn. Then we'd take ourselves over to the B & G coffee shop to sit there with eyes half-shut and the happy, incessant chatter still going on as if we had blown into town after a sensational national tour.

Early one March morning, Sonny and I were walking into a cold wind toward Broadway. My date at the Glass Hat would soon end. There were no jobs ahead, so Sonny, knowing I couldn't afford the Belmont Plaza rates, had invited me to stay at his place, a cubicle of a room at the Bryant Hotel. We were on our way there when I saw Dean crossing Forty-ninth Street with an older man. He waved at Sonny. "Come on over!" And we did.

Inescapable fate.

We were introduced. "Jerry Lewis, meet Dean Martin; Dean—Jerry." The first time in my life I was to hear what would be spoken around the world: Dean and Jerry.

The other man was Lou Perry, his agent. Short and slightly built, with a thin mouth and deep-set eyes, he gave me a quick glance, then listened quietly while Dean and Sonny talked about everything from broads to singing and work, and back to broads again.

When we shook hands in farewell, I thought it would be the last I'd ever see of Dean. Such an Adonis. And look at me, weighing 115 pounds—still fighting acne. Standing there in my bumpkin mackinaw jacket, T-shirt underneath and suspenders that held the pants two inches above my Flagg Brothers shoes. The heels made me five foot ten. When I took them off I lost the two inches, but I had a pompadour that brought me back up again. There was enough pomade on my hair to grease all the flapjacks in Hanson's drugstore.

So, tall and handsome, with my hair shining like Broadway itself, I find myself in Sonny's room a few nights later, the two of us tranquilly catching the flow while Dean spins a yarn, retracing his past, seeing himself in boyhood in Steubenville, Ohio. . . . Steel-mill town of immigrants and cheap labor and rowdy pleasures: a little house standing close to the Weirton and Wheeling mills; and a barbershop in the neighborhood where his father gives twenty-five-cent haircuts ten hours a day, and Saturdays, too. And his mother cooks big pots of spaghetti and meatballs, all kinds of Italian food, every evening a fantastic, mouth-watering meal. The smell of it—"Beautiful . . . the best . . . nothing like it in the entire world!"—Mom and Pop, and his older brother Bill, eating and gabbing at the kitchen table. Then the after-supper stories on the front steps of their little house. Pretty soon going to bed, listening to cats meowing on back fences and more cats joining in, the garbage cans rattling in the alley; the neighbors wrangling, their moans lowering into the dark Steubenville night.

He was born Paul Dino Crocetti on June 17, 1917. He quit school in the tenth grade—"It wasn't fun. I hated it, hated the system. All I wanted was to get out and go to work."

Sonny says, "Righto, Dean. You must've been profound in your early youth."

"Yeah, a real sonofagun." And he slides into it: delivering milk for his Uncle Joe, pumping gas at a filling station, working at the Weirton mill . . . sledging coils of hot steel, flipping them into boxcars and nearly getting killed when a four-ton coil dropped from a crane . . . Remembers one haunted afternoon in a broken-down, overheated poolroom, as gray as slate from the tobacco smoke. "I was chalking my cue, ready to take anybody on for a game, when along comes this kid, Ruzzi. He sticks his face in my ear and says, 'Do you wanta make some real dough?' Well, the next night me and Ruzzi and another buddy of mine called Slick drive into Cannonsburg, Pennsylvania, with ten cases of bootleg whiskey. Terrible hooch, man! The fumes could have run our car straight through to Los Angeles."

I laugh and applaud. Dean winks, makes a circle with his forefinger and thumb. I begin to suspect he likes me.

Now his eyes dim. A different note creeps into his voice. He says, "They're in jail . . . I could've been there myself."

Sonny coughs. "That's a drag, man. C'mon, tell Jerry about your ring career. You know, when you were just a regular kid like the rest of us Eyetalians."

Dean fakes a grimace and asks me, "You wanna hear that shit?"

"Yeah, I'll listen; sure, that's cool."

"Ok, pallie. Ask me a question and I'll tell you no lies."

"Well, ah . . . how many fights did you have?"

"Oh, about thirty. Mostly amateur stuff in West Virginia and Ohio. It wasn't that rewarding. They paid me off in Mickey Mouse watches. In the semipros I made ten–fifteen dollars a fight—bought Mom some extra pots for the spaghetti. Anyway, I quit the racket after taking a hard shot to the old beagle."

He gingerly touches his new-look nose. "Before the operation, it was five times bigger."

Sonny giggles and throws a pillow at him. "Schmuck, you could've been Jimmy Durante!"

Wham-bam, a barrage of pillows goes sailing across the room, and I'm bent over hugging myself smack in the middle of the whole rumpus. And life just then is a magnificent goof, moving in one rhythm, made of a single energy; we're clowning around like lunatics, but everything we do and say is positively the best.

And there are dreamy lapses in conversation while we listen to a tinny phonograph that spins 78s of Benny Goodman, Coleman Hawkins, Louis Armstrong, Tommy Dorsey, Billie Holiday. . . . We sit relaxed, reflecting off each other, our eyes hitting on internal images, our thoughts spilling over in pure honest enjoyment. And by now I've learned how Dean grew up and made his way through hard times.

He had a job at one of the toughest gambling establishments in Steubenville. The Rex Cigar Store. A front for the Ohio wise guys, a place where Dean clerked and sold punchboard chances over the counter, while in the back room a team of muscular hoodlums in gray fedoras watched suspiciously with their shoulders pressed against the wall as the gamblers shot craps, played blackjack and roulette. Lots of fast action, plenty of people who had come from poverty and threw big tips around to show everyone they had made it. Dean saw the potential. He studied the games. He became so good at them, the bosses hired him as a croupier.

"I pulled down between twenty and thirty bucks a day," he was saying to Sonny and me in the early A.M. "And at night I'd go to swinging parties with my pals. . . ." Well, Sonny is buzzing off in his chair, having heard all this many times before, no doubt, but I'm sitting like a kindergarten schoolboy, eyes and ears wide open while Dean goes on talking of one of his Steubenville adventures: partying one night at a roadside club called Walker's and being pushed up to sing a couple of songs, gin-drinking crowd giving him heavy applause and the band leader, Ernie McKay, offering him a job right then and there. That's how Dean got his start. . . . In Cleveland a few months later, singing with the Sammy Watkins band at the Hollendon Hotel, he meets a Pennsylvania girl named Betty McDonald—"Great figure," he reminisces. "I took her home to Steubenville and showed her off to all the guys who worked with me at the Rex. Yeah, she carried herself proud, man. Everybody said she looked like a movie star."

He went into his wallet, held up a picture of Betty; dark-eyed, long black hair, engaging smile, an Irish beauty in a white-lace wedding gown.

"We were married at St. Ann's Church in Cleveland and the next morning lit out on a bus to Louisville with Sammy and the whole band—"

"When was that, Dean?"

He smiles. "October 1940. Since then we've had three kids, two girls and a boy."

I say, "We have a little boy."

"Hey-hey, crazy! No, wait a minute—you married?"

I lock my arms, grin at him, sort of embarrassed.

He looks puzzled. "How old are you?"

"I was twenty this month."

"You look younger—like twelve."

And now Sonny stands up on shaky legs. He does a Leon Errol bit around the room in one turn. "What the hell time is it?" he yawns.

I glance at my watch. "It's a quarter to four."

First morning light filling the room, and I'm thinking that Dean has come along at the right time. I'm thinking he's going to be someone special: the big brother I never had.

[2]

On July 24, 1946, I pulled into Atlantic City to play the 500 Club, a flashy boardwalk spot that showcased unknown comics and singers. The place was owned by Paul "Skinny" D'Amato, so-called because of his pencil-thin silhouette. From head to toe he personified the jaunty, debonair nightclub operator. He wore London-crafted shoes, Parisian silk ties, and each of his made-to-order suits cost more than he was paying me as an opening act. But why complain? At a hundred and fifty bucks a week I could afford to bring Patti and Gary along. We stayed at the Princess Hotel, one block off the beach.

The first afternoon is retained in kaleidoscope memories of wild laughter trailing down from the roller-coaster ride; and the smell of sarsaparilla, hot dogs and buttered corn; the long, pleasurable walk we took on the boardwalk while lifting our faces to the sun; getting high watching Gary dig for shells, watching him splash in the surf and tumble in the sand—on that afternoon it seemed that nothing could go wrong. Sure as life itself, I felt that my luck would change for the better in this town.

Maybe the salty air had something to do with it, but as we prepared to leave the beach, I said to Patti, "Let's see what it's like in Acapulco."

She grabbed my ankle. I sprawled onto the blanket in mock horror, and she hitched up beside me, snuggled against my chest. "Oh, Joey, if *anywhere* is half as good as this, it will be wonderful."

At the 500 Club that night, I did my record act in front of two hundred tables and thirty customers. I bowed off to desultory applause, and there was Skinny waiting in the wings with a hypersuspicious smile. So I wasn't about to ask him if he loved the act. I recalled some pretty sage advice, my father saying: "The minute you start looking hard to please 'em, that's when you can't see your own faults."

"You're running a little short," said Skinny. "Give them more jokes, maybe a couple more impressions; just stretch it to twenty minutes. Other than that, kid, you did good."

"Gee, thanks, Mr. D'Amato. I'll get my records and pick something. I do a Deanna Durbin. That oughta—"

"Relax. Wait awhile—let's see what's happening out front. I want to catch the singer."

We sat at a corner table. Skinny's thumbs were revolving in a definite sign of agitation as this gut-stabbing sound ripped across the room.

By the second number I knew the singer was in serious trouble when Skinny almost soared out of his chair.

"I can't believe it—the guys sings as if his nuts are caught in a zipper!"

All the illogical pitfalls of running a respectable night-club suddenly crashed in on him. "The guy's bad . . . oh, my . . . he's so bad I'm gonna kill his agent."

"Maybe he'll get better."

"Yeah, kid, right after they operate on his neck. I can't wait around. I gotta get somebody else in here, and quick."

I thought of Dean. Instantly, without effort. We had

been corresponding. His last postcard had been sent from Chicago: *Working with Buddy Lester at the Rio Cabana. Buddy is great, but the spaghetti is lousy. Closing on the twenty-second. Open for a job on the twenty-third. Your pal.*

I took a shot. "Why don't you book my friend, Dean Martin? He's not working."

Skinny put a hand on my shoulder. "Tell me, just for my own edification, what's a Dean Martin?"

"He's a terrific singer. He's played some good places, like the Havana Madrid, the Rio Cabana, and, uhh . . . listen, you can call his agent, Lou Perry. He'll tell you."

Skinny pushed forward in his seat, anchored his elbows on the table, cradled his jaws and began meditating, wincing now and then as the noise from the stage kept battering his eardrums. At last—"Dean Martin, huh?"

I had him. "You'll see, Mr. D'Amato. Dean is not only terrific, but we've worked together."

"You have?"

"Sure. We do a lot of funny stuff." It seemed like years ago at the Bryant. Ah, such nonsense, such a nutty time. Only, it was all play, and all for free.

Skinny placed a call to Lou Perry. On the twenty-fifth, Dean arrived in Atlantic City—

That night he does his first show. He sings five songs, then gets off. I go on with my record act, and when I leave the stage Skinny is waiting for me, looking somewhat perturbed. He's muttering something about "cement waistcoats." The next thing I know, he's pointing in the general direction of his office.

And for five minutes tops, Dean and I are in there with him.

"Where's the funny shit?"

"Hmm . . ."

"I said, where's the stuff you guys were going to do together? If you're not doing it by the next show, you're both out on your asses."

So Dean and I retire to our dressing room. Our dressing room is a nail hammered in the wall. Two guys and a nail. And Dean speaks to the nail. "So what are we supposed to be doing together, pal?"

"I'm thinking, I'm thinking . . ."

In the alleyway leading to the stage, I say, "Here's the plan. You sing, and I'll put on a busboy's jacket. Then we'll grab some things out of the kitchen and make a lot of noise."

He says, "Where is that gonna get us?"

"I don't know. But if we don't do something funny, I'm gonna blow a hundred and fifty bucks."

The next show starts. The audience sits up, anticipating. All four of them. Literally, an audience of four, not including the maître d', nine waiters, five busboys, one cigarette girl and Skinny. If one of the customers snaps his fingers to order a drink, sixteen people are there in a flash, clomping all over him.

We do a three-hour show.

We juggle and drop dishes and try a few handstands. I conduct the three-piece band with one of my shoes, burn their music, jump offstage, run around the tables, sit with the customers and spill things while Dean keeps singing. That takes eight minutes. Then it takes another eight minutes to stagger up to the piano, and I don't know how much more time to remove the fat man from his stool so I can sit down. Finally, after I sit down, Dean gives me a withering stare. "Hey, kid, can you play that thing?" And when I say, "No," he says, "Then get the hell away from there!"

Screams from the two tables of two each, and on and on it goes. I'm looking gleefully at Dean, feeling the lightning, the whole world thundering down before us right there in that room.

And at four o'clock in the morning we leave the club,

head down the shadowy boardwalk kicking up our heels and cackling nonsensically because everything is so wonderful we can hardly believe it. Then, all of a sudden, about a mile past the Steel Pier, we find ourselves standing quietly by a rail, cigarettes lit and eyes peering into the inky-black sea.

Dean tosses his butt away. "It's really phenomenal."

"You mean out there—the ocean?"

"Yeah."

"Y'know, during the war I used to think of all those torpedoes zinging through the water in the darkness. Man, no wonder sailors get drunk."

"You ever been on a ship?"

"Oh, sure. The Staten Island Ferry. Five cents from the Battery to Hoboken."

"Wise guy. Anyway, when they book us to play the Palladium in England, we'll go by plane."

"Hey! It's a deal! And you wanta know what else?"

"What?"

"No bull, Dean. I have this feeling that pretty soon we'll be playing Hollywood, and the best clubs in New York and Chicago and everywhere. The main rooms! I tell ya, it's in the bag!"

He grins. "I don't know about that, pardner, but we're sure gonna have a lot of fun wherever it is."

"You bet. Wherever it is . . ." I echo softly. And after a while we start back to the hotel, whistling like a couple of goofs.

In the afternoon of the same day, I rented a typewriter and went to work shaping the act. After writing down the title, which I called "Sex and Slapstick," I laboriously typed out these words: *Since the time immemorium, there has never been a two-act in show business that weren't two milkmen, two food operators, two electricians, two plumbers,*

and for the first time here we have a handsome man and a
monkey. . . .

That was the premise.

And that is precisely how we played it. Not only onstage,
but whenever the mood struck. Everybody was fair game,
especially the unsuspecting targets we sighted at boardwalk
novelty shops, shooting parlors, all sorts of ethnic restau-
rants and the swarming beach itself.

For instance, at a booth in a Chinese restaurant I ordered
chicken chow mein, then stuck the noodles up my nose
while Dean nonchalantly sipped his Chinese tea. The
Chinese waitress watched with her tongue lolling out. Behind her, three other Chinese waitresses and the Greek
proprietor stood riveted to the floor until a guy in the
opposite booth hollered, "Waddya know, it's those two
meshugeners from the 500 Club!"

One afternoon it was the beach, a plan to do something
really crazy. In the midst of hundreds of sunworshipers, I
took off across the sand, kept going and finally dove into a
roaring wave. Seconds later, I called for help. Of course,
Dean was only a few yards away, churning toward me with
forceful butterfly strokes. A moment later he had an
arm around my shoulder. "Play dead. Don't move." He
dragged me to the shore.

It grew to more dramatic proportions when a lifeguard
pushed his way through the crowd. "Step aside—give him
some air, folks."

I jumped up. "If you don't mind, sir, I'd rather have a
malted."

His mouth fell open. "How's that again?"

Now it was Dean's turn. He looked at me curiously.
"What'll it be, kid? Vanilla or chocolate?"

"Chocolate, you dummy."

"I'm no dummy—you dummy. The name is Martin.
Dean Martin."

"Hi. I'm Jerry Lewis. Are you working in town, sir?"

"Sure. With you—you idiot!"

We skipped past the lifeguard, saying for all to hear, "Get dressed and see us at the 500 Club!"

Three nights into our engagement, the lines began to form. By the weekend the lines stretched down the boardwalk. So Skinny D'Amato raised our salaries to $750 and held us over for four weeks. Meanwhile, people from every part of the country were calling in reservations, some willing to pay any price for a ringside table. The press helped by whetting their appetites. Ed Sullivan raved about the act, as did Walter Winchell, Leonard Lyons and Bob Sylvester. They all touted us as the comedy finds of the year.

An added boost came from Sophie Tucker, the Last of the Red-Hot Mammas. She talked us up after one of our shows, telling a group of reporters, "These two crazy kids are a combination of the Keystone Kops, the Marx Brothers and Abbott and Costello." Heady stuff.

Sometimes, alone in my hotel room, trying to assess what had happened, thinking of what Dean and I had accomplished, of what we were capable of becoming, the adrenaline would pump so hard I'd jump around shouting, "There's no way to fail—no way!"

Then the undeniable fact, a sudden knowledge that we weren't a team yet. Not officially. Not with Lou Perry holding a manager's contract with Dean, which legally tied them together for another couple of years.

[3]

Lou Perry would have gone to hell and back for Dean. His loyalty was there from the start, but just when it looked as if the big payoff had finally come, he found himself out of the picture. To this day I don't know all the behind-the-scenes maneuverings that eventually put Abbey Greshler in full charge of the act, although I have a clear recollection of the initial rumblings.

The Havana Madrid had booked us for the month of September at a salary of $1,500 a week, split down the middle. Before leaving Atlantic City, we also signed an October 1 date with the Latin Casino in Philadelphia, getting double the price. Despite the money, Greshler expressed no great satisfaction over the billing, which listed Dean in the top spot and me as the extra-added attraction.

"You can blame this on Perry," he told me during a breakfast meeting at one of the boardwalk cafés.

I shrugged. "Well, it's not the worst thing in the world."

"Maybe not. But it's lousy. He'd better get his head out of the clouds, or everything's liable to go down the drain."

"Stop with the gloom," I replied; "nothing bad is gonna happen. Besides, I don't have any conflicts with Dean."

We looked at each other in silence. Then he said, "All right. I'll get Perry in line. Leave it to me."

So I went on my way, feeling the two of them would clear things up without much difficulty.

Now it's September. Business is booming at the Havana Madrid, but I'm seeing less and less of Perry while Greshler and Dean are spending more and more time together.

In October, toward the tail end of our Latin Casino engagement, Perry came into my dressing room. He said he no longer represented Dean, wished me luck and quietly went out. When the door closed, I sat for a while, remembering how he had pulled Dean through rough times, keeping the bill collectors off his back, and so forth. But I can't say I was sorry for the man. When Greshler offered him a lot of money to buy up Dean's contract, he took it. He threw in the towel without much fight. It was as though all the shared experiences, the solemn promises and the easy laughs had never existed.

So Perry was gone, and that October, as the billing of

Martin and Lewis went up on a nightclub marquee for the first time, at long last I had nothing to think of, to remember or to care about. I had my partner, I had big money coming in and I knew there'd be still greater times ahead.

In downtown Philadelphia there was a tailor shop that attracted many show people looking to buy custom-made clothes.

"Why do we have to get into tuxedos?" Dean was saying as we strolled along Walnut Street toward the shop.

"Are you kidding? If you go to the Bowery, you can always find someone in a gray suit lying in the gutter. That isn't funny. But *we'll* be funny if we're wearing tuxedos. You get it? They always howl when the rich guy falls on his ass."

He shot me a suspicious glance. "How rich do you think we should look, pal?"

The shop was in front of us. "Don't panic," I said. "It'll be over in a minute."

The tailor pulled a bolt of fabric from the shelf. He rolled it open on his worktable. "The finest mohair, gentlemen. Feel the material."

Dean ran his hand over it. "Not bad. How much are you getting for this?"

"Well, depending on the cut, like a plain or silk collar, the lining, with or without pockets—"

I stopped him short. "Let me explain. We want two tuxedos, made exactly the same. Rolled silk collars and a one-button front. As for the lining—waddya think, Dean—what color?"

A limp wave. "Anything you say."

"OK. We'll take blue . . . to match our eyes."

"Excellent. You'll be very pleased with our work. We cater to a discriminating clientele. Why, just the other day Fred Allen came in and ordered five cashmere jackets. A lovely man, wonderful human being . . ."

He was still talking about Fred Allen when the doorbell tinkled. "Excuse me, gentlemen. I'll be right back to take your measurements."

As he turned to greet another customer, Dean pointed to the bolt of material and whispered, "This ain't gonna be cheap."

"For Crissakes, Dean, it's only a tuxedo."

The tailor came back, rubbing his hands. "Well, now, I can have everything ready in two weeks. If you'll follow me, I'll take your sizes."

"I think you forgot something," I said dryly, observing Dean's distressful sighs. "What's it gonna cost?"

"We get two hundred dollars for this fabric."

"Two hundred dollars!" echoed Dean. "That's a lot of money for two tuxedos."

The tailor lowered his glasses to the tip of his nose and peered over them sheepishly. "You don't understand, sir. That's two hundred dollars apiece."

Dean hissed, "With or without the hangers?"

We left the tailor shop and caught a cab back to our hotel. In my pocket there was a receipt for the purchase of four tuxedos. Unknown to Dean, I had ordered the other two so we should have a backup and then kept his in my closet, hanging there in case he tore the one he bought.

The phone rang. I lifted an eyelid and squinted at the alarm clock. It was eight in the morning. Damn. Who would be calling at this hour? I turned the covers back and yanked the phone from its cradle.

My father's voice. "Did I wake you?"

For a moment I couldn't answer. My nerves tightened. In some incomprehensible way I felt guilty, as if everything I had become only made his life more painful, much harder to bear.

"No . . . I was getting up, anyway."

"You sound tired. Should I call back later?"

No, don't call back later. Talk to me now; what is it? What's wrong . . . what's right . . . what's anything?

I said, "I'm up. How are you?"

"Why complain? Listen, your mother and I want to come down to Philly to see the show."

"So come. What show?"

"The dinner show."

"All right. I'll make the reservations."

"Jerry, you'll have a good table for us?"

"Naww, I'm gonna put you in the kitchen."

He paused. "Well . . . wherever."

"Dad, you'll have a table up front, you know that."

"How should I know? You're a big celebrity now. Tens of millions of people are coming to see you—"

"So another two won't hurt. Anyway, how's Ma?"

"Good. She's feeling good."

"Is everything else OK?"

"Sure. Everything's wonderful. I've got four jobs this weekend."

"That's wonderful. Look, I'll see you tonight, and we'll—"

"Jerry?"

I held the phone away from my ear, looked at it, then answered with a slight edge to my voice. "I'm here. What is it?"

"Your mother and I are planning to stay over until tomorrow morning."

"Well . . . you'll stay at my hotel. I'll take care of it. And, uh . . . listen, Pop, if I'm not in my room when you get here, I'll see you after the show."

"We're leaving on the two-thirty train. Do you think you'll be at the hotel around five?"

I was dying to get off. "I don't know. I have to check with Dean. There's an interview . . ."

"Oh. All right. One way or the other, we'll see you."

He hung up.

I lay back, turned my head and stared at the window for a long time, searching for anything to look at but myself.

After closing in Philadelphia, it was on to New York and the Loew's State Theatre. Then in February we opened at Ben Madden's Riviera nightclub in Fort Lee, New Jersey, filling over a thousand seats every night straight into the summer.

Now, on a particularly beautiful afternoon, I stood on the beach in Atlantic City, one hand cupped over my eyes to block out the sun, and listened to the drone of a single-engine plane. It flew by, trailing a long banner which read: THE 500 CLUB WELCOMES HOME MARTIN AND LEWIS.

I chased it for a mile. I ran along the water's edge, yelping and cheering and pointing to the sky. "Hey! Look! That's me! That's me!"

[4]

Among all the nightclubs in the world, the Copacabana was the most legendary. Here were the famed Copa girls and star-studded acts. Here on any given night came the movie idols, the prominent athletes, the gangsters and high-society people—all here, looking to be seen, to be mentioned and gossiped about. And now the thrill of Martin and Lewis being added to the long list of great entertainers who'd played the Copa began to envelop me.

Mainly, there was this feverish belief that our act would go over bigger than ever in front of the New York sophisticates. To Greshler's credit, he believed it, too. Brazenness, cunning, mental toughness, willpower—those were his weapons, and he used them to the hilt on Monte Proser, who produced the Copa shows. Proser had scouted us at the Havana Madrid. He was not overwhelmed. I guess he figured the cost of his crockery was too high to risk having Dean and me around. But Greshler finally convinced him that we'd bring in enough business not only to pay for the breakage but buy a hefty piece of the Wedgwood china factory besides. Anyway, the little sonofagun got us booked as a nonstarring act under main attraction Vivian Blaine, a singer-comedienne who would score heavily later on in the hit musical *Guys and Dolls*.

One thing was certain. By now I had accumulated a substantial sum of money, and as soon as I learned the Copa appearance had been set, I made it over to Saks Fifth Avenue, dropped a fast five thousand dollars on presents, then rushed home to my Lehigh Avenue apartment in Newark, happier than a pig in shit.

And there was Patti, bent over the tub scrubbing Gary with a washcloth.

"Hi, darling. Be with you in a second." She cooed at Gary. "Daddy's home. . . . Oh, look at the big box with the pretty red ribbon."

"It ain't bad stuff in there," I said. "It's for you, sweetheart."

"Jerry—I can't imagine. What a surprise."

"Yep. I'm full of surprises."

She took the box into the living room. I reached down, tussling Gary's soapy hair, gloating with pleasure.

Now the expected cry. "I can't believe it! A mink coat!"

I plucked Gary from the tub, wrapped him in a towel and stood watching as she held the coat, softly brushing the fur, nestling her cheek against it as though the most inconceivable joy had just flooded through her.

"So that's why you've been gone all afternoon. Not a word, nothing said—you're too much, do you know that?"

"Yeah. Well, aren't you going to try it on?"

She whirled around like a fashion model. "It's gorgeous. It must be worth a fortune."

"What fortune? You're my fortune. Boy, I can't wait to see you wearing it at the Copa on opening night."

There was a pause, and a shush. The happy squeals of Gary as we folded our arms about him.

My whole body tingled with anticipation. In a few minutes the cue would start us down the aisle and onto the Copa stage.

Will they like us? It was my only thought as I opened the kitchen door a crack and peeked out at the crowd. A snarl of bodies, silverware rattling and champagne corks popping, waiters maneuvering from table to table holding trays aloft like acrobats on a tightrope. My father and mother were out there, also Patti, Irving Kaye, Greshler, Betty Martin, a host of relatives and friends—all waiting in the dimness.

Dean came up to me, grinning easily.

I said, "If we're gonna sneak out of here, now's the time."

"Any other ideas?"

"Well, I just hope we're ready for the Copa."

"You got it backwards. What you mean is, is the Copa ready for us?"

We did fifty minutes, going far over our allotted time. They wouldn't let us off. There was no doubt about it; if they could give that kind of response, then the whole world would respond. As we made our exit, hearing a last deafening roar, I yelled at Dean, "Get ready for the plane trip!"

Poor Vivian Blaine. She tried valiantly to overcome all the excitement that charged around the room, but it was

no use. Nobody could have followed us. She cut two numbers from her act and left the stage in tears.

A couple of minutes later a hundred or more people were
waiting to get into our dressing room. Between embraces,
kisses and handshakes, Monte Proser stuck his head in the
door and spoke to Greshler for a moment.

"What was that all about?" Dean wanted to know.

Greshler seemed puzzled. "We have to be in Proser's
office as soon as the crowd clears out."

He was shaking his head from side to side while staring
down at his desk. "I'd be a damned fool if I did nothing
about this show. It's coming off all wrong."

Greshler stiffened. "Wrong? Why, my guys took three
encores, standing ovations—where the hell did they go
wrong?"

"It's not them I'm talking about," Proser muttered, still
looking down. "Vivian Blaine is the problem. After what
happened tonight, there's no way for her to headline. So I'm
going with Martin and Lewis. I'm putting her in the opening slot." He looked up. "We'll talk tomorrow. Meanwhile,
I have to break the news to Vivian."

I tore my gaze from Proser and glanced at Dean. He had
a pipe stuck in his mouth, sucking it noisily and doing Eddie
Cantor bits with his eyes.

"Really, Mr. Proser," I stammered gleefully, "that's terrific, getting top billing and all—but a nice person like
Vivian Blaine . . . I feel bad about her."

He lifted a hand. "Nightclubs are nightclubs, and business is business. You have to give the customers what they
want; otherwise, you've got nothing to look forward to
except unemployment. In any event, I'll make up a new
contract for you boys. Don't worry, it'll be a good one."

It was our town. We owned it. We had everything but

the keys to the city, and I'm sure that could've been arranged if Abbey Greshler had placed a call to Mayor O'Dwyer. So a completely indescribable head-swelling time had begun. What with the Copa salary and doubling at the Roxy Theatre between the supper and midnight shows, my income had now soared to $7,500 a week. Offers came flooding in from top radio and television shows that wanted us as guest stars, and the finest nightclubs in America were bidding for our services. So were the people who held powerful positions in the motion picture industry.

Among them was Hal Wallis, a former studio chief at Warner Brothers. He had just formed his own company under the Paramount banner. He was a serious-minded, cultivated man, as I learned the night Greshler brought him to our suite above the Copa. After the niceties, he presented a rather detailed account of the films that bore his administrative stamp, almost all high adventure films starring the likes of Humphrey Bogart, James Cagney, Paul Muni, Gary Cooper, Errol Flynn—and who could ever forget *They Died with Their Boots On?* Then he got to the point. He wanted to do less of the dramatic stuff and had optioned a few properties with comedy themes.

"Unfortunately," he said, "none of the story lines calls for the kind of humor I saw tonight. But that doesn't mean we can't have something written."

Dean and I grunted.

Wallis continued, rising from his chair, "Let me give it some thought. We have marvelous writers, fellows who can shape characters to fit your style perfectly."

Dean said, "Good. Take your time, because the only thing that Jerry and I want is to be shown off right."

"Of course. I'm glad we agree." He looked at his watch. "Well, I must catch a plane back to Los Angeles first thing tomorrow morning. So if you'll excuse me . . ."

"Sure," said Dean. "It's been a pleasure. Hope to see you again."

"Yeah, me, too," I said airily, then went to the door to show Wallis out.

He hesitated. "I assure you, we're going to make a movie together. And soon."

If I remember anything, it's the blank expressions Dean and I displayed as the three of us said our good-byes. But the moment Wallis left, I leaped into Dean's arms, hollering, "This is it! We're going to Hollywood!"

And we both jumped up on the couch, laughing hysterically. The biggest thrill of our lives.

The Alfred Dunhill salesman placed a selection of gold cigarette lighters on the glass-topped counter. "I believe you'll find these to your satisfaction, Mr. Lewis."

An ultrathin number caught my eye. "Hm. How much?"

He inspected the little white tag. "This one is eighty-nine fifty."

"All right. I'll take thirty of them. With inscriptions. How fast can you get it done?"

"Oh, my. Well . . . will tomorrow be convenient?"

"Sensational!" I wrote out a check. "Now, I'd like to buy some cigars."

"Yes, sir, Mr. Lewis. The humidor room is on the second floor. The elevator is right behind you—"

I stepped into the room, with its gleaming mahogany floors, its paneled walls, its long rows of humidor bins affixed with bronzed plates, and the names: Winston Churchill, Groucho Marx, George Burns, Bernard Baruch, Nelson Rockefeller. . . .

The salesman came over. "May I help you?"

I pointed to the bins. "Do you have an empty one?"

"Well, yes . . . there's a rental fee, of course—and a two-hundred-dollar minimum order."

"No problem. My friend smokes that up in an hour. So we'd better make it a lifetime deal."

He gave me a curious smile. "As you wish. Now, what did you have in mind, sir?"

"I want the best Cuban cigars in the house. Big and juicy —like a dill pickle."

I ordered twenty-five boxes to get Irving Kaye started. The total bill, including some last-minute shopping in the luggage department, brought the whole megillah to $4,200. Sure, there I was at twenty-two, already owning two Cadillacs and a Jaguar XKE, and spending more on others than myself. Gold watches, bracelets, lighters, rings . . . it's easy to dump a ton of cash that way. But it didn't matter. I was feeling high and mighty and unstoppable, like a kid holding a fistful of tickets to the amusement park. I couldn't wait to try all the rides.

Meanwhile, Dean was having his own fun, playing golf out on Long Island and taking Betty to the best places, also throwing big parties at their swell ten-room apartment on Riverside Drive. Soon after they moved in, Patti and I were given the grand tour. What I remember most was that first look at Dean's bedroom closet, every square foot filled with handmade suits and tuxedos, racks and racks of shoes, ceiling-to-floor shelves containing imported silk shirts and cashmere sweaters—we'd come a long way and awfully fast since that day when Dean blanched at the thought of buying a two-hundred-dollar tux.

I caught him in a rare reflective mood. We talked for a while. At one point he said, "Betty's pregnant again. I hope it's another boy." Then a faint smile played on his lips. "Anyway, I'm planning to make this into a real home for her and the kids . . . sort of permanent, y'know."

Dreams and smoke, the human condition. As it happened, he didn't turn out to be the family man of Betty's dreams. He was and, as far as I know, still is a master of illusion. No one ever got to know him, not even Betty, because in those days I believe the only one he allowed in was me.

When he smiled everything was beautiful; he understood that I looked up to him as a big brother. He enjoyed playing the role.

Which now reminds me of an incident that took place in the Copa lounge. We were killing time until the midnight show. Dean was having a light conversation with the maître d' while I ran around getting laughs from the bar crowd. Suddenly above the yaks and cackles I heard this gruff-sounding voice: "Why don't you knock off that shit and be quiet?"

I halted in my tracks. A real bull. I figured he was either kidding or too drunk to appreciate who I was. So I threw him a stock line. "That's what happens when cousins get married!"

Now I see Dean wincing, and the maître d' has his head in his hands.

The bull slowly rose from his chair, snorted, sauntered up and stuck his finger under my nose. "That's not funny, you stupid sonofabitch. If you open your mouth once more, it'll be without your teeth."

I fell back three paces.

Dean came between us, trying to calm him down. "My partner is a little young. He didn't mean any harm—"

The guy paused. "Yeah, well . . ."

Given the breather, Dean grabbed my sleeve and pulled me aside. "Now, Jer, just say to the man that you're sorry, and it won't happen again. OK?"

I wagged my head, as contrite as I'd ever been in my life.

At which time he said to Dean, "OK. Only, you keep the little bastard away from me. Tell him he's lucky I've got a sense of humor."

A moment later Dean whispered in my ear, "For your information, schmuck, that was Albert Anastasia."

We did our midnight show, playing to an audience that included Mr. Anastasia, the Lord High Executioner of Murder Incorporated; Mafia chieftain Frank Costello; and other assorted underworld characters. I couldn't see them in the darkness, but I swear I could feel Anastasia's cold steel eyes hitting me like bullets throughout the performance.

[5]

If you are my age, it's a safe bet you'll remember 1948 as a year when television altered your life. Maybe you went to a neighborhood bar never before frequented, just to sit and drink a couple of beers while staring up at a magnified ten-inch screen beaming the Friday-night fights live and direct from Madison Square Garden. Or you had a rich uncle, the last guy on earth anybody would want to visit, except he was the only relative with a set, so on Sunday nights you were there anyhow to catch all those great new television variety shows.

Remember the first time you saw them? Of this I'm positive—if any two variety programs from those days come back to mind, then you've gotta say it was Ed Sullivan's "Toast of the Town" and the "Texaco Star Theatre," starring Milton Berle.

On June 20, 1948, the "Toast of the Town" gave its premiere showing. In a merry-go-round of talent, Dean and I appeared. Six minutes of hoofing, singing and sweating through the jokes, literally, because when we came off the makeup had melted down our collars from the high-intensity lights.

Later that year Martin and Lewis hit their stride on the "Texaco Star Theatre." Rehearsals started early one Sunday morning at the Henry Hudson Hotel ballroom on Fifty-seventh Street and Ninth Avenue. I got there before Dean, walking in to see Milton Berle, seemingly lost in thought, pacing back and forth with a red beret on his head, a thick towel wound around his neck and a corded whistle in his mouth.

A bunch of his people stood waiting for him to acknowledge them, making little sighs and whispered comments, some wandering from one spot to the other slurping coffee out of paper cups. Finally, this guy came over, saying he was Jay Burton, a writer for the show.

"What's Milton doing with the whistle?" I asked.

"He uses it to save his voice."

Milton stopped pacing. He turned toward me. At the same instant Dean ambled into the ballroom. His first words were thrown at Milton.

"Are we gonna be doing a show or playing football for you?"

Tweet-tweet—then, "Hi, fellas. C'mon, I'll introduce you to the rest of my crew."

A minute or so later he had us sitting on chairs at the far end of the ballroom. And sure enough, like Knute Rockne during halftime in the Notre Dame locker room, he made with the old pep talk. "We have a timed show here, boys. Tighter than my Aunt Jenny's corset. In other words, fellas, you must stick to eight minutes. Not ten. Not nine. I'm talking about eight minutes—on the nose. You got it?"

I looked at him. "Sure, Milton."

"Good. No ad-libbing."

"No ad-libbing."

"No extra schtick—"

Dean: "We got it, Milton. Eight minutes."

So Tuesday night comes and the cameras begin rolling. I tell you, we almost drove Milton Berle nuts. He couldn't move an inch without us being right there, climbing all over him. When he mugged or tried a joke, we'd mug and get the bigger laugh. And every time he tried to introduce the next piece of business, Dean would say something like, "Hold your horses, I'm not finished talking!" In a flash tap routine we left him in the dust, and for the coup de grace, just before a commercial break with Berle gasping for breath, standing slouched and helpless for the cutaway, I leaped in front of the camera, stuck my head smack into the lens and screamed, "Milton Berle! Big deal!"

It took him a while to get over it. But I guess in his heart he knew how much respect we had for him, even though his straight-faced good-bye after the telecast was, "When you maniacs are ready for a comeback, don't call me, call Bellevue."

Nowadays, of course, I occasionally see Milton in California or at one of the Strip hotels when we're both working Vegas. There's always a friendly embrace, always that warm pinch on the cheek. Then Milton will say, "Jerry, no ad-libs, no ad-libs."

Not long after the Texaco show, our nightclub scene extended to the West Coast, there to play Slapsie Maxie's in the heart of Los Angeles's Miracle Mile. And to designate any single place as the most fateful one, then Slapsie Maxie's stands out as the turning point, as the one that made all the difference.

There was a long roaring train ride across the continent, through towns and villages, wide endless fields, mountains that soared into the western clouds . . . Dean, Abbey Greshler, Irving Kaye and myself comfortably fixed in our first-class compartments, four nights and five days of playing cards, reading, sleeping and eating, and finally peering out the train window as we came chugging into the Pasadena station, each a little groggy but feeling a thrill of anticipation.

Mention the name George Evans to any publicity man worth his salt, and he'll tell you there was none better, none more creative. To wit: When Frank Sinatra was singing with the Tommy Dorsey band, it was Evans who rounded up the bobby-soxers and sent them into the Paramount Theatre, free—so long as they swooned all over the place for Frank.

Leave it to Greshler; he hired Evans to brew the same kind of magic for me and Dean, starting immediately upon our arrival in California. Well, after the great buildup, I was dying to meet this legendary Mandrake. But as we stepped off the train, Greshler turned to Irving and said, "See if you can find Jack Keller."

"Who's Jack Keller?"

"He's George's man out here. A real dynamo."

Irving headed down the platform, then looked back. "How will I recognize him?"

"First thing you do," said Greshler, "is look for a dynamo."

The next instant I was staring at this parade of press guys who came shouldering through with their cameras flapping, pads and pencils out, a whole mob scene in front of us. Leading the pack was a fat-bellied, unshaven, rheumy-eyed man in a wrinkled suit.

"Greetings," he said, taking a slight bow. "Jack Keller at your service."

As he raised a beefy hand to quiet the press, I jabbed an elbow into Dean's ribs and muttered, "Some dynamo. We come all the way out here to be welcomed by a bum."

Now Keller held both arms up. "OK, boys, here they are! Meet Lewis and Clark!"

He looked at us again, then at the press with affected surprise. "No, it has to be Stanley and Livingstone— O'Keefe and Merritt—Leopold and Loeb—"

My first introduction to Keller. An archetype of cynical masculinity. But he had the tender curiosity of a pussycat, and no man I have ever known possessed greater concern for what others thought and said. This from a former pool hustler and small-time con artist, a saloon character who could drink anyone under the table and walk away on steady legs. This was my friend; in fact, from the very beginning, as close a friend as I would ever hope to have.

Opening night at Slapsie Maxie's, ten minutes before we hit the stage: Dean and I stood behind the curtain, peeking out . . . that sight! The fabulous sight of a Hollywood crowd coming together, filling the room with glamour and chic; all that make-believe aristocracy, all that wealth, power and respectability. People in lounging attitudes at the bar, people sitting on top of the bar, people everywhere. I saw it, felt the whole huge meaning of it, right here, now, before a roll call of the most famous names in entertainment. Cary Grant and Joan Crawford arguing over a table, and Humphrey Bogart hollering, "I had a reservation!" while Edward G. Robinson sits peaceful as an owl with Bette Davis shouting indignantly into his ear, demanding that he get the hell out of her seat! And there's Ronald Reagan with Jane Wyman, the Jimmy Stewarts, the gaunt figure of Gary Cooper stooping over a ringside table . . . John Garfield looking up at him, syndicated columnist Louella Parsons trying to catch their attention. And I also recognized producers Sam Goldwyn, Darryl Zanuck, Jerry Wald—Hal Wallis!

To watch all that was once in a lifetime.

Then we went on and knocked them dead.

The next night you couldn't get into the club. Management was turning away five to six hundred people at each show, night after night. Such doings. The waiters were cleaning up—I mean, they were getting fifty bucks a head in tips, and I know some who made twenty-five thousand a week! And that's the truth.

Additionally, a million-dollar house band made our two-month stay at Slapsie Maxie's an easy romp. They grooved to the nonsense, intuitively followed every sudden idea, every improvised song or rhythm change of a dance routine, carrying us through perfectly, never missing a beat or a note.

Dick Stabile led the aggregation, which included his younger brother Joe, both of them first-magnitude sax players, and marvelous guys to boot. That was another fortunate break, because out of it came a long and fruitful association. During the next eight years, Dick's incomparable bandleading genius gave strength and substance to whatever we did musically in clubs, television and motion pictures. As for Joe, he put his saxophone aside in 1964 to become my business manager. He's still at it, my right arm and confidant, always there with his protection, love and loyalty. What more can a man ask?

But in recalling those fun-packed nights at Slapsie Maxie's, what's also relevant is that the euphoric lift was tempered by a change which began to affect Dean and Betty's marriage.

Jeanne Beiggers had come into Dean's life the previous winter, while we were down in Florida working the Beachcomber Club. She was nineteen then, blonde, beautiful, a reigning Queen of the Orange Bowl, not the sort of girl you'd overlook in a crowd. New Year's night, after the football game, she made an onstage appearance, taking a bow as Dean presented her with a bouquet of flowers. Love at first sight, they say, only I didn't know it until Jeanne showed up at the Copa, sitting ringside all starry-eyed, with Dean looking at her the same way.

They were together now in Los Angeles, head over heels

in secret love, keeping a safe distance from the prying eyes of Louella Parsons, Hedda Hopper and the other Hollywood hounds who at this point had picked up the starlit trail of Martin and Lewis: *Jerry Lewis whirling around town in wild shopping spree . . . Dean Martin finds Bel Air Country Club golf links to his liking. . . . Film producer Hal Wallis sets plans with Martin and Lewis for the team's first movie. . . . Betty Martin names the new baby Deana, waits breathlessly for Dean's return to New York City. . . .* Ah, Hollywood!

Hal Wallis more than made good on his promise, signing us to a long-term contract: Seven pictures in a five-year period at a hundred thousand dollars a picture. On top of that, he permitted us to free-lance one "outside" film a year. Abbey Greshler went right to work on the "outside" film. He believed he could induce a couple of well-heeled friends from Chicago to bankroll a company so we'd have the means to produce films on our own. The plan sounded better and better by the minute, for Greshler had this gift, a captivating and thrilling way of presenting things; here it was to draw us into believing we'd soon be the world's richest millionaires.

We swallowed the whole idea like two guppies in a feed pond and never saw the sharks. As chief officers of York Productions, Dean and I controlled most of the stock and were to receive a huge portion of the net profits. On the other hand, besides his normal agent's fee, we agreed to appoint Greshler executive producer of York films. Fine and dandy. Except it didn't work out so hot, considering that we didn't make a quarter from *At War with the Army,* our first York release. It seems Greshler neglected to tell us the difference between net and gross profits, among other things.

[6]

We went back to Philadelphia for another four-week stand at the Latin Casino, then returned to the West Coast for movie rehearsals. It was the beginning of a dark period of heartache for Betty Martin, which was brought on by the romance between Dean and Jeanne Beiggers. It also upset Patti no end because of her warm friendship with Betty.

"I don't understand," Patti was saying in our Philadelphia hotel room. "How could Dean do this to Betty?"

"What are you talking about?"

"You know perfectly well—sure as you're born. Don't deny it. He's been seeing this girl. Betty told me."

"I don't know about any girl," I lied.

"Jerry!" she cried suddenly, turning toward me with an exasperated expression. "Will you please talk to him? *Please,* my heart goes out to her—she's just had a baby, for God's sake!"

Something in her eyes. What were they seeing? What fears did they hold?

I said, "Forget it, it's nothin'. Anyway, Dean's personal life is his own affair. It has nothin' to do with you and me."

"Well," she said coldly, "if that's the way it has to be, then I won't have anything more to do with him."

And we sat there silently, weighing our thoughts. Presently I went over to her. "There's one thing I want you to know. If you turn your back on him you're gonna hurt me, because Dean's my friend. Do you understand what that means?"

She made no answer. I repeated the question, only now more emphatically. "Do you?"

And she said, "Yes." Then, in a low, brooding tone, almost lifelessly, "I'll do my best, if that's what you want."

A few minutes later we joined Dean and Betty for dinner,

and if anybody was to see us, they would've thought we were all having a gay old time.

In 1944 the CBS radio network got a new comedy series rolling. It starred Marie Wilson in the role of a dizzy blonde named Irma. Diana Lynn played the sympathetic roommate, and their two boyfriends gave the show a romantic twist. Five years later, with "My Friend Irma" still going strong, Hal Wallis acquired the rights from CBS to produce a movie version, casting Dean and me as the boyfriends.

But first we had to take screen tests. Dean came off fine as Steve Laird, the straitlaced, handsome proprietor of an orange-juice stand. All I had to do was fill the shoes of Al, a wisecracking, blustery type, the sort of character you'd meet at racetracks, which Jack Carson used to play so successfully in Warner Brothers B movies.

I struggled with the script, but the harder I worked at it, the more frustrating it became. I wasn't Al, and I knew it.

On the afternoon of the test they put a hat on my head and stood me before the cameras, saying lines like: "Got a deal for you, chicken—"

George Marshall, the director, tried his darndest to boost me over the hurdle. He repeated the test three times, patiently, not a trace of annoyance showing on his face. "Don't worry," he said. "In the next take, give it some more boldness, a stronger attitude. That's all I'm looking for, Jerry. Can you do that for me?"

"I guess so, Mr. Marshall."

After the fourth take, he slowly shook his head. "All right, let's wrap it."

A moment later we were alone. "Jerry, I'll be honest. It's a mistake to cast you in this role. You're not making it . . . not even *this* close." He spread his arms wide, then dropped them helplessly to his sides.

I grinned off stupidly. Then a pitiful request. "Mr. Marshall, tell me, what am I gonna do?"

A wan smile. "Look, we'll wait till tonight. Let's see the test. Maybe we can spot something that can turn this around."

That night I sat in the Paramount screening room with Marshall, Hal Wallis and screenwriter Cy Howard, creator of the original "My Friend Irma." They all watched, sitting together in a middle row, while I slouched down on a backseat beneath the whirring projector.

When it was over, you could hear a pin drop. They knew I had failed, that I had come off like an idiot.

I phoned Patti, who was still back in Newark, preparing to come out with Gary and take a look at the many pretty houses available for rent in Beverly Hills.

"How did it go, honey?"

"I loused it up. The test was terrible. You shoulda seen the faces. I'm comin' home, Esther. I'll pack in the morning—"

"Can't you give it another try? Maybe another test will change things."

"No, nothing will help. I'm just not cutting it."

Her voice got firmer. "Since when are you a quitter?"

The following morning I went to see Cy Howard at his office on the Paramount lot. We kicked the problem around and a couple of hours later created a new character named Seymour. I named him after the bike I had owned as a kid. And Seymour was the same kid Hal Wallis had caught at the Copa, the same one Cy Howard and George Marshall saw when they were at Slapsie Maxie's. What finally nailed the movie role was the scene in which I'm introduced as the eager, peripatetic nut hired by Steve Laird to help him run the orange-juice stand. Maybe you'll remember . . . a million oranges squeezed in a minute and a half.

That's what made it happen. I played myself, a mischievous nine-year-old kid. And from then on, with rare exception, I was never anything other than that on the screen.

To state it truly, I must've been almost out of my head with excitement when Patti answered the phone and heard all the crowing: "I passed the test! Get on the train! Tomorrow! You and Gary are gonna be staying out here a long time!"

A week later we rented a Spanish stucco house on Tower Road in Beverly Hills, at about the same time that Dean secured a Tudor-style residence for Betty and the kids, close to the Bel Air Country Club golf course. So there we were, the Lewises and the Martins. And those early years of unrelieved brooding, of deep doubts, the wonder and fear of who I was or where I would be going at last seemed completely behind me. I was actually living in circumstances far surpassing anything I had ever dreamed of. Now I could lavish my dreams on Patti, take her into the swellest stores so she could choose whatever her heart desired. I was happy just sitting down to write out the checks.

But if Dean was also going through that phase with Betty, nevertheless, he continued to feel ambivalent about their marriage, his responsibility to her and his increasing desire to see a lot more of Jeanne Beiggers.

Now, many years and events later, I'm not going to say anything further concerning the difficulties which finally led to Dean's divorce, except there were no great mysteries involved. Slings and arrows aside, it was really a simple case of incompatibility. As a matter of fact, the only thing that failed here was human nature, the incapacity of most people to truly understand themselves. And if you don't believe that, then you haven't studied philosophy.

Anyway, came September of 1949 and Dean married Jeanne Beiggers. The wedding took place at the home of Herman Hover, owner of a Sunset Strip nitery called Ciro's.

I was best man. Patti attended, though somewhat reluctantly, still smarting from the hurt she felt for Betty.

Good times, bad times.

My Friend Irma was about to open at hundreds of movie houses everywhere in the USA. A whopping advertising and promotion campaign had been set. Hal Wallis arranged a national tour—the kickoff at New York's Paramount Theatre. Dean and I signed to do six shows a day there during the first week of *Irma*'s run.

Due to accumulated pressure while making the movie and the tension over Dean's domestic problems, I decided to take an early train out, anxious to have a homecoming reunion with Buddy Hackett, Lenny Kent, Jan Murray and some other guys I'd been tight with before everything started to happen at the Copa. I could hardly wait to see their faces. There were so many Hollywood stories to recount, so many scenes to recreate over endless cups of coffee at Hanson's drugstore. . . .

Indian summer. Manhattan. I'm crammed into a Penn Station phone booth, sweating my ass off while cursing at the mouthpiece because not one friend has picked up on my calls. Finally, whacking the phone against the cradle, I stepped from the booth, then trudged up a flight of marble stairs out to the glary streets. A half-hour later, alone in a sumptuous suite at the Sherry Netherlands Hotel, the frustration really started to grind. Weary as hell, I collapsed into a dead sleep with my clothes on.

Now, late afternoon, under a refreshing shower, I figured there would be enough time to raise Buddy and the rest of the guys for a great party at Lindy's that night. All the while I'm scheming up practical jokes to play on them, and thinking, too, of the surprised looks when they received their presents. . . .

So once more I give Buddy a call. Again, no answer.

Down the list it goes. Incredible. Mothers and fathers answer, children answer, wives and girl friends answer, but not a single person has any idea where my pals are. No, they're all out and can't be reached.

The air was stuffy as I walked along Sixth Avenue, staring vacantly at people who passed me by, some turning their heads in recognition, some calling my name before moving on and getting swallowed in the lights. Suddenly, there was Radio City Music Hall, the marquee a blaze of red neon, the crowds standing behind ropes, smiling, exchanging pleasantries and waiting eagerly to be let inside.

"Do you wish to see the movie, Mr. Lewis?"

I peered at the usher—young and skinny—seeing myself in a uniform just like his only six or seven years ago. "Sure. Uh, listen, can you get me a ticket so I don't have to stand in line?"

I fished some change from my pocket. He was back in a flash with the ticket. A moment later I rode an elevator up to the balcony section, got off, stumbled to a seat in the last row and watched a picture called *Bandwagon*. But after a while the technicolor screen broke and shifted into a million scattered lights. I reached for my wallet and began thumbnailing the crisp stack of bills, thirty of them in hundred-dollar denominations. And I thought: if this is what it's like to be a star, then who needs it?

The next day I dropped into Hanson's drugstore. The place was filled. At one of the tables sat Buddy Hackett, Jan Murray and Milt Frome. I walked up to them. "Hey, where were you guys last night?"

Milt gave a double take. "Jerry Lewis! Grab a chair, *chatzkele*. Sit down."

Then Jan spoke up. "Where were we? What a question. Why didn't you tell us you were coming in? Last we heard, you and Dean weren't due for another few days."

"Yeah," Buddy giggled. "We thought you were still out

there, celebrating your success with the big-shot Hollywood stars, and drinking champagne, and getting to all kinds of wild parties with beautiful starlets. Heh heh heh . . ."

"No lie," chimed in Milt. "Admit it, Jerry. I bet it feels great to be doing all that. It's certainly a lot better than working the mountains in front of fat old ladies and drinking Dr. Brown's Cel-Ray."

Gradually, they stopped the ribbing. Then we began swapping jokes, carrying on like nothing had changed. They acted as though I was still the same nutty kid.

Just before I left, I gave each of them a gold identification bracelet.

But I didn't tell them I had spent the previous evening at Radio City Music Hall, all alone in the balcony, eating caramel corn which kept getting stuck in my molar.

The long Broadway stretch glistening with sunlight; crossroads of America full of people. Dean and I at an open window looking down at the cheering crowds, smiling back at them and waving and drinking in the frenzied intensity of all those fans who've gathered in some indefinable way to give us this moment—hard to express—we feel as if tears are about to burst from our eyes, and could kiss the world and laugh until everyone in it without exception is laughing right along with us. That's how it was the whole gorgeous afternoon on that September day when *My Friend Irma* opened at the New York Paramount.

And that's what good publicity is all about.

The reviews helped, too: *Martin and Lewis . . . effervescent, beguiling, ridiculous, sublime, maddening, slick, sharp, infectious, downright zany, brilliantly funny, simply something else again . . .*

Essentially meaning: the dailies and trades thought we did pretty good. *My Friend Irma* was a box-office smash, raking in a fortune for Paramount and putting our names up in lights.

Around then we also entered into negotiations with each of the three major television networks, being that we were hot to trot in that direction for a proper reason.

Because earlier that year Dean and I went on the air with a tightly structured radio show sponsored by Chesterfield. Among the guests: Tallulah Bankhead, Bing Crosby, Bob Hope, Jack Benny, George Raft; some were nervous, not knowing what to expect from us—

As example, we had Ann Sothern on the show. She shook so badly the microphone picked up her trembling. We had to put rugs under her feet.

Not Tallulah, though. What a contrast! Right from the beginning she let us know there would be no cocking around—"Otherwise, gentlemen, you can go fuck yourselves"—that's the kind of gal she was.

After ten weeks, Chesterfield canceled us. Our first professional bomb. No excuses, we had it coming. For one thing, sticking to the script cramped our style. And secondly, Dean went a little overboard—at a time when most sponsors were very conservative, frowning on any entertainer who would dare poke fun or make light of his association with the product.

Chesterfield certainly fell into this category. When Dean persisted in smoking a pipe or Lucky Strike cigarettes before a studio audience of three hundred people, the account exec's hair follicles rose higher and higher. The hard fact, as I see it, is that this was the reason why Chesterfield decided not to renew our contract.

But with the success of *Irma,* who needed radio?

Yes. Our luck was holding, and we kept rolling along at an insane pace.

[7]

I bought a California ranch house on North Amalfi Drive in Pacific Palisades. A dream house, with toddler swings in the backyard, a swimming pool, lemon and orange trees. Rooms enough to raise an army of kids. And oh, God, did we want kids. But after our firstborn, Patti was told by a number of doctors that she couldn't have any more. It was horrible. Neither of us accepted it. Then she underwent several operations and finally proved the doctors wrong.

So life goes. Between operations we adopted a baby, another boy, whom we named Ronnie. Now, as I remember the day when we brought him home, seeing all that sweetness bundled up in Patti's arms, seeing Gary constantly peeking at his face, awestruck, so incredibly happy to know he had a little brother, just then I saw nothing else.

One evening our new friend Tony Curtis dropped by, and we chewed the fat but mostly stuck to the subject of movies. He wanted to break away from the inane pretty-boy roles foisted upon him by his producers at Universal. . . . "Truth is, Jerry, I'm sick of wearing tight uniforms and having to look so damned honorable all the time. But those guys don't listen. They can't see me playing something nutty for a change."

Well, it was perfectly obvious that Tony had a natural bent for comedy. So I said, "Tell you what, I'll write a funny part for you, and we'll make a movie right here."

"You mean a home movie?"

"Exactly."

He grinned. "Very good. Long as I get star billing."

"Sure, Tony. Anything for a pal."

I was highly interested in the technical aspects of filmmaking, already owning a wide range of professional cameras, plus elaborate sound and editing equipment. So the next morning I began putting down cinematic ideas on paper. Strictly satirical stuff, literally an exercise in fun.

The initial effort was entitled *Fairfax Avenue* (reborn out of Billy Wilder's *Sunset Boulevard*), featuring Tony, Janet Leigh, Jeff Chandler, Vince Edwards, John Barrymore, Jr., Shelley Winters and about everyone else in our tight-knit group. After that we did *A Streetcar Named Repulsive, Come Back, Little Shiksa, Son of Spellbound, Watch on the Lime* and *The Re-Enforcer,* a twelfth-rate detective story with Dean himself playing the arch-criminal Legs Lasagna, whose best lines were: "Send up-a da broads," and, "I wanna talk-a to my lawyer . . . Seymour."

We made another movie that ran behind schedule because Errol Flynn grabbed the maid's buttocks, then tried to make a three-point landing on her bones.

After completing each movie, we'd pull ourselves together and hold a gala premiere, the likes of which you'd witness only at the plushest Hollywood openings. On my front lawn, a battery of revolving klieg lights that stabbed the night sky; at the curb, scores of limousines jammed bumper to bumper, hundreds of guests following a red carpet through a roped entryway leading into a spacious playhouse I had built in back of the house especially for such occasions. I'll tell you, those were the days, unlike any I ever had before or since.

Those antique films are stored under wraps among hefty piles of scripts, notes, sketches and undeveloped story lines. They contain some wonderful lessons, so many good things that I didn't know were good at the time. Yet there's no need to look at them again, because I would be embarrassed now to see how amateurish they really were.

Still, the things I did while in the company of my buddies were artfully planned so as to win over their loyalty and affection—I wished it without actually realizing what I might have to give up in return. At the time, I was Charlie Moviestar in beautiful real life. Everything around me seemed like a ripe plum ready to be picked. Many a night I'd get into my XKE Jaguar and speed down Sunset Boulevard, blasting the horn for no particular reason except to feel monumentally important. And all the nameless nobodies on both sides of the street would watch me shooting through, looking swell, insanely handsome and maybe a little bit stupid, for all I know.

That night, driving along with Jeff Chandler—Brooklyn-born and pegged for stardom off his performance in *Broken Arrow* as the Apache chief, Cochise—sitting there next to me when suddenly in the glittering swirl of traffic he said, "You should catch the Will Mastin Trio, they're breaking it up at Ciro's."

I nodded, recalling the act, which I had seen at Loew's State, Mickey Rooney topping the bill and the Will Mastin Trio opening. They did a solid ten-minute turn. Best of all —the kid in the middle, out there dancing on atomic feet, then git-gat-gittling a Danny Kaye number so perfectly I would've sworn Danny himself was up there in blackface . . . So I go to Ciro's with Jeff, and after the show he brings me backstage to meet his friend—you guessed it— Sammy Davis, Jr.

And after we met, our own chemistries took over.

Away from the club, with its dressing-room atmosphere of gushing sentimentalities, Sam and I got to know each other well. There were serious talks, months of real closeness. I loved Sammy. At the emotional center of it all I could see his problem clearly. A problem of circumstance —born black in white America.

One night at my house I had him look in the mirror. He looked hard and long. Then a grim smile as he turned around. "Well . . ."

I said, "You're black, Sam. Nothing is gonna change

that. And if anybody tries to make you feel that's bad, let it be *their* problem. Besides, I wouldn't have you any other way."

It's important to remember how tough it really was for black entertainers in those days. As late as 1950, they were not permitted on the casino floor of the Vegas hotels. They had to come in at the stage-door entrance and go out the same way—an insufferable policy which I became aware of and fully understood only while Dean and I were playing the Sands.

We had the Step Brothers on the bill with us, Prince Spencer, Masso, Flash and Al Williams—a great act, brilliant dancers and a favorite of the crowds. On the second night after we opened, I stopped by their dressing room to say hello. It was hot as hell in there, absolutely stifling. "Hey, you guys," I said, "why don't you take a breather? Go out and have some dinner, or something."

Glum expressions. At last Prince Spencer said, "Well, you know, ah . . . we're not allowed."

"You're not allowed? What kind of crap is that?"

"Man . . . aww . . . Jerry, it's the *rules* . . . see, what I'm sayin is, 'cept for the dancin', we ain't nothin' around here."

"Oh, yeah?"

I barged into Jack Entratter's office. He was the Sands entertainment director and, by all means, a man of considerable refinement as well as intelligence. He listened with measured deliberation when I told him about the situation.

"So what are you going to do, Jack?"

"Not a damned thing. I don't set the policy; that's done upstairs."

"Then get it undone."

"Come on, Jer. You gotta be kidding. Half the gamblers

out there are from Texas, Oklahoma, Louisiana, Missis-
sippi—y'understand?"

"Uh-huh. So you go right ahead and ask upstairs if they
want a second show tonight."

"What do you mean?"

I hissed the words out. "I mean, Jack, if the Step Brothers don't have dinner in the hotel dining room, at any table
they pick, you're not getting Martin and Lewis onstage
tonight or any other night."

I walked to the door, hesitated, then looked back at him.
"One more thing. I'm sure you won't mind them gambling
in the casino if they want."

That was the breakthrough, because in quick order the
Step Brothers were given carte blanche to eat, drink and
gamble at the hotel like everybody else. Meanwhile, my
name went on the Sands "shit list" until the boys upstairs
saw that business pumped along as usual, indeed got even
better with Dean and me playing there, which goes to prove
the Almighty Buck answereth all things.

Martin and Lewis was a money machine that seemed
never to break down. Money poured in from nightclubs,
radio, television, personal appearances at arenas and audi-
toriums crisscrossing the nation, and from making the
sequel to *Irma* (*My Friend Irma Goes West*), besides doing *At War with the Army*.

Plenty of pockets were getting filled. But there was a
big mysterious hole in our own.

In a nutshell, under Abby Greshler's management Dean
and I went broke.

Today, I have no more understanding of Greshler's maneuverings than I had back then. But I can state unequivo-
cably that getting rid of him was the smartest business
move we ever made, the eventual costs notwithstanding. In
there among the losses was a sizable chunk of dough that

we ought to have made from *At War with the Army* for York and its umbrella company, Screen Associates, which Greshler had formed with his Chicago pals.

It was all worth losing because after we dumped Greshler, the MCA organization (second only to William Morris in the talent-agency field) came aboard to represent us, and immediately things turned around for the better.

Jules Stein was MCA's president, a multimillionaire philanthropist whose charitable endeavors kept him so busy that he left the daily top-level decisions to vice-presidents Lew Wasserman and Taft Schreiber, both different in temperament but each possessing keen business judgment: Wasserman the tall, smooth, lean-figured type; and Schreiber an austere, moon-faced man who'd never be seen wearing anything other than expertly tailored suits.

They operated out of a Beverly Hills colonial white-brick building, in an elegantly furnished office with thick, rose-tinted carpet, velvet drapes, huge walnut desk. Wasserman sat behind it on the day Dean and I signed a renegotiated television contract to do the "Colgate Comedy Hour" show for NBC. Months before, Greshler and NBC program chief Norm Blackburn had worked out the original agreement which put Martin and Lewis into four Sunday-night shows spaced over the fall and winter season of 1950–51. At a hundred thousand dollars a show, it took only a split second of time for us to stick our signatures on paper. Greshler had us believing that we had pulled off the greatest coup in television history. But history inexorably moves forward. So when Wasserman looked at our contract, he swiveled in his leather chair, looked again, then said, "How could you have signed this?"

Dean, warily: "With a pen."

"Why, what's wrong?" I interjected.

"The terms," he said. "A paltry sum. You've been hoodwinked, boys. NBC's got you for peanuts."

A couple of weeks later we were back in his office, and Wasserman had the new contract in his hands. He said, "Everything's set. You do the first show for one hundred thousand dollars"—and rose dramatically to announce—"thereafter NBC wil pay you one hundred fifty thousand dollars per show. In other words, the grand total comes to five hundred fifty thousand dollars, less MCA's commission, of course—"

And that was just for openers.

[8]

Work. Ralph Waldo Emerson called it the high prize of life, the crowning fortune of a man. To me this is a marvelous maxim because work has always been good for my soul. I'm really at my best working eighteen hours a day, seven days a week. No less the case back then; at age twenty-four my mind was incapable of conceiving the idea of stealing a moment to rest. What rest? I was so full of energy that if anyone, including Dean, had warned me to slam on the brakes, I wouldn't have listened, anyway.

Dean and I came in by train for the Colgate show. Dawn lights passing in the outer yards of the Pennsy Station; then the long, dark tunnel and the familiar blur of iron stanchions and staircases, tangles of people snapping in and out of view, the whole entourage in our private car stirring, stretching, grinning—you know, that great sensation you get upon arriving in New York.

The porters run up in a pack answering my cries to start pulling stuff from the baggage car. It's comical, Irving Kaye back there on his haunches squinting at labels, double-checking a mountain of trunks, suitcases, valises and assorted boxes—some forty-odd pieces. The bulk of them belong to me, with just two suitcases and a golf bag belonging to Dean. A perfect example of the difference in our individual natures. Like one kid having a compulsion to hoard a million sticks of bubble gum because he's afraid that one morning he will wake up and find all the bubble-gum factories shut down. But the other kid, though liking bubble gum every bit as much, isn't particularly worried about the external industrial complexities. He enjoys life regardless, almost indifferent to what may or may not happen tomorrow.

But rather than bore you with psychological overtones, the cogent fact remains that I looked after all the business details while Dean played golf. By those ground rules we lived, and on that basis our partnership thrived.

The early fifties, then—every day a Fourth of July, with fireworks bursting everywhere; unreal, breathtaking and mad. The "Colgate Comedy Hour" was that and more!

Lou Brown was the bandleader. He grew up in Brooklyn, the son of a paperhanger—came to music playing piano at Mountain bungalow colonies, weddings, bar mitzvahs, cellar nightclubs, and developed into a real virtuoso working pit-band gigs on Broadway. A grinning, unpretentious guy, so terrific that we hired him to accompany us on the road.

Meanwhile, the show rehearsals built to a frenetic rhythm Monday through Saturday, all day and half the night, with hardly enough time to take a leak in the john, much less run out for a quick nosh at the Stage Delicatessen on Seventh Avenue.

Roly-poly Max Asnas owned the place. He would greet you with the most flabbergasting non sequiturs, like: "Take a chair. Life is life, one good earthquake and the whole city will fall—try the pastrami."

Terrific. Then back to work.

In the wee hours I'd arrive at my suite in the Essex House, tired as hell, ignoring all but the most important telephone messages.

Well, one night Jack Keller buzzes my room and says, "Lou Brown is in the lobby with a friend, some guy from the Latin Quarter band who'd love to say hello."

It takes a lot of willpower, but I tell Keller to send them up. A minute later here comes Lou and behind him the friend, wearing a shlumpy tuxedo further rumpled by this obvious bulge underneath the jacket. And he says, "Gee! Everything's happening—you're the *real* Jerry Lewis!"

I find myself staring at his doleful, droopy-eyed kisser which somehow reminds me of a constipated beagle. He says, "I'm Sammy Bidner. You wanta hear me play a tune?"

"On what?"

"On my saxophone."

And Lou says, "Whip it out, Sam."

By God, I watch him reach into his jacket, and presto—there's the cutest little saxophone I've ever seen. A midget sax! And there's Sam blowing a fast chorus of Jimmy Durante's "It's Just One of Those Songs"—ta ta te . . . ta ta ta ta—his fingers squeezing the tiny valves like a Hindu snake charmer, his eyes rolling and sweeping about in utter abandonment.

In the midst of his performance, from giddy exhaustion I reel toward him, grab both of his lapels, rip them clear off and twirl them over my head, while Sam stands there with his eyes wide and wild and his dwarf sax still going ta ta te . . . ta ta ta ta. . . . .

Only thing to do after that was to apologize for the ripped jacket, then make amends. So before he and Lou called it a night, I stuck three hundred-dollar bills in Sam's front pocket. "Get yourself a new wardrobe at Leed's clothing store. They carry a smart line. You know the place?"

"Certainly. Broadway and Forty-sixth—"

Where I had met Sy DeVore in the real early days while browsing through the suit racks, hoping maybe to spot something under thirty dollars. And Sy waited on me, full of chatter and jokes, and eventually we fell into a conversation about show business. I didn't buy a suit from him that day, but I never forgot how nice he treated me. Six years later, practically single-handed, I set him up as Hollywood's leading tailor. In 1949 alone I bought 100 suits from him at $250 apiece, also 135 cardigan sweaters and more pairs of slacks than I could count. Frivolous trivialities which nevertheless found a way into print. Soon a great reputation was born. Sy DeVore's. He developed a worldwide one.

Now to get on with Sammy Bidner.

It's a night or two after I sent him to Leed's. There's a knock on my door—Sam, with his off-the-wall looks and sudden display of mysterious dark glasses sneaks into the room. Two enormous paper bags are stuffed under his arms. He says, "Jerry! You got a minute?"

"Yeah. What's that—a band of little pixies?"

He minces up, says, "It's something to give you a lift before the show."

I appreciate the thought, though I'm not too excited because the shirts or ties or whatever the hell else he has in those bags ain't gonna lift me very far. Until I see—

"Indian nuts! Charlotte russes! Boy! The best food in creation! Don't touch it! Just let me look!"

Sam laughs with obvious relief. I step back now and study him gravely. "You're a maniac."

He shrugs. "I heard that."

"So, tell me, would you like to play on the Colgate show?"

"You bet your ass!"

"Then you're on it the next time we come to New York."

And Sam has been popping up ever since, whenever I

need him as a musician in shows and pictures. But I must admit, what makes him so dear to my heart (I've gone around boasting about this for years) is that he's my connection for Indian nuts, which come exclusively—private stock—from a dried-fruit and nut store on the Lower East Side. If they ever cut me off, I think I would die.

Saturday night. A big powwow going on at the Essex House—all the writers, directors and producers bunched around, sweating over sketches, bits and jokes, production numbers; everybody anxiously discussing what to keep in, what to toss out; the whole thing appearing sensational and hopeless at the same time. Meanwhile, every nerve is frazzled, and the awful smell of stale cigarettes smoldering in greasy plates makes this final meeting before actual air date of the "Colgate Comedy Hour" a pleasure to be done with. Satisfied or not, by tomorrow night we'll know what the rest of America thinks.

Wearily, I see the guys out, close my door, then go to the window and look at pinpoint lights in the distance. All my emotions rise as I ponder about Patti, the kids, my parents. . . . The old Irvington nights suddenly howl in my eardrums, so long ago when I'd wonder whether I would ever grow up and be happy with my life. . . .

I flip on the TV, sink back in a chair, emitting a long sigh. It's three o'clock. I stare groggily at the tube, try to follow the action of some silly adventure movie. At last, I fall asleep.

To say the first "Colgate Comedy Hour" was a success is to put it mildly. We launched the show Sunday night, September 17, 1950, from eight to nine at the old Park Theatre off Columbus Circle. According to our Nielsen rating, it was a stupendous hit. But most of the reviews put too much emphasis on Jerry's abilities and not nearly enough on Dean's. For instance, the *New York Times* television critic, in his morning-after column, said I was the team's "works," then referred to Dean as a "competent" straight man. Competent? What an inglorious word. So what else is new? Most television critics were the same morons then as they are now.

To set the record straight, I'll use a sort of metaphor to explain exactly what Dean's end of our onstage partnership represented. Imagine a day at the circus. . . . There, at center ring, is the flyer winging his way high up on a trapeze while thousands watch his every move, not realizing that if it weren't for the catcher below, the flyer would be nothing.

And Dean was my catcher—the greatest straight man in the history of show business. His sense of timing was flawless, so infinite and so fragile it almost looked as if he didn't do anything at all. Which, of course, was the magic, giving form and substance to the act. It's what made Martin and Lewis work. The truth is, I would never have done as well with anyone else.

[9]

Within a span of fifteen months we had made *That's My Boy* and *The Stooge,* were working on a picture called *Sailor Beware* and assigned to start *Jumping Jacks.*

The same formula, same comedy logic—keep it zany and get it in the can on time. After all the running around dealing with studio people who were saying and doing things I didn't understand, by the fourth picture I began to feel like a streetwalker on Saturday night.

They'd place me in front of a camera—"OK, Jerry, make your little funny faces"—and after they were finished and had walked away, I would be left standing, of no further interest to them until the next setup. I wasn't going to have that. I wanted to know how things worked.

One afternoon they found me poking about up on a catwalk above the sound stage. I had to know if the cat-walks were made of two-by-fours. Were they built on a temporary basis? Who hung them? The carpenters? The grips? Who?

And down below, the director's yelling, "Get your ass on the set!"

The next morning there's a nine o'clock shooting call. I'm in the miniature department at eight, watching thirteen-inch submarines being photographed for a Cary Grant picture. "Gee, I don't understand—will they look full size on the screen?" They suggest I go over and see Chuck Sutter in the camera department, he'd explain everything. So I go there, and Chuck shows me a twelve-inch lens, then demonstrates how they utilize it in the tank. Swell, but I still don't know how they get the right effects on the sky and sea backings around the tank. So Chuck sends me off to the transparency department to look at the backings. Then I go upstairs to admire the artwork. Now it's almost nine-thirty and the assistant director is having a conniption fit—"We need you in front of the camera, *please!*"

I spent weeks in the production department. No one could find me. And on the sound stage, by the camera, it was me again, saying, "Excuse me, but how does that turn? What's moving? The part in front . . . Oh, it's a glass piece, a prism. Ah-hah. And how does the boom swing up? Can you tell me?"

"Well, Jerry, it's counterbalanced with mercury."

"Very interesting. But how come you don't push the boom?"

"I can't. Union rules. That job goes to another guy."

"I'll be darned," I say and ask, "What about the lights?

In the dressing room before the 1970 Telethon with MDA's president Bob Ross and its director of Public Health Education "Moose" Delgado

With Moose

With Dr. Michael DeBakey at Methodist Hospital in Houston

With Sammy Davis Jr. and (below) . . .

. . . Johnny Carson on the Telethon

The night Frank Sinatra brought Dean to the Telethon, Labor Day, 1976

The Bellboy, *1960*

The Nutty Professor, *1963*
(PHOTO BY BILL CRESPINEL)

Me and The Shnoz—Jimmy Durante

With Peter Lawford and Sammy Davis, Jr. on the set of
One More Time, *which I directed in 1970*

Helmut in The Day the Clown Cried

Hardly Working, *1981*

King of Comedy, *with Robert DeNiro*

Slapstick, *with Marty Feldm
and Madelaine Kahn*

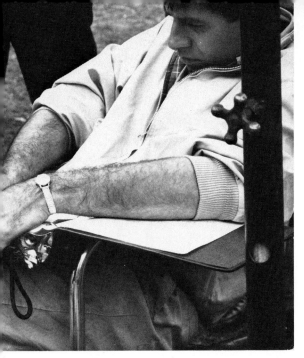

Writing . . .
(PHOTO BY BILL CRESPINEL)

. . . and shooting

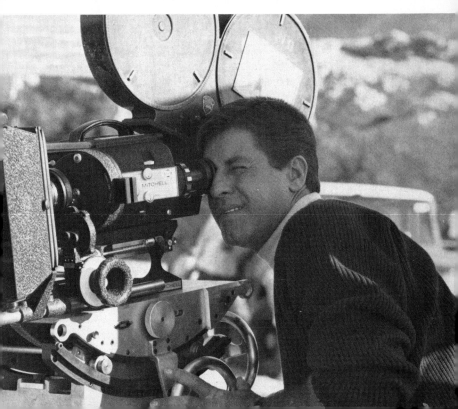

Lonnie, Charlie, and Lillian Br

Ronnie, Patti, Gary, and me at Brown's
in the mid 1950s

Charlie and Lily, Dad and Mom at my Pacific Palisades home

My parents' 50th wedding anniversary: Mom and Dad dancing, Patti standing behind me

whole family. Clockwise: Gary, Patti, me, ...ie, Anthony, Scott, Joseph, Chris

With Gary on the Jerry Lewis Show, 1968

From the top:
Irving Kaye

Joe Stabile

Jack Keller

With Sam and Joe and Claudia Stab

Do you need so many?"

"Yes."

"Why?"

"Because the set needs four hundred footcandle."

"Footcandle. You're putting me on—you have candles you bring in with your feet?"

"No. That's a light measurement."

And the cameraman would finally smile and say, "You'll do all right, kid," then pat me on the back and stick his face into the lens, laughing.

Meanwhile, I'm learning the film business between takes, the way I learned about burlesque from hanging around backstage.

The nitty-gritty details about the making of *Three Ring Circus* are not important, except to say this was the picture that infuriated Dean when Hal Wallis okayed Don McGuire's screenplay which relegated him to a secondary role. At least Dean thought so, and when I looked at the script, I had to agree. Indeed, we gave Wallis a what-for and then some, until he finally smacked his brow and said, "All right, I'll send it back to McGuire for a rewrite."

But after McGuire doctored the script, I could plainly see it hadn't improved much. To compound matters, during the filming Dean kept blowing his top at me and everyone else, saying he was fed up to the ears playing a stooge. It got pretty hairy. There were days when I thought Dean would ditch the whole package. It almost happened. One morning he arrived an hour late on the set and stared daggers at me. "Anytime you wanta call it quits, just let me know."

I said, "Come off it, willya? What the hell would I do without you, anyway?"

He grunted. Then a disgusted wave of his hand and he

strode toward his trailer. It developed into psychological warfare for the balance of the picture.

Then an entirely different matter to contend with. A family melodrama, replete with mysterious confrontations, grinding suspense and imminent peril. The endless story of Jewish guilt. The action starts sometime in 1952.

I'm at the Pasadena train station, waiting there for my parents who are coming in from New York to spend a couple of weeks at my house. Suddenly I see them negotiating their way through a crowd. After the first warming hugs, once again it's the self-conscious stares, the clearing of throats—"How ya been, you sure look good, lemme take your bags—"

I ask, "How's it going, Dad?"

"Same old thing. And you?"

"No complaints. I'm working."

"So I hear. You look tired as hell."

We proceed to my car. Sometime later, driving along Sunset Boulevard, my mother gives him a nudge. "It's so pretty out here. Maybe we can investigate an apartment—"

He says, "My God, you talk like I'm retired. I've got bookings in New York, the Mountains, Philadelphia—*forget* California; I'm not ready for the woodpile yet."

A year goes by. Then my father calls me to say he and Mom have decided to move out to California. I feign calmness and tell him I'll send the airplane tickets, and also arrange to have their furniture shipped from New York.

Finally they arrive—two weeks before the furniture. They're at our house one week when he says, "California sucks. We're gonna go back to the Mountains." At this point my mind goes haywire. "Well, if *that's* what you want, let's say good-bye. However, before you leave, you should know I just spent nine thousand dollars to give your goddamned furniture a vacation!"

He looks at me. "Jerry, the streets out here are deserted. There are no buses. You can't get a cab. And furthermore, how's your mother gonna go shopping?"

I fold my arms. "Why didn't you say so in the first place? I'll get you a car."

We end up laughing, and everything is fine. The furniture comes, and my parents move into a perfectly beautiful apartment in Beverly Hills.

Meanwhile, I've called Mr. A. L. Roache, chairman of the board at General Motors, ordering a custom-built Cadillac. I mean, *one of a kind:* it's built like a tank. Shatterproof glass and steel. Cost me a fortune, but who cares? I'm so worried my father might run into somebody, with this Cadillac at least *he* won't get hurt.

At last the car is ready. A magnificent four-door sedan, incredibly shiny, the most gorgeous upholstery and trim; you can't imagine the extent of satisfaction I get when they roll it out of the showroom. I can't wait to slip behind the wheel and drive over to his place. But I also can't imagine going there without first buying twenty-five yards of red ribbon to wrap around the car—

That afternoon I pull up in front of his apartment house, tie the ribbon over and around, front and back and crossways, and tie a great big bow on the hood—

All of a sudden I hear him yelling from his apartment window: "Hey, son, what is that!"

I yell up: "Happy birthday, Pop!"

And he yells down: "How come it's not a convertible!"

Don't laugh—you can go crazy from this.

Such complications—my parents, all the incongruities of their love for me . . . Was it a loan? A gift? Or some kind of punishing test to ascertain the exact degree of feelings I had for them? I couldn't understand that. I knew only there was an upbringing, a way of seeing things. *Mother:* "I brought you into the world . . . I took from my mouth to give you . . . I went without clothes . . . How come you never call?" *Father:* "You listen to your mother—"

Not that I would deny this, but enough already! I was twenty-eight and married, with children of my own.

I was being pulled in so many different directions that I almost came apart. While Dean and I were cranking out movie after movie and following them up with promotional tours and all the other stuff, as far as Patti knew I could've been off somewhere on a different planet. To alleviate the loneliness, she had her mother move into our home in Pacific Palisades. Mrs. Colanico was a beautiful, quiet woman, friendly and patient, a big comfort to Patti. Just her being there helped to smooth over some very sticky problems of my own.

Though Patti had converted to Judaism, she soon began to regret her decision. Her heart wasn't in it. She had converted solely to please me. Simple as that, and yet the harder she tried, the harder it became to avoid her conscience. As time went on, I realized what a terrible thing I had done to her. All those promises—no crucifixes in the house, no New Testament—boy, what I put her through.

And it gives me an added pang of sorrow now to remember confronting my parents and telling them Patti had returned to Catholicism. They were disappointed, naturally, but what could they say? "We're thrilled"?

So when all's said and done, I felt like a soldier coming home after losing the war.

And that's the honest truth.

BOOK FIVE

As I've said, thirteen is my lucky number, has been ever since Grandma Sarah gave me her bar mitzvah present —the gold Star of David.

But while making my thirteenth Martin and Lewis picture, *You're Never Too Young,* I began to feel that our luck as a team was running out. Dean, to whom I had felt a brother in the past, now seemed like a stranger. It was all one essential problem that could not be reconciled beyond an uneasy truce. Off the set we went our separate ways. Even when working, it would have been disastrous if I as much as suggested a funny line or variations of actions in the shooting script without getting him to think the idea had popped out of his head in the first place. One method was to mark the change on the margin of a page, then show it to him and say, "You know that water-pistol idea you gave me last week? I think it's great. . . ." And underneath the script I'd have my fingers crossed.

Maybe the core of our difficulties was the unsolvable problem every straight man has to face. Dean had spent years listening to the incessant prattle of Jerry this and

Jerry that; Jerry was so funny—Jerry swung from the lamp
. . . And Jerry Jerry Jerry . . . I don't care who you are,
sooner or later it's going to wear you down. In Dean's case
especially, because in his heart he knew *he* was the reason
we were successful.

Thus the rub: a human comedy. The very same follies
of life that made Dean and me successful inevitably drove
us so far apart we stood at opposite poles, each feeling
betrayed and hurt beyond repair. Chalk it up to stubborn
pride, also give self-doubt its proper due, then infuse it
with other emotional traps such as mock humility, pseudo
ignorance, blind desire. . . .

One day I received a telephone call from Charlie Brown,
offering to hold the premiere of *You're Never Too Young*
at his hotel in Loch Sheldrake.

"Oh, Uncle Charlie"—here I hesitated—"tell me more."

A gush of nostalgia swept over me. I saw the old busboy
days, the drab kitchen chores and those gleeful moments
when I submerged my identity and became Frank Sinatra,
Danny Kaye, Igor Gorin—I thought on that; and all at
once, looming up like the sun had burst through a cloud,
there was the sight of me returning as a sort of hometown
hero, the big international celebrity and King Shit of the
Catskills!

"Keep talking, Uncle Charlie—I love the idea!"

I brought it to a meeting at our York Productions office.
Line producer Paul Jones, director Norman Taurog, the
Paramount publicity chief, and Jack Keller were all there.
I told them that Charles and Lillian Brown would give
us the royal treatment: gala festivities before and after
the premiere, including a whole weekend of cocktail parties, dances, press receptions, continuous entertainment;
and a ribbon-cutting ceremony opening the new Playhouse
that the Browns had built in our honor. To cap everything,

all transportation and rooms for the studio executives, cast, publicity and media people would be picked up at no cost to Paramount.

Settled low on the couch, snapping his pencil at a pad on his lap, Hal Wallis looked ecstatic. And the group alongside bent forward with great enthusiasm. "Terrific deal! Can't go wrong! This oughta save us fifteen–twenty thousand bucks."

Next morning I sounded Dean out. He glared at me, as though nothing could be more ridiculous, saying, "You should have consulted me first."

"I'm consulting you now. Give the word and we'll do it. If not, we won't."

He took a breath, long and slow. "Actually, Jerry, I really don't care where we hold it."

As far as I was concerned, that was his tacit approval. So the plans moved forward, with Uncle Charlie and Aunt Lil working busily on the other end, readying the grand proceedings. But the day we were supposed to leave for the premiere, Dean's road manager, Mack Gray, came to me and said, "Your partner isn't making the trip."

"What—are you putting me on, Mack?"

"Look, Jerry, I'm relaying this straight from Dean's mouth. He said he's tired; he's going to take Jeanne on a vacation to Hawaii. What else can I tell you?"

There were three miserable days of traveling by rail into New York as I raged at the wall growing higher and higher between Dean and me. Not even Patti or my children were able to console me; they didn't know the extent of my despair, and I couldn't bring myself to explain it to them. We arrived at Penn Station on June 9, 1955. The atmosphere was charged; reporters swarmed about, asking why Dean had missed the junket.

"No comment."

"Then where is he? Can you comment on that?"

"No. You'll have to ask him."

A mass of confusion, a dozen or more cries and mounting pleas: "Have a heart! C'mon, Jerry, you're not helping us!"

"If I commented, it wouldn't help me."

We stopped overnight at the Hampshire House, then drove up to the Mountains. Along Route 17, bursting into my eyes was a string of billboards with pictures of Martin and Lewis slapped across, proclaiming our joint appearance at Brown's Hotel.

Gloomily, I hunched back against the car seat, gazed out the window through a drizzly rain at my old stomping grounds. Uncle Charlie and Aunt Lil stood in the driveway, Welcome Home banners displayed over their heads on the portico, the guests charging from doorways and exploding into cheers. It was beautiful. It shook me, making me grasp Patti's hand.

"Momma, what am I going to tell them?"

A brave smile. "Whatever you think is best."

Brave faces. She played her part to the hilt, and somehow I got by acting as the silly little kid who never wanted to be anyone else. For the entire weekend I clowned around, playing a bellhop, a busboy, a waiter; and through all the parties and receptions I kibitzed with the guests, even while climbing a ladder to unveil the Dean Martin-Jerry Lewis Playhouse. But after two hours of entertainment following the Saturday night premiere, the silly little kid stood before a phalanx of newsmen, no longer laughing or having anything more witty to say because he was in tears: "I don't know the right words. Maybe the lawyers wouldn't want me to talk about the problem . . . so I want to thank you for saving me the embarrassment by not asking questions I can't answer. . . ."

Then the long walk-off with Patti, feeling the grip of her

fingers against my elbow and realizing she was my strength, the one person in my life who made everything worthwhile.

The train going home. Always a train going somewhere.

An expanse of sky. Copper-colored mountains stretching across the desert. Night coming on. A song rising from time past, so faint above the hum of rails, above the chatter and noise of passengers. Going home with the song drifting, blurring . . . lost. A sudden wave of loneliness, and sleep.

Then morning. Waking up to see the California foothills under fabulous sunlight, seeing it clearly, without having to struggle with the sadder reality, the knowing feeling that tells you something important and good is finally ending. And to know, beyond a shadow of doubt, that the team has nowhere else to go. That it's time to quit, and soon, while there's still air to breathe in.

Trapped as Dean and I were in a maze of multimillion-dollar contracts with Paramount, York Productions and NBC, it would've taken a whole city of Philadelphia lawyers at least two to three years to untangle our legal affairs. Nonetheless, the day after I got back to California I walked into Lew Wasserman's office and said, "Please do something, anything, because I can't continue working this way."

He stroked his chin. "What about Dean?"

"How do I know? We don't talk to each other. Just get me out of my commitments, and I'll be happy."

"But, Jer—"

No buts. I kept pressing until Wasserman agreed to take up the matter with Paramount, saying also that he'd inform Dean of my decision.

A few days later, the Paramount board of directors gathered around in their New York conference room. Plenty of arm-waving, head-shaking conclusions. Then a collective thumbs-down. Jerry Lewis must fulfill his contract. Case closed. Maybe Dean's letter to them made the difference. Because he wrote, "I'm ready, willing and able to go back to work."

And we did.

Pardners: the story as adapted by Sidney Sheldon from a 1936 Bing Crosby flick, *Rhythm on the Range,* was representative of our previous films, basically running to gags, pantomime, some songs, a touch of romance, feigned terrors and a happy ending, if nothing else. But each and every day on the set seemed longer and harder to get through.

A jumble of scenes, a picture of me arriving at the studio: hurrying on to makeup and all that; emerging from my trailer; talks with director Norman Taurog and waiting for setups, lighting, camera angles; the sound of a clapboard: "Quiet . . . We're rolling . . . and *action!"* Grimacing under my ten-gallon hat, attempting to roll a cigarette, twirl a rope, mount a horse—"It's a take!"— Then walking off across the lot back to the trailer and sitting there, drowsy, indifferent, thinking of nothing and nobody while Jack Keller and Irving Kaye hover close, checking to make sure I'm OK. . . . "Why don't you guys leave, I want to get some rest."

By July the bottom had dropped out. I lay in bed, staring at photographs of Patti and the children. Faces filled wtih innocence; they were the center of my life, governing my every action, all my thoughts. Yet I could never say or do enough to make up for the time spent away from them. In the last couple of months I'd come home to find the house darkened, everyone asleep. And I'd sink down exhausted next to Patti, muttering through clenched teeth, "Talk to me. Please, honey, talk to me," waiting vainly for her to tell me I was right, that Dean was wrong. But now, as always over the past year or so, there were no answers, no sign, only a detached silence and a whispered good night as I'd lie there, seething.

Living unbearably within myself, I moved to a decision by calling a friend, Henry Luster, a psychiatrist in Beverly Hills. "You have to help me. I'm going off my rocker. Can I see you today?"

"Yes, of course. Let's make an appointment for two o'clock."

His office was nice and modern with a masculine look to it, catercornered with two recessed walnut bookcases; the collected works of Freud, Adler, Jung, Reik, and more volumes by Proust, Camus and Sartre—*Origins of Psychoanalysis* . . . I ran my eyes over the titles, then turned to Henry. "Well, do I talk to you from here or from the couch?"

He chuckled. "Why don't you just explain what the problem is?" gesturing to a chair by his desk.

I sat down, lit a cigarette and told him the whole story.

When I finished, he said, "I think it would be a mistake if you were to undergo analysis."

"I don't follow you, Henry. What is that supposed to mean? Be specific."

"Well, if we peel away the emotional and psychological difficulties, there might be a danger." He looked at me carefully. "The danger is, your pain may leave, but it's also quite possible that you won't have a reason to be funny anymore."

And that was that tune. I was out of his office in twenty minutes, marveling at the wealth of understanding I had gained from those words.

[2]

Early in my career the most important thing I learned about the boys from Chicago is that once you gave them your hand, you had to live by it. If it meant you had to show up for a drink with a couple of hookers or show up to sign a couple of autographs at a dinner, or whatever— you'd better be there, baby: *you shook their hand!*

But the man who taught me the true value of a hand-shake was Y. Frank Freeman, the president of Paramount Pictures. This giant of industry wore honor as some men wear fine clothes. For seventeen years we had a personal understanding, everything based on trust.

In July of 1955, Dean and I got into an IRS tax bind. It placed us against the wall for $650,000. I went to Y. Frank Freeman and told him my plight. He didn't want to know the details. He reached for his pen and wrote a check for that amount, made out to Jerry Lewis, drawn on the Bank of Atlanta, in the personal account of Y. Frank and Margaret Freeman.

After the ink was dry, he eased back in his chair and said with that soft southern drawl of his, "We ain't gonna have to sign any paper, Jerry. Not after all these years. If you shake my hand, I'll give you this check. Just tell me when I'm gonna get it back."

"I need sixty days, Mr. Freeman."

"Counting from when?"

"From now."

"What time is it?" he asked.

I looked at my watch. "Three o'clock."

He bent forward, wet his finger and started to flip the pages of his desk calendar. "Let's see . . . sixty days from now puts you into September thirteenth, my friend. I'll just pencil you in for three o'clock."

I managed to take care of the IRS, but I never told Dean the circumstances of how the check was written. He knew only that I would handle it. He'd say, "You're the business head, pardner. You do it."

On September 13, at ten minutes to three, I was back in Y. Frank Freeman's office, waiting to return his $650,000.

His secretary announced me on the intercom. And the voice came through: "Well, send him in."

He was standing by his desk. "You're early."

"I'm sorry, Mr. Freeman, I know how busy you are."

He smiled pleasantly. "It's nine minutes to three. Do you realize what kind of interest you can pick up in nine minutes, Mr. Lewis?"

I barely maintained a straight face. "Would you please take this check so I can go back to work?"

His arm went around my shoulders, and as our eyes met he said, "Jerry, you did right. You kept your bond."

A few weeks later, the phone rings: Y. Frank Freeman on the line. "I hate to impose on you, Jerry. But I have a favor to ask."

"Impose? I've been waiting a month to be imposed. What is it?"

He goes on to say that the *Los Angeles Times* would be sponsoring a benefit for the poor children of Los Angeles on November 10 at the Shrine Auditorium. As chairman of the committee, he wanted to know if Dean and I would appear.

"Of course."

The reply comes back, kiddingly, "How do I know, Mr. Lewis, that I can depend on you and your partner to be there?"

"Mr. Freeman, you can rest assured that Martin and Lewis will be at your benefit. Don't worry about it, we'll do your crappy little show."

"I love ya, Jerry."

I hung up. And I'm suddenly frightened. I had never committed ourselves to anything without first clearing it with Dean. I remembered what had happened when we held the *You're Never Too Young* premiere at Brown's Hotel. What if the same thing were to happen at the Shrine Auditorium?

I went directly to Dean's dressing room on the Paramount lot. The instant he opened the door I said, "Hey, pal, I hate to OK this without your approval, but something important has come up."

"Is it a contract?"

"Sort of."

"OK, then sign it. You do it, anyhow."

"No, this is a little different. Y. Frank needs our help at the poor children's benefit on November tenth."

"Sure, he's got it."

I took off my jacket and pulled up a chair.

"Dean, hold on, now. This doesn't involve money or contracts. I'm not concerned about any of that shit. This is Y. Frank, and . . ." I spelled it out. "You see, this is the man who helped us to stay alive by lending us the six hundred fifty. Do you understand what I'm saying?"

"Hey, man . . . I told you. It's OK."

"Well, I'm gonna ask you to do something for me, so I can rest easy. I want you to stick your big grubby Italian paw in mine and agree that you'll do the benefit for Y. Frank."

And Dean stretches out his hand, saying, "Jerry, for Crissakes, I know how important this is. You got it."

And I'm free as a bird. I'm fine.

I'm at the Shrine Auditorium on November 10, as scheduled. Only, Dean wasn't there.

I made a limp apology to the audience that he had a bad case of laryngitis. Then I did twenty minutes and fled.

The next morning Y. Frank telephoned me. He said I shouldn't take it too hard. These things happen; don't worry, everything was still OK. But no. There were all those ads, the billing, the promos, and something more. I had let Y. Frank Freeman down.

On November 11, I walked into Dean's dressing room.

"You crossed me, Dean."

"What are you talking about?"

"You must be kidding. You gave me your word that we'd do Y. Frank's show."

"You're out of your mind. I don't know a thing about it."

"Where were you last night?"

"When did my life become your business?"

"I didn't mean it that way. I mean, I sent an interoffice memo by messenger, with a copy to your dressing room, a copy to the Lakeside Country Club, a copy to your valet and a copy to your wife. So you mean to tell me that you didn't know we were supposed to be at the Shrine at eight o'clock last night?"

Without batting an eye, he said, "Nobody told me there was going to be a benefit."

He looked around and spotted an envelope. He opened it, then took out a folded sheet of paper. On the clean side he started to scribble something, all the while muttering, "Listen, Jer. I need two prints of *Living It Up*. Can you handle this?" And gave me the paper.

It was the memo I had sent to him.

It was filled with the empty spaces of our days together.

[3]

One more time: a picture called *Hollywood Or Bust*. Paramount hired Frank Tashlin as director. He had already gone through the ringer with us the year before while directing *Artists and Models*.

Tashlin, a big burly guy who carried his body around as though it was a strain to move from place to place, had a mind that moved at lightning speed. His knowledge of comedy far surpassed that of any director I had ever worked with. What I learned from him couldn't be bought at any price, because there is no college in the world where they can teach you how to think funny. But first I had to learn a painful lesson—how to behave.

I wouldn't tell Dean what I thought of him, so Frank Tashlin took all the flack. For six weeks I laid it into him, grandstanding, playing the king, reacting intemperately to his directions before each take. And during that time, through one tantrum after another, he withstood the onslaught, amazingly, with a forbearing equanimity. Meanwhile, everyone on the set became irritable. Even former light-heavyweight champion Maxie Rosenbloom, who played Bookie Beeny in the picture.

One day I needled Maxie with a garbagy impression of a punch-drunk fighter, every other word a profanity, the whole thing meant to belittle his former trade. He should have hauled off and knocked me through a wall, but he simply backed away like I didn't exist.

Then the day came when Tashlin couldn't stand my antics any longer. He stopped the production cold, gathered the crew around him in a circle and accosted me.

"I want you off the set."

"Ho ho."

"I mean it, Jerry. Off! You're a discourteous, obnoxious prick—an embarrassment to me and a disgrace to the profession."

I looked about, the blood draining from my face. I could see a hundred or more people watching; it was a bad dream, a nightmare.

"Hey, Tish, whoa—calm down. When did you get the right—"

"Jerry, as director of this picture, I order you to leave. Go. Get your ass out of here and don't come back."

It was the longest walk of my life. I went home sobbing and spent the whole afternoon staring into myself, seeing all my efforts ending in despair, wasted, adding up to nothing but failure.

That evening I called his house. He wouldn't come to the phone. I tried reaching him again and again. Finally: "Yes, what is it?"

"Tish, I'm sorry. I can't tell you how sorry I am. I was wrong. All I ask is, please, let me come back."

A brief hesitation. "Will you behave?"

"Yes. I won't give you cause to be angry with me anymore. I promise."

"OK. Report to work in the morning. The shoot is at seven o'clock."

"I'll be there at six. And Tish . . . thanks."

"For what?"

"I don't know, maybe for saving my life."

I kept the lid on, doing whatever Tashlin wanted; no more hassles, everything in gear. But inside, the pressure was building, building—the vital lie, the lie that still stuck in my throat; the hostility I felt toward myself for not admitting that Dean's and my partnership was a sham. Yet a fear of what lay beyond became the knot which chafed at my dependency on Dean. I had to break out of it; otherwise, I knew it would eventually kill me.

On May 18, a Wednesday night, I served as toastmaster at the Screen Actors Guild testimonial dinner for Jean Hersholt and remember it as a high because the funny stuff went over big. After the ceremonies, as I walked to my car, stopping momentarily to light a cigarette, a sudden rush of nausea hit me. From what?—probably the excitement of performing . . . perhaps the spongy roast beef

I had eaten . . . ahh, it didn't matter. The nausea had disappeared.

The minute I walked through the door, Patti said, "What's wrong? You're as pale as a ghost."

"I'm all right. It's nothing." I moved toward a chair, breathing deeply. My legs had turned to jelly.

"I'm calling Dr. Levy," she said.

I nodded. Then a searing pain shot across my chest and I collapsed in the chair.

Fifteen minutes later she had me in Dr. Marvin Levy's office.

He took an electrocardiogram. I lay there on the table with clenched fists, panting, biting down on my lip. The pain was unbearable.

He called in the nurse. "Get a hypo ready." Now to Patti: "I'm sending him to Mount Sinai Hospital."

She was bending over me, whispering, "I'll go with you," and clutched my hand as the nurse gave me the hypo.

My father's voice: "Jerry, I've come to see you."

He was looking through an opening in the plastic tent that surrounded my bed, his head cocked a little to one side, frowning and saying, "What happened to you?"

"Not a thing," returning his gaze through misty eyes. "I'm taking a vacation. . . ."

His face pushed further into the tent. "Do you know what you're doing to your mother?"

If my life had depended on it, I could not have spoken another word. I simply closed my eyes, pretending sleep, seeking desperately to lose myself in the euphoria of medication.

Muted murmurs at the door. I heard the doctor say, "It's a coronary strain. He needs a few days' rest."

The door closed.

And that was that.

[4]

At the Paramount lot later that month, I tried for the miracle.

I stood looking at Dean, hoping, praying. I said, "You know, it's a helluva thing. All I can think of is that what we do is not very important. Any two guys could have done it. But even the best of them wouldn't have had what made us as big as we are."

"Yeah? What is it?"

"Well, I think it's the love that we still have for each other."

He half-closed his eyes, and his head lowered. There was a long silence. Then he looked up. "You can talk about love all you want. To me, you're nothing but a dollar sign." He may have wanted to say more. God knows, he probably could have gone on for hours about all the real and imagined injustices I had heaped upon him during the past couple of years. Maybe he would have, if I had stayed to listen. But I didn't.

It was dark when I got home. Entering the study, I sank into an armchair, yielding to a sudden and uncomfortable sense of intrusion, as if I were in a strange house, looking around at someone else's possessions. A leather-bound volume of the *Pardners* shooting script lay open on the table. I glanced at it, somehow got past the first page, then pushed it aside. I lit a cigarette; the smoke curled up into the light.

Patti stood in the doorway. "Are you hungry? Can I fix you something?"

"No. I only want to talk. It's important."

"What is it?" She had a nettled expression on her face. It meant: "If you're going to drag out the same old stuff, I couldn't care less."

"Please . . . sit down."

She sat stiffly on the couch opposite me, waiting.

When I finished telling her that I had made an irrevocable decision to split with Dean, she stared off as if she had heard nothing.

I stood up, took her by the arms and shook her gently. "Honey, I'm talking truth! I'm going to call MCA in the morning. Then I'll call Paramount, and my attorney, and the accountants; what I'm saying, Momma—I swear to God—I will never work with him again."

A shudder went through me. I was wide open. She could see clear through me to the back of my collarbone.

"All right," she whispered. "Now I will talk."

A tear ran down my cheek. I said, "You know, Esther, I'm gonna have to push a lot of money like over a crap table to all those people."

"I know."

"And we may have to sell the house and take the kids out of private school."

"It doesn't matter," she said. "We will live where you live. If it's on Fairfax Avenue in a two-bedroom apartment, that'll be all right, too. And you know what, sweetheart? Private school isn't all that great, anyhow."

Moving my hand slowly, I touched hers with my fingertips. We held each other close, listening to our own thoughts in silence, and I swore that I would never lie to myself again, to the day the lid of my coffin closed over me.

A bank of lawyers, accountants, corporate executives and my business manager sat in at the meeting. Dean wasn't there because he didn't provoke anything. So I attended without him.

And now MCA chief Lew Wasserman was evaluating things, speaking intensely—I couldn't wait for it to be over. Yet the ambivalence—

His voice droned on and on: "Here's your potential for

the next year and a half. Seven million—apiece. Here's such and such . . . Films . . . Television . . . Nightclubs . . . Concerts . . . Good heavens, Jerry, compromise. Live with it. What in the world is perfect? You can't, you can't, you can't—"

But I had to.

Dean and I are finished, but we aren't done. There are engagements to keep, including the two weeks at the Copa, our last shows together.

What time is it? What day? What year? And who and where am I? The fragment of a memory stirred. Then another. One by one they returned. I rubbed the back of my neck, sank down on the pillow; warm bed, home, the family near. *Yes. Here I am, now, this moment, liking myself, proud of what I think, and I won't give it up. Never. Not even if I have to learn how to walk all over again.*

BOOK SIX

I HAD planned a vacation to help me take my mind off things. So we went to Las Vegas with Jack and Emma Keller.

On August 2 the four of us checked into the Sands Hotel. And the next few days we had a ball. We went to shows, played blackjack and the roulette tables, lounged in the sun, did a little shopping, sang and whistled down the streets arm in arm like real tourists; it was great! I put everything on hold. In limbo. But in the back of my mind the most important question of all had not been answered: Now what do I do?

Then came August 6. It was about six-thirty in the evening. I had just finished packing, ready to go home, when the phone rang.

"Hello."

"Jerry? This is Sid Luft."

"Hi, Sid. How's Judy?"

"She's what I'm worried about."

"Why? What happened?"

"She's got a strep-throat infection. She can't sing. So I'm asking, would you go on for her?"

"Sid! Hey, I'd love to, but I'm practically on a plane—"

Sid Luft was Judy Garland's husband and personal manager. A real charmer, he could sell pizzas to Gino. "We're in trouble, Jerry. You can postpone the flight. Come on, kid, for old times' sake—"

I clamped my hand over the receiver, looked furiously for Patti—"Honey!"—then got back to Sid. "Listen, I wouldn't know what to do. I mean, I haven't done a single in ten years."

He kept pushing, cajoling, boosting my ego, calling on my sense of professionalism, my friendship with Judy, throwing in everything but the kitchen sink. Patti walked in from the other room. Cupping the receiver once more, I said to her, "Judy Garland's sick, and Sid Luft wants me to go on for her—"

She gave me a quizzical smile, as if to say, "You're going to say yes, aren't you?"

I shook my head, frustrated. "Momma, there'll be a thousand people in that room—"

She said, "Do it! You'll be fine."

After a long pause: "Sid? It's OK. I'll do it."

Patti took a dark blue suit out of my bag and began pressing it with a traveling iron. I watched her, feeling strangely calm, almost inert. As she draped the suit over a hanger, all of a sudden I remembered. "Black socks—I didn't bring any with me."

She said, "Wait here, darling. I'll borrow a pair from Jack."

I looked up. "He's got small feet."

"Cut the tips off," she laughed.

Ten minutes later, now dressed with cut tips, I took a Saint Anthony medal that Patti had given me and slipped it into my pocket. In another pocket, I put a picture of my children.

It was a little after eight o'clock. The dinner show at the Frontier Hotel went on at eight-thirty, and I still didn't

have thought *one* about how to pull off an hour onstage
without an act.

Judy opened her dressing room door. She pecked me on
the cheek, then folded her arms around my waist. "Thanks,
Jerry, I'm so glad you're here." Her voice sounded like
Tallulah Bankhead impersonating B. S. Pully, so I knew
this night she was for real.

"Yeah, well, I didn't have anywhere to go, anyway.
Now, shut your mouth and listen. Just sit on the stage
while I work. The people came to see Judy Garland. And
if they don't, they're gonna be pissed at whoever is up
there."

"The hell," she said. "This is your night."

"I know, baby. That's why I need you to get me through
it."

The honey-toned, brassy rise of "Over the Rainbow"
pulsed across the jam-packed show room. Then a spotlight
and her chorus boys singing the introduction—*Miss Judy
Garland*.

I walked onto the stage. There was a big swell of oohs
and ahhs with ripples going through it, and sudden shouts
building into relentless applause. I saw Patti at her table,
hands clasped together as if in prayer. The applause got
stronger . . . warm, intimate, impenetrable. It was almost
impossible to think—

I grabbed the microphone and said the first thing that
came into my head: "I don't look much like Judy, do I?"
The laughs came. The news about my breakup with Dean
was still fresh, and the crowd made me feel that everyone
wanted to show they still cared. I walked to the wings and
led Judy out. The house came down with roars as we
hugged each other. And as she sat on the lip of the stage,
I did a show. The adrenaline kept pumping through fifty-

five minutes of nonstop clowning. I couldn't believe it was happening, that I was making it alone, without Dean!

I didn't know how to get off. The crowd wouldn't let me. So I turned to Judy: "What do you sing as a finish?" She said, " 'Rockabye Your Baby.' " And I sang it, actually got down on my knees and belted out the song just as I remembered my father doing it—and Dad would have liked to believe that I thought Jolson came after him. I was never better on any stage ever in my life!

When I got back to the dressing room, it was one big yell. Patti came running, all at once laughing and crying into my arms. She was there; nothing else mattered, only the joy of that moment.

And the next morning we left Vegas for home.

Three days later, I'm at a recording studio in Hollywood. . . . Arranger Buddy Bregman bends over a music stand, his hand poised while eighteen musicians wait on his cue. Suddenly a switch is thrown in the control booth—"All right, stand by. . . . Here we go. . . . 'Rockabye Your Baby with a Dixie Melody'. . . ."

Decca released it in November. And believe it or not, they sold over a million copies before the year was out!

Nineteen fifty-seven was my year. I was thirty-one, a motion picture producer with a sumptuous office on the Paramount lot, and everything I touched had turned to gold. I made *The Delicate Delinquent* for a little under five hundred thousand dollars, and it figured to gross six million. In 1957 I also produced *Rock-a-bye Baby,* which brought in more carloads of money. Besides all this, "The Jerry Lewis Show"—my first major television effort as a solo performer. Then the TV guest shots, the picture tours, lecturing, comedy workshops and more. I raced through life like Jesse Owens. Dean or no Dean, I had a need to live like this. I wanted every day to have thirty-two hours. Therefore the drive, the striving for perfection, not letting up for a minute because I was still afraid that the world would stop turning if I didn't hurry.

[2]

A quarter of a century gone since the split with Dean. A thousand things have happened, some not terribly important, others monumental in that they more or less led me straight along the path I chose to take. But to stay on it, I had to commit myself to a raw truth.

Before the split I was a pretty shallow guy. Yet I'd like to think there was some good stuff down deep, because you just don't grow up one day and become a better man. You have to take who the man is within and bring it out—the part that was buried. Human nature can't change overnight. We don't suddenly become better by simply saying, "I'll be dedicated," or "I'll be honest." One is either dedicated and proceeds that way, or one doesn't; one tells the truth, or one lies.

I've been looking through my Creed book today. It's a profusion of thoughts and reflections written over the years. Words to live by. Such as: "Restlessness is discontent and discontent is the first necessity of progress." Thomas Edison said it first, and I thought enough of those words to write them down on June 4, 1961.

Another: "I shall pursue my principles without calculating the consequences. . . ." Franklin Delano Roosevelt. That was entered in my Creed book on November 10, 1959.

And from Ayn Rand's novel *The Fountainhead:* "Throughout the centuries there were men who took first steps down new roads armed with nothing but their own visions. The great creators—the thinkers, the artists, the scientists, the inventors—stood alone against the men of their time. Every great new thought was opposed, every great new invention was denounced. But the men of unborrowed vision went ahead. They fought, they suffered and they paid. But they won. . . ." Placed in my book at the age of twenty-two, and burned into my consciousness from that time till now.

One more: "Fame is a big beautiful balloon surrounded by a lot of little boys with sharp pins. . . ." Jerry Lewis; the date unknown.

The sad thing about words is that there are billions and billions of them in a million books which express every conceivable thought pertaining to life on this planet. Sad, because after eons we haven't learned much about anything except how to blow each other apart a little bit quicker.

Yet I believe there is room to turn all this insanity around somehow, some way. Why not by humor? As far as I know, it's the cheapest and most harmless commodity humans have ever possessed. Until somebody proves to me otherwise, I contend nuttiness is the only wide-open channel to sanity left in a world filled with madness. That's why I also wrote in my Creed book: "Humor—a marvelous instrument. If used properly, it can suffocate a lot of ugliness out of people."

Across the years, behind the footlights and vast arenas of entertainment, there were key people who stood tall in the midst of pygmies. When in need, I turned to them. Often as not, they fed my mind and soothed my heart. But when I ached unnecessarily, they wouldn't participate in that kind of bullshit.

One of them is Jack Keller. His eyes flash devilishly; his face wears a battered smile that comes suddenly and spreads into a V-like look of bemused cynicism. The Old

Trapper, as I affectionately called him—and a curmudgeon if there ever was one. He didn't believe in children. He hated Democrats. And, boy oh boy, could he drink! On St. Patrick's Day every year he'd crack open a bottle, and his liver would run for cover. On ordinary days he could put two or three quarts away, but you'd never know he had a drink. Yes, I can see and hear him as though he were standing here this very second, pouring himself a triple shot and saying (Jackie Gleason-style), "As long as it's liquid we will imbibe . . . and if it's solid, we'll stomp on it!"

Jack contentedly guzzling his scotch in the wings of the London Palladium Theatre. It's early 1958, a dazzling opening night with half the Royal Household, including Her Majesty, sitting among the masses. I edge over to the curtain, peek out and find myself whining pitifully to Keller, "I'm gonna bomb. I feel it, I'm sick." He looks at me askance and says in a gravelly whisper, "That's normal." Now, Marino Marini and his Neapolitan Quartet bow off, and Lou Brown whizzes by me to take his position at the piano. There's a worried flutter in his eyes. . . . And for a long second there's fear, the fear I have of laying a Godzilla egg in front of the Queen!

It had been five years since I played the Palladium. My debut there with Dean was not a roaring success. Attribute it to bad timing or what you will, but back then a wave of anti-Americanism had swept over England. Wherever you looked, there were visible signs of the controversy. Posters and slogans hung on walls of buildings, ghoulish displays presenting the caricature of President Eisenhower, his famous grin blackened by little electric chairs strung across the teeth like barbed-wire fence. And below—FREE THE ROSENBERGS!—a battle cry brought into London by worldwide propagandists who believed that Julius and Ethel Rosenberg were not guilty of selling secret atomic data to the Russians. Maybe so, but I knew next to nothing

about the case. In fact, you'd be hard pressed to find anyone less politically oriented than I was during those days.
I just wanted to make people laugh. The Rosenbergs were
not my fight.

But one fight I'd have loved would have been with a
couple of would-be American representatives who had left
Great Britain a short time before Dean and I got there.
Namely, Roy Cohn and David Schine. Though they weren't
a comedy team, we could never have been so funny.

Anyway, we went on and did our act in a cold atmosphere, with the odd sensation of being viewed by a hang-
man's jury.

In the middle of a routine a voice rang out: "Boo!" and
"Yank, go home!" Then some twenty more voices began
to chant the same thing—

The London papers made a big hullabaloo out of it the
next morning, blasting Martin and Lewis as though we
were "that *other* comedy team."

So now, here I am once again at the London Palladium.
Only this time alone, solo, single, by myself—table for one,
please—and the butterflies weren't just in my gut but in
my vest, pants, jacket and tie. I had been nervous all my
professional life. But scared? The first time! Then from out
of the blue another first . . . Keller, probably feeling all
those vibes, put his arms around me and pulled me close
with so loving a touch I thought, as he squeezed, Jesus
Christ, the Old Trapper does have a heart. Now we're
looking practically nose to nose, and he whispers, "Go
out there and do the best you can with the shit you got."

I cracked up. I only hoped it would rub off on the audi-
ence. Then I heard, "Ladies and gentlemen, the London
Palladium is proud to present the star of our show, Mr.
Jerry Lewis," and I was on.

I did sixty-five minutes, reaching far back, further than
when I'm looking to put a one iron next to the pin. At the
finish of my performance the applause was incredible. The

audience moved their heads from me to the Royal Family, and the more they applauded, the more the Royal Family applauded. They all stood as one, giving me the first standing ovation of my career.

When I exited backstage, the Old Trapper's eyes were shining. I grabbed him and planted a kiss on his forehead. No kid at Christmas could know the excitement I felt. As I pulled away, silently waiting for approval, he, too, was silent for a beat. And finally he broke it with: "Well, you fooled them again!!!"

That was my Keller.

He had an astonishing intellect, though you'd never know it until you challenged him. Like I said, he hated Democrats, being a hard-core Republican to the very depths of his soul. According to Keller, all our international troubles had begun with FDR. So one day he says to me, "You like Roosevelt, don't you?"

"Yes."

"Then you're an illiterate."

Undismayed, and still holding my ground, I replied, "He took us out of the Depression, you putz."

"Yeah, right into World War Two and Yalta" (referring to that historic meeting with Churchill and Stalin in intricate detail, which sounded as though he had been there, too, listening with great disgust to everything being said). "The sonofabitch sold us down the river, and someday your children's children are gonna suffer the consequences."

This only adds salt to my wounds. "Well, Jack, that shouldn't bother you because you don't have any children."

"That's right, you illiterate bonehead. So why do I have to pay taxes for schools when I don't have any kids going there?"

"I don't know. And, anyway, let's not talk about it because you're the same moron who told me you ate shit on a shingle. I never heard that expression in all my life. But if I like what you like, I'm brilliant."

"Exactly."

"Then why don't you get my name in the papers?"

"Any schmuck can get your name in the papers. You're paying me to keep it out."

Go answer that one. So I say, "Never mind. Just tell me —your expense sheet this week—two hundred and sixty-five dollars for stamps?"

"I write a lot of letters."

"Two hundred and ten dollars for magazines?"

"If you open your mouth once more, next week it'll be three hundred!"

"So what did you beat me for this week?"

"I had one of my best weeks."

"How can you steal and tell me?"

"Because I love you. There are people around you who steal and don't tell you. I'm a man with some quality, a Republican through birth, by conviction and purpose, and I shall always abide in everything the Republican Party stands for. And do you want to know why?"

"Why?"

"Because it has *right* on its side!"

"So how much are you going to steal?"

"All I can until my house is paid for!"

"You have the house in Canada, and you're still gonna steal from me?"

And he said, "I got to put in a garden. . . ."

And who's going to argue with that? Certainly not an illiterate . . .

He was a book all by himself, and I wish he could be around today so everybody could read him. I told him that once in so many words. I said, "Jack, is there anything you haven't done? I mean, you've hustled your way through all kinds of crap like a raging bull. Yet you sit here now at peace with yourself . . . satisfied. You really do amaze me."

He said nothing, but I knew from his expression that he had found something most men search for all their lives but could never find.

Part of it, I figure, was what Keller saw as sugarcoated phoniness. He knew the difference between saint and sinner, and recognized those qualities in himself, which enabled him to fit into any situation, any gathering anywhere —and contribute something every time.

He used to say, "If you feel you're about to make a move that you won't be proud of, don't do it." And, "Better you should fall flat on your face than bend too far backwards and wind up on your ass." And, "For Christ's sake, Jerry, if you're gonna make a mistake, make it loud and noisy. A small goof will only embarrass me."

This brings us to a time when I sure as hell had to choose the way I wanted to go.

There was a surprise party for Louella Parsons. I got an engraved invitation and threw it into the wastebasket. Patti retrieved it and said, "Why can't we go? It'll do us good to get out for a change."

She was right. We had been infrequent nightclubbers and hadn't indulged much in the Hollywood swirl since 1958, when we bought the old Louis B. Mayer estate on St. Cloud Road in Bel Air. A veritable palace it was, so big, in fact, that it took us better than a year to discover all the rooms. At the final check, so help me, there were seventeen bathrooms. On the front door we placed a gold plaque: *Our house is open to Sunshine, Friends, Guests, and God.* In this house I felt that position and wealth didn't have to alter my life.

It was home.

Well, I never should have left it to go to Louella Parsons' surprise party. I can remember everything: the crowded private room at Chasen's Restaurant, the movie stars sit-

ting around—Bogart, Cagney, Peck, Hepburn, Gable, etc.
—and in walks Louella as though it's an ordinary Tuesday
afternoon and she's dropping by for a cup of soup. "Surprise! Surprise!" "Oh, dear . . . My darlings, is this all
for me?" (The only one-liner that took three minutes.)
She starts into the room, gussying and sighing like Clarabelle the cow, the entire throng of stars glad-handing her
with a standing ovation as she heads toward her table,
where Patti and I happen to be seated. I mean, our behinds
were planted squarely on those chairs. All she could see
was that.

So she gives me a look. "Why, Jerry, is there something
wrong?"

"No, Louella. Everything's fine."

"Oh, well, I thought you might have broken your leg.
You weren't standing."

I stared straight at her. "Louella, that was you who came
in, not Her Majesty."

She turned crimson under her makeup. Patti kicked me
under the table. Then we finished our half a meal and left.

A couple of days later, predictable as ever, Louella raised
back and unwound an item in her column. It was an indiscriminate rip. She called me rude, brash, obnoxious and a
self-centered bore. Anyway, it didn't upset me. I knew she
was a barracuda who would not hesitate to rip the hide off
anyone. So whatever I did to her that night, to me it was
a moral victory.

The tag line came from Keller. He told me that a few
people who had attended the party had phoned him to say
they wished they had my guts. Naturally, he added some
choice four-letter expletives simply to put what happened
in the proper perspective. "You're supposed to be such a
smart businessman. You know the importance of the press,
but at times you can't even do *wrong* right."

"You want me to be different, huh?"

"No—because I hate what you do, but I love why you do it."

[3]

Through all the years that Jack Keller was my friend, he never asked me to do anything that would hinder my best interests. And certainly no request ever for himself. So he caught me off guard the day he said, "I need a favor. It's not for you; it's for me this time."

"Name it."

He said, "A friend of mine is in trouble and needs some help."

That was Jack. He finally asked a favor for himself that went to another. Thus, at the ripe old age of twenty-two, I had a meeting with a man who really thought I could be the answer to a mystery plaguing mankind for thousands of years.

His name was Paul Cohen. Handicapped, a victim of muscular dystrophy since childhood, Paul had taken the initiative to contact Keller and ask if I would see him regarding an organization he was preparing to set up to combat the disease. I agreed eagerly.

The previous year, while working the El Capitan Theatre in Hollywood, I got to know about the effects of dystrophy through an associate. One of his relatives—a nephew—had been struck down with it; a lovely child withering like a winter's leaf in the early springtime. And to see him this way . . . I made a few inquiries, waited and watched, helplessly.

Then something disastrous happened, something very personal. The effect almost wiped me off the face of the earth. My mind still can't escape from that experience. There's only one way out. One exit. It's the day we find a cure for muscular dystrophy. Until then, as the philosopher Epicurus said when pressed to explain why he would not discuss the motivation for his work, "I have given most of my life to light, allow me to give this part to the shade."

My discussion with Paul Cohen took place in New York. He got right down to cases. His organization consisted of a small group of patients and the parents of children similarly afflicted. He said, "We need research into the causes of dystrophy. So far it's virtually nonexistent. We're in the Dark Ages; nothing has been done to develop an effective method of treatment."

Paul spoke with passion. Tall, husky, Oscar Levantish face, he had a superintelligence, an acerbic wit that hacked away all the technical folderol—so intense as he talked at length and admitted, finally, how much he counted on me being a spearhead figure for the Muscular Dystrophy Association.

I said that before accepting the responsibility, I would like to see a specialist, with pioneering work in the field. "I'm sure you understand, Paul; I need to know."

"By all means. I'll get in touch with Dr. Milhorat, my personal physician. There's no one more qualified."

That afternoon I was ushered into Dr. Ade T. Milhorat's office. He smiled up from his desk. "I'm happy you've come. Paul tells me he's been trying to get you involved in our fight."

"I hear it's a tough one."

"Yes. The invisible enemy, you know. Hah! Go fight shadows—"

"Well, I just want to find out if I can help."

He gestured. "Here. Sit. I'm afraid it's a long and discouraging story."

And he began: "Imagine, if you will, a relay race of some fifty miles around a mud track in which the baton is passed from one runner to the next. It could take forever before a race like that is finished. Meanwhile, how many will be left in the stands watching? Oh, it's a bad business, all right. We doctors stumble and fall, the children die and the mud triumphs over us all.

"But there's always hope," Dr. Milhorat continued. "And I'm pretty sure we're going to win. I'm optimistic, anyway."

"That cheers me," I said grimly. "What will it take to speed up the race a bit?"

He joined his fingertips and peered over them. "Three things. Time, money and luck. The three necessities of life."

"Time and luck are your department. Now, what about money? How much is needed? Cause I might be able to do something there."

"Well, Jerry, at this stage it could be perhaps a few thousand, or maybe millions, or ten times that. You see, it's a question that can't be answered. The invisible enemy again. Now you see him, now you don't. Frightening. Hah! To think we've come so far in medicine with so many new drugs, new techniques and equipment—all useless against the disease."

"So where's the hope?"

"God only knows. We have to keep trying. A hundred years ago we didn't even have a name for the disease. In fact, the leading neurologist of that time—Guillaume Duchenne—could do no better than call it a creeping paralysis." As he talked, he drew out some papers from his desk drawer and thumbed through them, found what he was looking for and said, "I'll show you what we're up against. Take a look at this. You'll learn."

He handed me a list of thirty or so doctors; their credits, degrees and affiliations. Summaries of their work reduced to cold agate print, like "Alfa Tocopheryl Phosphate and Energy Transfer in Muscle"; "X-Y Chromosome Factors";

"Vitamin E Content of Tissues in Progressive Muscle Disease"; "Creatine Tolerance Tests." Those tests entered under Dr. Milhorat's name, dated 1937, when he and associate H. G. Wolff reported them at Cornell University Medical College in New York . . .

"What exactly does this mean, doctor?"

He smiled briefly. "It means that's about all there is. A coterie of dedicated men pushing forward the research for answers, ranging from the profound to the simple. Sorry I can't be more specific than that."

He took out a letter and handed it to me. "This is from John O'Brian, a patient of mine. A Harvard man. He himself has muscular dystrophy. Yet that doesn't stop him from being one of Washington's top lawyers. Anyway, as you can see, John enclosed his check for fifteen hundred dollars because he has a *conscious* feeling for humanity—to others, to the less fortunate victims. It's a gesture . . . highly appreciated, I assure you. He sent it along with the letter after I returned from Europe and was informed by the Armour Packing Company that their research grant had been terminated."

I sat staring at him. Fifteen hundred dollars! The Colgate people were paying me that just for buying milkshakes—

"Well, doctor, you've given me a lot to think about, and I thank you."

"Quite all right, Jerry." He hesitated. "If you would like to get another opinion"—chuckling—"I'd recommend Dr. Huston Merritt. He's professor of neurology at Columbia College of Physicians and Surgeons. Brilliant fellow, I might add. He's made some promising inroads in the study of muscle physiology."

My visit with Dr. Huston Merritt was short, but not sweet. "So, let's not delude ourselves," he said, rising from his conference-room chair. "However, if you're that determined, Mr. Lewis, I think you'll go out and do a good job."

I said, "A *job?* I'm talking about opening my heart. If I do it, it won't be a job."

Down the Columbia steps I went. Jack Keller was standing with my chauffeur at the curb.

"How did it go, Chiefie?"

"Wonderful. Get your fat ass in the car."

I slammed the door, dropped my briefcase on the seat and slouched back, still smoldering over Dr. Merritt's ending remarks.

"We'll barely make the airport," said Keller.

"A goddamned job, is it? Well, he don't know what this kid can do!"

"I presume you've got yourself booked for another battle, my prince."

"Yeah. The biggest one yet!"

Between 1948, when I first met Paul Cohen, and until 1956, it's all random memories and a clear image or two. How far off those times: the eternities of shows, the fund-raising affairs, the benefits and dances, the work going into it for muscular dystrophy on all fronts in scores of communities across the land.

I see myself now, alerting the public of the need for their aid. I see Dean there at my side, sharing the same goals. And somewhere along the way I can hear him saying, "You talk so beautiful, I wanta put my arm around you and smack you right in the eye." Then somewhere else yelling, "We'll lick this thing, pardner! You and me! You make the speeches and I'll pour on the charm!"

So we did, starting December 1950 on the Colgate show, clowning around filling time at the end of the program, when suddenly I ad-libbed a pitch to the video audience: "Will you people out there each send us two dollars? One for Dean and one for me." Wow, the sponsor really got hot over that, but meanwhile the money came in all week long, and we turned over about two thousand dollars to the MDA research fund.

It's only money.

I recall a Halloween party given at the home of Mrs. Hal Wallis in Van Nuys. Forty-eight boys and three girls were there to meet Barbara Stanwyck, Alan Ladd, Betty Hutton and other celebrities. Dean and I made the introductions. Little dystrophic children getting autographs—and stalwart Alan Ladd, his hand trembling, signs his name for a wisp of a child caged in metal braces. Later, he takes me aside. "I'm appalled. So many of them . . ." He has a drink in his hand, and he's crying.

In 1951 we did a sixteen-hour telethon, carried by only one station, WNBT New York. The organization raised $68,000, and things began to look up. Then a special Thanksgiving holiday, a television-radio simulcast held at Carnegie Hall. Two hours of entertainment, with Jack Keller coordinating the details and tirelessly assembling the program; a salute to the National Association of Letter Carriers. Porch lights were lit all over America, and mile by mile the mailmen walked, in town and city, in sunshine, cold or rain, to collect money so that one day we could tell some poor kid, "My child, you'll walk again." I said that night on the air, "It's a disease they don't know about. They don't know where it comes from, or what to do when it does arrive. The only thing these kids want is hope. So give them something to look forward to—"

When all the envelopes were collected by 100,000 letter carriers, and the donations tabulated, we had raised a total of $3,500,000, by far the largest sum in the organization's existence.

But I couldn't for the life of me lay back, saying I lit a

candle and made a speech, so now I can go home thinking
I've contributed enough.

In 1956, when my partnership with Dean had all but
disintegrated into dust, there was another telethon, our final
one together. We maintained a cosmetic posture and somehow got through a twenty-one-hour extravaganza which
gave a big push toward the construction of a research center
to be known as the Institute for Muscle Disease. We came
on over WABD, Channel 5 (Dumont network), with
broadcast pickups from Bridgeport, Connecticut; Wonderland Park in Westchester County; Mineola, Long Island;
and Brown's Hotel. From the stage of Carnegie Hall I stood
applauding Milton Berle's emotional plea to the audience,
while Dean looked on, his collar open, tieless, peering
ahead so you'd never suspect how deeply he had been
touched.

It took place twenty-six years ago. And every year since,
more and more has happened. No easy road, I'll tell you,
but there were never any low points with regard to my feelings about eventually finding a cure.

I'm walking on.

[4]

Beginning with the first Martin and Lewis picture, I had
consistently racked up big profits for Paramount. So in
early 1959, the studio negotiated a long-term contract with
me. Fantastic terms, the price staggering. I would star in
fourteen films over the next seven years and get ten million dollars.

Y. Frank Freeman, God rest his soul, put all the elements
together. It was his farewell gesture before retiring from
Paramount, providing a watershed deal in a career that had

already given me abundant security. But he did much more than that. During those uncertain times with Dean, when fear held on tight, Y. Frank embraced me with his concern, his understanding and his prayers. He had nothing to gain except my respect, gratitude and affection.

After he stepped down, the studio was not the same. Oh, the pictures were shot, all right, and the dollars kept bubbling forth, but no longer under his warm, soft light.

In January 1960, I completed *Cinderfella,* a natural money-maker for the Christmas season. I packaged it that way, the whole thing Christmas oriented, down to the record album and full-blown holiday campaign.

Suddenly Paramount chief Barney Balaban hits me with a different approach. He wants to release the film in July.

I said, "Barney, it'll die a miserable death in July."

And he said, "What do we do without a Jerry Lewis movie for the summer? That's our big push."

And I said, "I'll make you one."

He bites his lower lip, saying, "What do you mean, you'll make me one?" adding sadly, "You don't have enough time."

"Barney, if I deliver a print by the end of June, you'll have a summer release." So he thinks about this for a minute in jut-jawed silence and then says, "I dunno, Jerry, we need a picture for our exchanges the first of June."

"OK, you'll have it."

"Well," he says, "if you're willing to take the risk . . ." Meaning, of course, that Paramount didn't want to be my partner. So I told him I'd put up my own money, and with that Balaban says, "Very good. . . . Yes. . . . You have a deal!"

That night I flew out of Los Angeles to Miami, scheduled to open at the Fountainbleu Hotel on January 17. En route, an idea came to me. The vision of a bellboy, the entire role played in pantomime, the character a symbol of protest against people who regard bellboys, elevator operators and, indeed, all other uniformed workers as faceless dummies.

Immediately after arriving in Florida, I went to Ben Novak, owner of the Fountainbleu, and enticed him into allowing the film to be shot at his establishment. Then, during my engagement, which ran through January 30, I wrote the script, staying up eight days and eight nights. Not one wink of sleep. I turned out 165 pages like some kind of drugged madman, alternately writing and hallucinating scene after scene. As my own director, I had the added task of hiring actors. Fortunately, Milton Berle happened to be available, so I wrote him into the picture. Also, from bygone Catskill days, Jimmy and Tillie Girard, Eddie Schaeffer, Herkie Styles, Sonny Sands, Harvey Stone . . . my sidekicks Lou Brown and Jack Keller in it, too, and half the population of Miami Beach had applied as extras.

On February 8 we started shooting. A month later the picture was wrapped. Then, during an engagement at the Sands Hotel, from March 10 into the middle of April, I cut the picture, scored it, dubbed it and shipped it in May to Paramount for distribution. Sounds a little far-fetched, I know, but those are the straight facts. What's more, to my great satisfaction, *The Bellboy* opened on time, grossed ten million dollars U.S.A.—and I had no partners!

Comedy is a serious business. You spin off a comic value, and all of a sudden you're in a heavy moment. It's remarkable, tough to come by. After fifty years in this racket, I ought to know. I've always played my idiot character as I myself see life—a big dark storm that once in a while is brightened by a rainbow of laughter. So any comic creator who can turn a negative to a positive is my kind of comedian.

Stan Laurel, for example; he was a pure comic genius, the archetypical man in trouble, an underdog going up against the guy in the black top hat. It's the old hiss-the-villain thrill. . . . That top-hat guy, ugh, phew, he's the millionaire bank president who holds the mortgage on your house. Get him! Knock his hat off with a snowball!

During the last three or four years of his life, Stan gave me so many valuable insights, passing his knowledge of comedy along with loving care. Discussions in which he'd tell me of the old times when he played the English music halls, and of his career with Oliver Hardy . . . *Stan and Ollie,* what a team! When I think of the different attitudes they were able to project in the moil of utter chaos, it brings a smile to my lips, even now. They were so fantastically original, so appealing, that I'd often stay up all night running and re-running their two- or three-reeler films. Each viewing showed another facet, some new twist or turn. "Ring the bell, Stanley," and Stanley pulls the bell out by its roots. "Well, here's another fine mess you've gotten us into! Let me do it." So Ollie sticks his hand in the hole where the bell used to be and, of course, gets a shock, then blames Stan. . . . Chimerical and endearing, like an old souvenir.

While finishing *The Bellboy,* quite by chance I ran into Dick Van Dyke. He told me, "Stan Laurel is in bad shape. Nothing serious, but kinda sad." This cryptic remark fed into still another, until suddenly I had the picture. Stan living in virtual seclusion; a great man sitting idly or walking about with one foot tending to drag a little because of a stroke.

"Why don't you give him a call?" ventured Dick. "I'm sure he'd love to hear from you."

Thing is, I was at a loss what to do, never having met Stan before. So I said, "He doesn't know me. It could be awkward for the both of us."

"Don't be silly. He's the same wonderful guy we grew up with. Believe me, there'll be a lot to talk about."

On a Thursday morning of that week I called Stan, saying how much I admired his work and would appreciate his opinion regarding a script I'd written. He thanked me and said it would be a pleasure, sounding exactly like his film voice, soft, almost girlish, a wisp of merry old England in it.

"Sunday is visiting day. You can see me then." He made it seem as if I'd be visiting him in a hospital.

He and his wife Etta lived at the Oceana Hotel in Santa Monica, occupying a small apartment on the second floor. It had a nautical look: model whaling boats, coral and conch shells in glass cases, a brass ship's clock on the wall, an old-fashioned pewter lamp suspended over his desk and at the far end of the living room an expansive window that overlooked the ocean.

He pointed. "It's a nice pool, much bigger than Liberace's . . ." all the while peering out, as if engrossed by nothing else. Then he turned toward me and said, "I spend hours here hoping mermaids will surface. But they never do."

Etta, a charming blond-haired woman, smiled at her husband and ran her fingers across his back. "Come, Stan. Sit in the kitchen with Jerry. I'll fix tea."

We sat down. "I'm curious to know what you think of this," handing him *The Bellboy* script. He glanced at the title. "If you've written a part for me, I'm flattered, but unfortunately I can't go back to work right now."

"Well, I wanted—I mean, the picture has already been shot. I'm in the midst of cutting it, so I thought maybe you'd go through the material and make some comments."

His watery blue eyes twinkled. "Happy to, Jerry. Yes, I can look it over during the week. Now, let's visit."

It was a stimulating four hours. He talked and reminisced about his experiences as a young comedian in the theatrical company owned by his father, Arthur J. Jefferson. "Everybody called him A.J. He was quite a man, taught me the fundamentals of comedy . . . I can remember a vaudeville sketch he had written which played the big houses around Northern England and Glasgow. After a month's run one of the comics in the sketch gave Dad a hard time, so he fired him and I became the replacement. Anyway, we got to know each other real well that year. Then I went out as a single. Then America. And I tell you, Jerry, whatever I was able to make of myself, most of it I owe to him."

Fathers and sons. I told Stan of my own family beginnings. He listened, nodding his head, understanding, sharing the similarities of our backgrounds: the hard knocks, the frustrations, the love and pain that went into the kind of life we had both lived.

"I'm past yearning to lead the life of a vagabond," he said, now looking at Etta blissfully. "But the English music-hall tour Ollie and I took in 1954—our last professional appearance together—well, it was really something, is that right, Etta?"

"Oh, indeed," laughing—and to me, "The boys had a ball. They were so happy. Full houses, everybody dying to see them. And they finally cemented a relationship on the tour, one that Stan wished for but couldn't achieve until then."

"It's true," he said. "We were never close before that. When we made pictures, it was like a well-oiled machine, all work and no play. After work, though, we didn't socialize. I hardly saw him between pictures. We were very unlike by nature. Outside the studio, he loved golf and I loved the cutting room. I could stay there practically every night editing and doing all the technical stuff, sometimes working twenty-two hours a day at the studio. Ollie wasn't interested in that. But whatever I did was all right with him. He gave me my freedom as a sort of exchange for his own. So . . ."

Stan sank into thoughtful silence, a silence that pierced me like pinpricks. The parallels, such parallels . . . He murmured, "You know, Ollie was like a brother to me."

I took a beat, then asked, "It's been a couple of years since he died, am I right, Stan?"

"It was 1957. Had a stroke, then complications. Near the end he couldn't speak. The last time I saw him, it was all pantomime. He looked at me and his eyes said, 'What a fine mess *this* is.' "

I laughed to keep from crying.

For three days after the visit I slaved away at the editing of *The Bellboy*. Mind into matter . . . I could not forget Stan's saddened eyes, his apparent loneliness. No statues for him in the Hollywood fog, but neglect and vast indifference to his contributions by the industry. Perhaps Stan found it easy to accept this, though I couldn't make myself believe it, not for a second.

The following Sunday I visited him again. Ida met me at the door, took my hand and held it affectionately. "Stan's not feeling too well, but come in. He's expecting you."

He limped out of the bedroom, carrying a stack of letters. "My fan mail," he grinned. "Imagine, I still hear from kids all over the world."

I said, "It seems to me that you've got a big job trying to answer them. Maybe I should come back another time."

"Nonsense. Everything in its proper order, I say. I'll simply put these letters on my desk—neat, everything neat, in its proper place—and then we'll talk."

The talk—now, in my head, it's a thousand little forgettable things, because Stan and I covered so much ground. Nevertheless, there were some priceless moments, neither bitter nor sweet, just remembered for their meaning. . . . He said: "Look to tomorrow when you may be able to do something . . . and when you stand before an audience, don't take them for granted. Comedy is not a contest. It should be appreciated. So if they don't get it right off, help them. . . ." He said: "I tried to make people laugh. It was my job, my only job. I wasn't out to change society or impose moral lessons on the conscience of the world. That's for others: the preachers, the politicians and what have you. I only wanted to have some fun and give a little back. . . ." He had marked my script, made notes on the margins, and at the bottom of the pages there were explanations, brilliant observations. . . .

I asked him to work with me. I offered him a position with my company as technical adviser. I offered him $150,000 a year.

He turned it down. He wouldn't believe I really needed him. There was no way I could convince him it wasn't charity.

Before leaving, I asked if he would come to my house and have dinner some evening. He sighed, giving me that helpless Laurel smile—like, "That's a good idea, but"— and said, "I would rather not leave the apartment. When you get to know me better, you'll understand why."

"Well, tell me now."

He remained silent for a while, then answered in a dry, controlled voice, "I don't wish to have anyone see me in this condition. I want the people to remember me as I was, especially the children. . . ."

So that was our talk one Sunday afternoon in Santa Monica, years and years ago.

He was a kind, warm, sensitive man who requested nothing from anyone, other than to allow him the pleasure of spending his last days looking at the ocean, and dreaming of days when laughter was brighter and friends were closer.

He loved the water. He loved friends, too. But they didn't stay with him as the surf did. And the surf didn't particularly care what his status was, how many films he had made or how much money he possessed. It gave him the priceless gift of devotion.

It was always there, whether he did or didn't show a need for it.

[5]

Autonomy in film, as well as any other endeavor, is a tough rap because it requires integrity. I've had to sleep with *that* every night. Very painful, sometimes terrifying. No matter how I've tossed and turned, there's no getting away from it.

The Nutty Professor, my fourth film as director-writer, happened out of a desire to do a comedy version of the classic horror story, *Dr. Jekyll and Mr. Hyde.* I had the whole movie envisioned, but the professor himself, Julius Kelp, took a long time to jump into my skin. Mainly because I couldn't find his voice.

Then, early 1962, on a train going from Los Angeles to New York, while I sat in the parlor car having a drink with Jack Keller, this little guy walked up wearing eyeglasses so thick that I swear he looked like a frog peeking out of two Mason jars. He cleared his throat: "Ah, ah, ah, ah-hem, are you the show business fellow?"

I said, "Yes, I am. Who are you?"

"Haggendosh, Furnace Pipeline and Storm Window Company, Cleveland. I, ah, ah-hem, you make this trip often for shows and skits and sketches?"

"Yes, I travel back and forth."

"Oh, marvelous. Ah, say, are you going to have breakfast in the, ah, morning or, ah . . . the . . . ah, ah, ah . . . my card, sir. Haggendosh, that is."

I bought him drinks for two hours; never took my eyes off him.

Then I headed to my drawing room and looked straight

into the mirror: "How do you do? I, ah, ah-hem, I think it's you. Ah, ha-ha, marvelous. Actually, yes. Good."

And there he was!

Many people thought the flip side of Professor Kelp— the hateful character, Buddy Love—was a vengeful attack on Dean. Untrue. No, Buddy Love was a composite of all those rude, distasteful, odious, crass, gross imbeciles whom we can spot instantly at any large gathering. We know him only too well. He's the insensitive putz who slams the door in children's faces on Halloween. He's the miser who thinks Christmas is humbug, the walking time bomb who kills Presidents, the "nice boy next door" who rapes a lady in the street. He's all those things. But he isn't Dean. He's Buddy Love, infinitely for himself and disliking all other humans.

I made him a glaringly destructive force, despicable to the core, as a balance against the loving professor. Creating the role had me in a sweat, especially when I saw images of Buddy Love creeping out from inside me onto the page. A crying horror!

It got even worse during the actual filming. I kept pushing the Buddy Love sequences to the end, procrastinating my ass off, dreading to see him come alive on the screen. I remember shooting the scene where Buddy squatted in a corner facing the laboratory like a terrified animal, feeling an inconceivable loneliness, oblivious to the camera and the crew until, finally, I said, "Cut!"

The Nutty Professor was a departure for me in all departments: writing, directing and performing. A Jerry Lewis movie without the familiar image. It raised serious questions in the front office. I had to answer to the guys who put the financial pieces together, then dropped the responsibility of making the picture into my hands. They were concerned. They thought a large portion of the audience (meaning the kids) wouldn't understand it. "It may scare the hell out of them," said a studio executive as we walked from the screening room.

I answered, "Did you ever hear of Snow White? Remember that chase through the forest after her life was spared by the woodcutter? That didn't hurt Walt Disney any."

Came summer of 1963 and I went on a personal appearance tour to launch the movie, hitting thirty-five cities during a span of forty days. Despite lukewarm reviews by the critics, we broke box-office records everywhere. Then into New York for an all-out spree, romping on the stages of local theatres, giving scores of interviews, posing for pictures, taking hundreds of my own and even finding time to slug down a mountain of egg creams on Lexington Avenue and Fifty-third Street, where the hot-dog-lunch crowd milled about in amazed disbelief.

That night at Newark's Robert Treat Hotel I held a press conference, saying things like, "The kids love me because I get paid to do what they get punished for doing," then fielded a lot of questions, dead on my feet but staying there afterwards just to work my way around the room and greet the local exhibitors.

Unaccountably, a small man wearing an outdated pinstripe suit came over and said in a dockyard voice, "Hey, Jer, I been waitin' a long time to tell ya I'm sorry."

Another humorist, no doubt. "OK, pal, I'll bite. Why are you sorry?"

He said, "For bustin' ya wid a two-by-four in fronta da Adams Theatre when we wuz kids."

"Wha—Jesus Christ! Hey . . . waddaya know."

I saw the whole scene, that ferret-faced look of his which I'd long forgotten. A night of high drama, sudden violence, while I was working after school as a part-time usher at the old Adams in Newark, the year they arrested Gene Krupa for marijuana. He had played there that night.

"Yeah, I remember."

"Well, anyway, I wanta wish ya luck wid da movie. And just t'make things right, me and da fam'ly chipped in to give ya somethin'."

I thought he was going to pull out a gun. Instead, he handed me a check for twenty-five dollars, made payable to the Muscular Dystrophy Association.

I took it wordlessly and firmly shook his hand.

The limousine going back to Manhattan, inching along sluggishly in traffic. I rubbed my collarbone, smiling to myself. Sure, I had yanked the kid from his seat for making noise, then turned him over to the manager, who threw him out of the theatre. . . . *He was waiting in the street with eight or ten of his buddies. . . . Them against me and three other ushers . . . And he hits me with a board. . . . I'm lying in the gutter, sewage pouring into my mouth. I try to get up, see him holding the board and running like a jack-rabbit between cars. Then I see the oncoming truck. I scream, "Look out!" He stops on a dime. The truck roars down the block. The kid makes it to the opposite sidewalk and disappears. . . .*

The little bastard just broke my collarbone, and there I was yelling through the pain, "Look out!" I didn't want him to get hit by the truck. I didn't want him to get it like that.

I thought of Buddy Love, my created monster, and realized that if he lived within me, I always had him under control.

France, 1965—rumbles and recognition. A mob scene at Orly Airport, and a thrilling reception it was, the greatest satisfaction I had ever known in my career.

The whole visit to Paris was unbelievable. After sixteen

years in motion pictures, having put my heart and soul into it, only to find myself denied the recognition I so desperately wanted from the critics of my own country, here the critics honored me as director of the year for my "artistry and imagination" in making *The Nutty Professor*.

A coronation of sort, and my crown was sweet revenge.

[6]

From 1959 to 1962 I had more or less stayed away from television, limiting myself to a few guest appearances, one straight acting role (in a remake of *The Jazz Singer*), a master of ceremonies assignment at the thirty-first annual Academy Awards and the telethon for MDA. Other than that, I focused strictly on films and nightclubs. There were no compelling reasons to get back into the television rat race again. I didn't need the money or the grief, so why do it?

Besides, my family had expanded to five boys, each one healthy and demanding of his father's time. Sure enough there was Gary; then Ronnie; followed by Scotty, Chris, and Anthony. No applause necessary, it was my pleasure.

Anyway, the winter of 1962 came, and it so happened that Jack Paar went off the "Tonight" show. Until NBC could find a suitable replacement, several people filled in for Paar as temporary hosts. Since I had a hole in my schedule (meaning nothing else better to do), I thought it might be fun to give the show a whirl. So they put me on, and I wound up doing it two weeks.

The odd thing: a great majority of viewers were astonished to see that the nut could talk. And to corroborate this fact, NBC received an avalanche of letters from all parts of the country, thousands of delighted comments about the sensitive and intelligent way I handled the guests. Which coincided with my sentiments exactly. (What did they expect me to do, pee on them?)

As a result of the "Tonight" appearances, two of the three major networks locked horns over me. Jim Aubrey, head of CBS, flew out to Los Angeles wanting to tell me *his* story. "Look," he says, "we'll give you sixty minutes in prime time. Name your figure and it's a go."

I say, "That's very generous of CBS, Jim, but for what I want to do, sixty minutes ain't enough."

He says, "An awful lot of people would love to have the opportunity—"

"That's them, whoever they are. I'm not interested in them. I'm a rich, famous, handsome, young Jewish movie star, and when I'm ready—when I feel like it—then I'll do a show. But it's got to be live, no prerecording, no delayed broadcast, none of that crap. It's live or nuthin'—"

So Aubrey fumfers a moment more, saying, "Come off it, Jerry, we're talking about prime time. I mean there's such a thing as sponsors, you know. And then we have the station breaks, ah, the various contingencies and multiplicities—"

I just stare at him and continue, "Let me put it to you simple, straight, on the line. I must have creative control or it's no deal. I will use who I want to use as guests, I won't sell what I don't believe in and, most important of all, I will not settle for less than ninety minutes of *your* prime time."

"My God, man, be reasonable. We don't have ninety minutes to give."

"OK. There's nothing more to talk about."

A week passes, and suddenly in pops Mort Werner, the NBC programming chief. With a soft, almost musical lilt to his voice, he offers me a ninety-minute slot on *his* network. "Take your pick, Jer. We'll give you either Tuesday or Thursday night."

I say, "Thank you, Mort, but no thanks. The middle of the week is out. I want Saturday night."

"I'm sorry . . . just can't help you there. We've already scheduled a block of movies for Saturday nights."

As he left I gave him a nice good-bye and wished him luck with his movies.

While all this is going on, unbeknownst to me there's more smoke blowing in my direction. I finally get the drift when Leonard Goldenson, lord and master of the entire ABC-Paramount network, comes to my door a week later and says, "Jerry, soon as you hear what we have in mind, I know you'll join our team."

Now, Goldenson is the moving spirit behind the team. He's family (so to speak), and we've been friends for a long while. Therefore, we sit earnestly to discuss everything in a big conversation which inevitably leads to Goldenson's assurance that not only would I have Saturday night clearance to do a show, but to cap it off, I'd have two hours instead of ninety minutes. "From ten to twelve," he says, issuing a kindhearted smile, anxious to make the deal and catch a flight back to New York in a hurry.

I slow him down a bit. "Just one other thing, Leonard. The money is fine. And I'm satisfied that you'll give me full autonomy. However, the run has got to be for five years; no options, understand, because I'm not about to go week by week worrying whether the Nielsen ratings are falling or what some disgruntled old lady might say in a letter to standards and practices."

He whistles under his breath, then fakes a light jab under my chin. "You sonofabitch, we're not the Chase Manhattan Bank. That's fifteen million smackers—cash—just for you to entertain the people forty times a year for two hours."

"Leonard, it's all in the cards. If you want the show badly enough, you'll give me five years. Otherwise, forget it."

Gradually he pulls himself together. "You win, you *meshugener.*"

And when he places his hand in mine to seal the bargain, what it represents in actual terms is a cool seventy-five million dollars.

The startling magnitude of it, perhaps an illusion which would never materialize, the illusion so subtle and intricate it lulls me into its web as time goes round.

It was now the summer of 1963—Patti pregnant again, really hoping and psyching herself up for a girl. She did the nursery in pink; frilly little touches in all different shades of pink. The drawers were stuffed with pink dresses, kimonos, booties, hats, sweaters and blankets. Cuddly little pink teddy bears sat on the pink dresser; all sorts of pink rattles waited in the crib. Not only that, we even had a pink ribbon tied around our dog's neck, and at one point I almost painted my Mercedes pink—so you know how much we both wanted a girl.

I was also building up steam for the ABC show, besides getting ready to shoot a film called *Who's Minding the Store?,* the title prophetic, considering that I was continuously on the move and didn't know how much help I had been to Patti at the time. When it came right down to truth —about giving, about spending an extra moment or two with her to discuss the children or some other concerns she may have had over the day-to-day routine of family life— if she got eight minutes from me it was a lot. Early mornings I'd start out the driveway, leaving those responsibilities behind me. Why doodle around at home when there were more important things to take care of? The house would be there when I got back, but only if I kept putting out the product. I'd say to myself: "Well, whether it's right or wrong, that's the way it is—if I don't come first, they haven't a prayer." But somewhere down the road a heavy guilt would mushroom inside me, like a gigantic storm attacking, smashing angrily against my thoughts. . . . Storm-lashed memories of the kid alone, the feeling of neglect, the fear of abandonment, of being cut adrift and discarded in the wake.

Nevertheless, I kept working, harder and harder, sometimes right around the clock, skipping sleep entirely. No time for sleep. No room to lie down and think of anyone but myself.

Then came a summer evening when more than a thousand representatives of ABC and its affiliated stations gathered at the Beverly Hilton Hotel to rally in support of my show, all in the cause of drumbeating a September 2 premiere: Saturday night *live*. Attending were the usual Hollywood kingpins, trade union leaders, members of political and church organizations; and tables were put aside to accommodate my film company associates, Jack Keller, Irving Kaye et al., and also my parents.

Everything was perfect, except the seating plan. An innocent goof, I'm sure, but still a costly one, leading to further trouble in my family affairs.

Patti and I arrived at the hotel, where a battery of security guards hustled us safely through the lobby and into the main ballroom. Mom and Dad were dancing among a whole crowd of people. She was wearing a pink gown, he sporting a pink carnation in the buttonhole of his tuxedo. They saw us and stopped dancing.

As we approached (warily), Dad said, "Do you know that we're sitting alone with strangers?"

I said, "What are you talking about?"

He said, "The least you could've done was put us in with some of your crowd."

I turned to Patti and let out a low groan. She stared back at him.

Then Mom stepped forward. "Let's not start arguing.

This is supposed to be a happy occasion"—then, offering her cheek to Patti, added, "I'm thinking pink, can't you see? And anyway, tonight my boy is having a wonderful celebration in his honor."

I showed a frozen smile as Patti gave her a quick peck, then said, "We better get to our table." Which resolved nothing, as no amount of words could satisfy or articulate the hurt all around. So I worked my way past the dance floor with Patti, holding on to her hand but feeling only my own confusion. . . .

We made it to the dais, sat together behind a table covered by gilt-lettered cards bearing the most distinguished names of ABC-Paramount. I looked at her and finally, after a thick silence, bent sideways in my chair and turned my attention elsewhere.

Unbelievably tense.

Suddenly it was September, and my private griefs got sidetracked by the constant sweep of show business.

I bought the old El Capitan Theatre (on Vine Street above Hollywood Boulevard), then hired a crackerjack crew to refurbish it, top to bottom; the stagehands, electricians, carpenters and set designers worked as one to get the place ready for my premiere, which loomed closer and closer, while I looked after every detail. When completed, without bragging I feel safe in saying we had the greatest television studio ever. The best electronic system, best control booth, best seating; the entire theatre a magnificent gem. Over two million dollars went into the job. There were cameras upon cameras: at the ramp, at center stage, a big one set on far stage left, a mini-camera stage right, one above eye level on the podium and another in the balcony with a protection camera in the back. The carpeting was a luscious red, the balcony seats gold, the lights rainbow-colored. As for the band room, it looked like a honeymoon suite at the Ritz, not the shroudy Fairfax Avenue CBS kind with its ratty floors.

So all was well. And on premiere night I stood in front of that theatre, as proud as though I had built the Taj Mahal.

But it wasn't all that grand. From the opening cue— "You're on the air"—there developed a series of raging battles between me and ABC over the choice of guests, the use of language, the racial references and social commentaries. It rose up and crashed over me before I had a chance to get my bearings. Like any other show, mine needed time to develop, to get the rhythm going, the flow sure and smooth until it reached level ground. However, high in the ivory towers of ABC, strings were being pulled as "The Jerry Lewis Show" moved from its starting block.

Not unlike some of the NASA pre-Apollo flights, there was the countdown, the lift-off; we soared, teetered and went flat on our ass.

On the thirteenth week we did the final show for ABC. They paid me off and paid plenty. I sold the theatre back to them and made a profit there as well. Then it was time to face my peers. After all the hoopla—the press, magazines, television interviews and so forth—that Hollywood and the rest of the public had heard about for months on end, how was I to tell them that I blew it? Blame ABC? Hardly! Blame the crew, staff, technicians and writers? Of course not! I simply took out a full-page ad in all the theatrical periodicals. Only one word appeared:

"O O P S!!!"
jerry lewis

So you've got the picture. Except for one more thing. You won't find any pink in it because the Lewis family had another boy. . . .

Joseph.

[7]

I was in my office writing a script, the radio on . . . when the announcement came, breaking in tersely through the speaker: "Shots were fired at President Kennedy's Motorcade today in downtown Dallas. . . ."

A few minutes later I knew the worst had happened, the worst evil of all. I didn't move from my chair, just sat and stared, railing at the world and cursing the cruelties of Providence. Slumped there, listening to bulletin after bulletin . . . waiting until the first shock waves subsided.

It was in Chicago, shortly after Dean and I teamed up. We were playing an extended engagement at the Chez Paree and living at the Ambassador East Hotel.

One night around 2 A.M. I'm getting ready for bed, and there's a knock on my door. I go to answer it, and this young fellow is standing there, saying in a broad Boston accent, "Because I live next door I'm sure you think I want to borrow some sugar."

"No, I didn't think you wanted sugar at this hour, but if you want my autograph, I don't have any pictures here."

I invited him in and we started to talk—it was my first introduction to John F. Kennedy.

He had seen our show that night. Later, he stopped at the hotel desk and found out that my suite was adjacent to his. Anyway, he was now running for Congress and would be giving a speech at the Executives Club in Chicago the following morning. Could he read it to me? I said fine. It was a dry, bland speech, something about "America Today"; something on the importance of America's future, too many people existing for today, the now. . . . I recall one particular line: "Whether you understand it or not, the *now* is twenty-five years from now, and this country has to be ready, the people have to be ready. . . ." It lacked punch. I told him if he gave that speech at the Executives Club, he'd be back in the Navy quick. He agreed, then asked if I could put some humor into it. So we worked on the speech. I punched it up with a few gags, scribbling them between his typewritten lines. One gag he especially liked. "If I do it," he said, *"I'll* be appearing at the Chez Paree."

Oh, yes, he loved a joke, as much as I loved to tease him. I'll give you a for instance, a little cameo of a practical joke I played on him one afternoon at the Ambassador East. . . .

As I got off the elevator thinking mischievous thoughts of one kind or the other, here he comes walking down the hall looking stunningly handsome. I say, "John, you'll never believe—there was a chick ringside last night, I can't explain—a combination of Lana Turner, Ava Gardner and Betty Grable—the most fantastic chick I ever saw in my life!"

"Hm-hm . . . but can she cook?"

I pressed on. "Let me just send her in to you to say hello."

"Well, Jerry, I have an appointment. However . . . I'll be back between seven and seven-thirty this evening." And he gets into the elevator.

At seven-fifteen I have this chambermaid from my floor —big, fat, shining gold tooth, a wart on her chin, no eyebrows, the ugliest chambermaid in all Chicago—stationed at his door as I open mine a crack and signal her to knock.

John opens his door, and she says, "Mr. Lewis told me you'd be in and you wanted to look on me."

I heard him start to plotz. She was out of there in three minutes, heading toward my suite.

I said, "What happened?"

"Well, Mr. Lewis, he gave me twenty dollars to go away. Now, if you give me fifty more, we can have us some real fun."

A straight-faced nod as I hear John laughing in the other suite. I think he laughed through the night. You could hear him through the walls.

We'd stroll around Chicago bantering about show business and sports, going from street to street, crossing Michigan Avenue with its big hotels and stores, occasionally shouting into blustery winds. And John would walk straight ahead, never blinking, as though he were at the wheel of his old PT boat.

I remember him writing bits and pieces on great American heroes. He kept them filed away in his suite. Years later, when I read *Profiles in Courage,* I realized the book had to have started there—Chicago—while we both were young and getting our acts together.

He had been a senator for a short while when I caught up with him next. I was working the Melody Fair Tent in Hyannis and visited him at the Kennedy compound, his family retreat. There, we spent many an idle hour watching sea gulls, formations of clouds, blue water that looked like a Winslow Homer painting; out on those waters we'd sail, John at the wheel, grinning, enjoying himself . . . I remember him saying once, "I can never get enough of it."

Bad back and all, he also played golf. Played it well. I joined him a couple of times on the course, but only to ride around in a cart while he trekked the green. He golfed and I searched the grass for little white balls that had gone astray. I thought—what a dumb game this is.

Jack Keller had taught me how to play sometime around 1950, then made me give it up because he felt I didn't have the mental equipment. Mind you, Keller had been a professional, one of the few left-handed pro golfers in tournament play. At the age of nineteen he shot a 58 at the Town and Country Club in Minneapolis, which to the best of my knowledge still stands as a course record.

One day in Los Angeles, Keller took me to a practice range for a lesson. I teed up the ball, swung hard and watched it dribble off the tee to die in the grass a few yards away. A disgrace! I threw the club at it, stomped up and down, and carried on plenty. Keller grabbed me by the collar. "What makes you think in the depths of the stupidity that you call a brain"—furiously shaking me—"what makes you think you were to hit that shot any better? Until you can walk out here like a gentleman and meet the challenge, I don't ever want to see you play this game."

That's why I stayed on the sidelines during John Kennedy's golf games. Almost twenty years passed before I took up golf again, deciding to meet the challenge and attacking the learning process with abandon, every day for four solid years, never missing a day; weather, pain, rain, no one to play with, it didn't matter, I had to be good and got better. My official handicap came down from a beginner's 24 to a formidable 8, and less than two years later I was playing to a 5! By then Keller had retired to Sidney, British Columbia. But I kept sending him my scorecards, maybe just to let him know he had given me a gift I shall cherish the rest of my life: the game of golf, and how to be a gentleman and sportsman while playing it.

Since those early outings, a lot more has happened. Kennedy took office as President in 1961. The next spring, I had a meeting with Paul Cohen and other board members of MDA. As things stood, except for limited radio spots and one telethon over the past three years, there had been virtually no national publicity. Hence, it had become tougher to recruit fund-raising volunteers, which in turn made it tougher to come up with big bucks to fight muscular dystrophy.

I told the board, "I know some people. Let me see what I can do."

As a first step I placed a call to New York Supreme

Court Justice Samuel J. Liebowitz. A champion of the underdog, Liebowitz gained fame during the Scottsboro trial back in the early thirties. I got him on the phone and said, "Judge, I know the government has given research grants to many organizations, to individuals, people like Jonas Salk. Well, that's what I want for MDA. But how does one get up like Jimmy Stewart did in *Mr. Smith Goes to Washington* and ask for dollars to cure muscular dystrophy? I wouldn't take advantage. I'd just state my case the best I can."

"Jerry," he said emphatically, "it's the law of the land. Any tax-paying citizen has the right to go before Congress and request a grant if it's in the public interest. Of course, I recommend that you wait until Congress is in session."

"When is that?"

"After the Easter holiday. But you may not get on the agenda. It could be next year, perhaps a year later. It depends. These things can't be rushed."

Two minutes late—a lot. I had a 9:30 A.M. appointment with the President of the United States. I realized he had more important matters to think of than the one I was bringing to his attention.

"I apologize, Mr. President. I couldn't remember your address."

John Kennedy laughed. "By inclination or design? Anyway, it's good to see you, Jerry."

Here we sat, the two of us, John at his desk in a reflective attitude as I told him of MDA's needs. "There's just one thing I can come up with, and that's to go before Congress and ask for one hundred million dollars. They do it for foreign aid and everything else, so let them help my kids get out of their wheelchairs."

He answered slowly, weighing his words: "I don't believe you would want the government for your partner. You'd only inherit a rancid can of peas."

"What does that mean, sir?"

"Simply this: if the money is appropriated by Congress, then never again will you be able to run your organization as you now run it. No longer. You couldn't do a damn thing without the government's approval." He rested a finger against his cheek. Then in an undertone, "I'll do what I can, naturally, if this is the course you wish to take."

"No," I said, slowly getting up to say good-bye. "You've convinced me. Forget the request. Thanks, but don't help."

The last time I saw John was at his birthday party in 1963. He had called about a month earlier, saying, "I know you're not a spring chicken anymore. Do you have enough energy to do a benefit?" He wanted me to do a "one-man show" for his birthday. . . . The only way I could have said no was if I had lockjaw. . . . And there at the Washington Armory a sea of faces, at least five thousand people seated at tables, including Vice-President Johnson, kings, queens, dignitaries from all over the globe, not to mention the entire Kennedy family . . . What do I say first? I knew my craft and was sure of the program I had prepared, but since ancient days at the Greek forum the performer had to have that first line, the first anything to help get him off the ground. . . . And it hit me maybe ten seconds before I was introduced: "Tonight I am told the honored guest as well as the birthday boy is John Kennedy. Well, folks, I'm taking no chances. Electrician! Throw that spotlight on the head table—" And as the light caught John, I said, "Will the real President of the United States stand up!"

He stood, tall and handsome, taking his white handkerchief out of his pocket, smiling and waving it at me like a Navy coxswain sending flag signals. . . . The audience

went wild with laughter and applause. I was home free.
What a night. . . . What a man! After the show we had
a couple of drinks at his suite at the Mayflower Hotel. . . .
Before I left he gave me a gift. A plaque. It was hanging
on my office wall when the bulletin from Dallas screamed
out that dark November day.

The plaque is a tangible reminder of his ideals. It reads:
*There are three things which are real. God, Human Folly,
and Laughter. Since the first two are beyond our compre-
hension, we must do what we can with the third.*

[8]

One day early in my career I'm shopping on Beverly Boulevard when suddenly here comes Clark Gable out of a restaurant. As you can imagine, whole groups of people stared
at him. Nobody moved until Gable got into a black limousine to be driven off somewhere. Then a block away, still
window-shopping, I heard excited voices and saw those
very same people laughing and pointing at me. "Hey, Jerry!
Make a face! Wow, are you funny!"

So—they were in awe of Gable with their titters and
arm nudging and rubbernecking, but they seemed to have
recalled something silly on my face which made them infinitely more happy, just to look at the sight of that jerky
Jerry!

That's when I knew I was a star.

For sixteen years I had been ringing up consistent studio
profits, one of the few stars whose name spelt "Guaranteed
Bucks" on a movie marquee, and you can credit Barney
Balaban for admitting to the press, "If Jerry wants to set
fire to the studio, I'll give him the match."

Of course, I didn't follow through. Instead, I ended my association with Paramount. Things had changed. The policies were harsher. There were a lot of incompetents in the front office, and their decisions began to affect me directly. As a good illustration, while doing *The Family Jewels* I had to go over my cost sheets on a set we were building. A one-room interior—couch, dresser, a few pieces of Salvation Army furniture—but all I could see was a mysterious designation: #842 charged to picture #15637 . . . or whatever. Anyway, alongside the numbers there's a whopping figure of $12,000.

An outrage! Somebody's trying to shuffle dollars, and I gotta find out who. So I go to Mr. Who and say, "Explain this to me, because I don't understand it."

For an hour Mr. Who sits there shaking his head. It's as though I'm talking to Internal Revenue.

He says, "Well, there's the union."

I nod.

"Then you have to account for the insurance."

I smile.

"Then you have miscellaneous. . . ."

And I say, "What's with miscellaneous?"

No answer. It turns out miscellaneous is Miss Cellaneous. She's a real looker, but I decide she ain't gonna be in my picture anymore. I'm gonna make her into somebody else. I'll make her lumber, hammers, paint, brushes. But no more Miss Cellaneous. Because she's grabbed my money and is now living in South America with Martin Bormann.

I needed someone to watch my back. I felt like the fighter who walks back to his corner after having 90 percent of his body socked six inches within it. He says to the manager, "How'm I doin'?" And the manager says, "He ain't laid a glove on ya." "Oh, yeah!" says the fighter. "Then you better keep your eye on the referee, because somebody's kickin' the shit outta me!"

Well, I called Joey Stabile, who'd helped me over the years. At first he wasn't that sure he wanted to work for me. Our friendship meant more to him than anything. But I had no fear of placing it in jeopardy. Not from day one, when we met at Slapsie Maxie's. He was my kind of guy, scrupulously honest and dependable. Though a little out-distanced by his brother Dick as a musician, he also had a real talent and gifts of his own. He was a skilled crafts-man, a master builder. He could construct anything from a birdhouse to the finest luxury home and give you the right count on every nail and board that went into it.

So when he finally joined my company, Joey functioned as though he had been in the film business all his life. He dug around at Paramount; got the right count on every buck that had gone to Miss Cellaneous, every couch bought and charged off to my production company. Joey's discov-eries overrode my loyalties to Paramount. After completing *The Family Jewels* I did a film called *Boeing-Boeing,* then got out of there in 1965 and signed a contract with Colum-bia Pictures. And soon the cameras were rolling again on another Jerry Lewis comedy—*Three on a Couch.*

[9]

Work. It was my avocation, my pastime, my enjoyment, one and the same. I never asked myself if it was bad or good, or selfish, or wasteful. I just knew I needed to work. So trivial a task as picking up the newspaper on a Sunday morning was an imposition. Let somebody else do it. I had more important things in mind.

Meanwhile, right under my nose there's a hot-rod music craze going on, top volume, amplified and blasting out of loudspeakers like the guns of Navarone. Yes, the Beatles and the Rolling Stones were creating electrified sounds that switched a whole new generation of kids over to the discovery of noise.

And there's my son Gary bopping away on a set of drums in the house, not so loud as to wake the neighbors, but still it's rock and roll, and I'm checking on him at least occasionally to see what the hell he might be getting into. Remembering anyhow when he was younger, about eleven, throwing a pitch to catcher Roy Campanella at Chicago's Wrigley Field, the entire Dodger team and my movie crew watching on a lovely afternoon . . . Gary having the thrill of a lifetime while we filmed sequences for *The Geisha Boy*. I stood looking, dreaming big dreams of his future, my own world crowded out, forgotten. . . . He was pitching no-hitters, winning the World Series, getting the Cy Young Award, enshrined in the Hall of Fame. . . .

He was playing those drums when I looked up at a framed newspaper clipping telling of that workout at Wrigley Field, with Pee Wee Reese, Duke Snider and quiet, warm, wonderful Gil Hodges commenting that I handled myself well enough on the diamond to make the big leagues. . . .

I hung it on the wall because it made me feel like a hero to all my sons.

They were growing. They had their own dreams. And now, objectively, I realized I was on the outside, not involved with their individual strivings, frustrations or most intimate fears. I did my duty. I loved them as much as any man could love his sons, but in the long haul it was Patti who really brought them up. She entangled herself in all the little superficialities—the skinned knees, the chipped teeth, the jealousies and disagreements—one minute to the next. It was Patti who actually got Gary started in show business. She encouraged him, got him the drums and

bought the equipment for his group. They called themselves The Playboys. Then they cut a record . . . "This
Diamond Ring," a smash hit that sold two million copies.
Gary was voted the number-one male vocalist by *Billboard,*
and the number-one leader of the best new rock-and-roll
group of 1964 by *Cashbox.* Publicity flashed around. The
group rode on its crest, which took them into the colleges,
theatres and nightclubs. . . . They made it big. Their
songs—"This Diamond Ring," "Save Your Heart for Me,"
"Everybody Loves a Clown"—and their first album, *A
Session with Gary Lewis and the Playboys,* were getting
played on every Top 40 station, night and day.

Gary came to me with a royalty check in his hand, as
though nothing unusual had happened. He said, "Father,
I just got this check for three hundred fifty thousand dollars. I want to split it with the four other guys. What do
you think?"

He was paying them five hundred dollars a week.

I said, "They get a salary They get it fifty-two weeks a
year, whether they work or not."

His weight shifted from one foot to the other. I knew I
was putting him through an ordeal, because I had been
through the same kind of thing myself.

"Well, how much do you want to give them?"

"Down the middle, even shares to all the guys."

"Are you sure this is what you want?"

"Yes, Father."

I stared at him, then grumbled: "I think you're the worst
businessman I've ever met. But you'll do what your heart
tells you."

I was so very proud of what he had become.

That was 1965, a year of transition and adjustments. In
retrospect, the events are hard to place chronologically.
They get mixed up with later events and excitements so
innumerable I can't keep track. With pinpoint accuracy,

though, I can refer back to a night when, in a split second, a fraction of an inch made the difference between all my yesterdays and tomorrows.

The date, March 20, closing show at the Sands Hotel— and I took a pratfall off the piano doing a flip. Now, when you take a fall, you have to commit yourself. No rearranging things in midair, no hesitation or you can get hurt. Well, I committed, saw the microphone cable, twisted out of control and landed on my back—165 pounds slamming against this little plug attached to the cable. I was numb, but got up and finished the act.

Lou Brown walked me backstage. "That was some fall. You landed like a rock."

"Yeah, I think I hurt myself."

"I wouldn't be surprised. You oughta call the doctor."

"Aw, it'll go away."

Next morning I put in thirty minutes trying to get off the bed. The pain was horrendous, almost paralyzing, and it wouldn't stop.

I stood this for two hours, then went to Dr. Bill Stein, an orthopedic man in Los Angeles. He said, "There are problems. Before I can tell you what they are, I'll have to examine the X rays thoroughly."

I came back two days later, and he told me I had chipped a piece out of the upper spinal column. He then fitted me with a neck brace to relieve the pressure, started me on codeine and empirin, and said, "Don't remove the brace until you have to."

So there it was, a metal albatross around my neck, morning, noon and night. I tried, or would try, to get along without the brace while working at the studio. But the longer I remained free of that accursed contraption, the more my poor aching body cried out for it.

A year later I began seeing a number of neurologists— all to no avail. The prognosis was uniformly bleak. Not a single optimistic note among them. I'd have to live with the pain. Fibrous tissue (a pretzellike scar) had pressed around the nerve roots within the spinal column, causing irreversible damage. Therefore, the pain could be relieved only by heat, massage, rest and medication . . . the use of a drug more powerful than codeine and empirin.

It started simply enough with me taking one Percodan a day.

One little yellow tablet, containing a semisynthetic narcotic analgesic called Oxycodone hydrochloride. A real painkiller. It comes in bottles or blister packs, with labels clearly marked—*WARNING: May be habit forming.*

[10]

It's been said that a boat is a bunch of wood surrounded by water that you pour money into. Something about a boat, though. For some men it's *the* great escape, sitting there on the aft deck beneath a wash of stars, so untroubled, peacefully contemplating the purr of an engine and the exquisite calm.

I didn't understand that feeling until 1961, after completing *The Ladies' Man* at Paramount.

I went to Mission Bay with Joe Stabile, looking to rent a speedboat and do some water skiing. Naturally, the marinas had a wide selection of boats: dinghies, ketches, yawls, sloops, sailboats and yachts. But nowhere could we rent a speedboat. So I bought one.

Joey ran her all over the ocean, gunning the RPM's higher and higher while I rode the skis, loose as a goose, sometimes soaring above the waves at what seemed like fifty miles per hour. But the best part . . . putting the boat ashore, sitting quietly with our Cokes and sandwiches, then taking my first bite—"Jesus Christ! I never thought food could taste so good! Now I understand why people live on boats."

Joe grinned. "Maybe we can load yours up with pepperoni and go around the world."

I eventually got myself a forty-one-foot cabin cruiser named the *Pussycat*. It came equipped with every conceivable electronic device. I mean, gizmos upon gizmos—lights blinking, sonar screens blipping, blips that would tell you if the fish were jumping and the lox was in the refrigerator. Truth is, I rigged up a Videocom camera on the bridge, with monitors port and starboard, to scan the Pacific behind me. Secured to the mast was another camera shooting the horizon ahead. Luxuries like that. And the money didn't mean anything. I spent it on pleasure, on having the family along to share the same pleasures. The children loved it. They were either fishing or just working around, keeping *Pussycat* spotless. Sometimes, while down below checking their bunks as they slept, I'd think—All these years of searching and wanting . . . now, just seeing them safe and sound on the *Pussycat* makes up for everything.

As it turned out, I had four big boats: *Pussycat, Pussycat II, Princess* and finally *Princess II*. She was the most elegant, a sixty-eight-foot yacht with gorgeous lines, lush, finely honed; actually rivaled the very best ocean liners for comfort.

Its predecessor, *Princess I,* resembled it in design, and I would've held on to her a lot longer except that an unfortunate twist of bad luck took things out of my hands.

I'll never forget the date: July 19, 1966. We set out from San Francisco, heading south along the Monterey coast toward San Diego. Aboard, my secretary Carol Saraceno, my assistant director Hal Bell, maintenance man Joe Proux and engineer Art Gannon. At about midnight, while I'm in the lounge half-dozing on the couch waiting to relieve Joe Proux at the helm, he suddenly barges in, saying, "Hate to tell you this, Jerry, but there's a break below the waterline. We're flooding, and I don't think the pumps can handle it."

I looked. Sure enough, the water was rising fast in the engine room. Ten seconds after that I got on the radio, raising Maydays. I had no idea if anyone heard us. Over and over I called our position, and from midnight till five in the morning no one responded.

Meantime, Art Gannon kept shooting off flares every ten or fifteen minutes. You'd see a quick burst of yellowish light, the ocean shining and then falling away into darkness again. An incredible sight, and frightening . . .

The Monterey coast is five hundred miles of rocky shoreline. The surf smashing against those rocks could pound you into chopped meat if you tried to come in. By 5:30 A.M., it seemed as though we were goners. I watched my children's belongings float across the saloon; toys and things disappearing under swirling water. The night was fading. Through the mist we saw the dim outline of land, perhaps a mile away. I gave orders to abandon ship.

None of us at the time knew that a thirteen-year-old boy had spotted our flares and alerted the Coast Guard. We only knew our lives were at stake, that *Princess* was doomed to break up and go under. Joe Proux, Art Gannon and I hastily lowered a rubber raft. Carol Saraceno came running, schlepping her purse: "My makeup is in here. If I'm going to die, I want to die beautful."

And there's Hall Bell standing against the rail, his eyes frozen with fear.

It was like a newsreel, the five of us huddled in the raft, drifting by torturous degrees to safety . . . to a tiny dot on God's earth, the only accessible place along the entire jagged coastline between San Francisco and Los Angeles. A miracle!

We waded ashore. A group of Coast Guard officers immediately brought us to waiting automobiles which drove us to a café some two miles from the beach. There, we were given coffee and blankets.

Around eight o'clock the same morning I stood on the beach, aimlessly throwing pebbles while watching *Princess* start her long slide into the deep. Then, after one last desperate glimpse, I walked away.

Later on, I discovered the fault lay in the construction of *Princess*'s hull. A former engineer who had worked on the boat gave testimony at my insurance hearing, showing blueprints that called for one-inch slugs instead of the one-half-inch slugs that were used. He had told the inspector they wouldn't hold. So I collected on the insurance, but it didn't make me feel any better because in the final measure of things it was my ship, and she died.

When the *Titanic* went down, do you know where the captain was? On deck, after dinner, dancing with Mrs. Jones. Meanwhile, the *Titanic* strikes an iceberg. Watertight doors don't make it, and five compartments are slowly filling up. Now, the British Admiralty calls for the responsible party to step forward and confess. *Seaman:* "Not I, sir. I was busy getting a new job on a ship coming out of Southampton." *Admiralty:* "Yes, yes, of course, you may stand down and be dismissed." *The captain:* "But you see, sir, I was on deck dancing with Mrs. Jones." *Admiralty:* "We don't give a shit. You ruined our fucking little boat there, Captain. Do you notice the fruit salad on your hat? Do you see where it says Captain, you piece of shit! Into the slammer—the old Bailey for you, sir."

And he's still there.
The Cap-i-tan.

[11]

Irving Kaye had been smoking those Dunhills and smiling
and lugging my suitcases all over the world for nearly a
quarter century, but now his step had slowed, the urge to
travel had left him. Nevertheless, I couldn't think of any
easy method to retire him gracefully. I'm saying to myself,
"Poor Irving, what'll he do if I put him out to pasture?
He'll hate me—I can't do it." And I'm beginning to hate
myself for thinking about the day when I'll have to tell
him, "Irving, it's been great, but you need a rest."

One day he walks into my office not saying a word, with
his hands clasped in front of him, head jutted a little forward in an aggressive pose or look of anxiety; stands awhile
as I finish a phone call, then slides into a chair.

I say, "You're acting strange."

"I am?"

"Yeah. What is it? What's with the face?"

"It's my face. It's not bothering me. Is it bothering you?"

"Starting now, yes. Something's wrong, so you may as
well tell me because I'm gonna sit here till you do."

"Well, I don't want to work anymore."

"Anymore? When did you begin?"

"I'm getting old, Jerry."

"You're not so old."

"I'm pushing seventy. What's left? Five—ten years?"

"Don't talk foolish. There's plenty of mileage in that
tank of yours."

"Yeah yeah yeah. Listen . . . am I in your will?"

Which, indeed, he is. I took care of that long ago.

I say, "Irving, everything is in order. You don't have to worry."

"Good," he says. "So how about an advance?"

"Advance?"

"Sure. On the will. Statistically, I'm gonna croak before you do, so I'd like to have it now."

And today we're talking about forty-two years since he stuck a toothbrush in his pocket, then rode the rails with me to Buffalo, to the old Palace Theatre. . . . Going there in his always clean but rumpled suit, puffing his cheap cigar, head down, eyes skimming the pages of *Variety;* and you could tell by looking at him that he was going nowhere but home, to whatever town had a theatre, lights, crowds and a deserving spot for him backstage.

My caring friend—he's the same man I met in 1939, except for minor changes, like the once surefooted prance that's now slowed to a shuffle. But he still gets around to see when I'm playing Vegas or anywhere else, so long as it doesn't run him over eighty dollars to get to. And if I dog the show, you can bet he won't come into my dressing room. I'll hear from him later, telling me, "You better get your act together, or you'll wind up back on those straw-seated trains to Loew's Oblivion—"

He always told me the truth, and I guess I love him most for that.

BOOK SEVEN

W H Y is it that when a child is born, only the limbs, eyes, fingers and ears are counted and considered? Why not the mind? It's the machine that governs the very existence of life. Why then is it not treated with greater care and appreciation? Why aren't people made to understand that from the first moment when the mind functions it begins to register all the emotions: fear, joy, hope, faith?

If the child can breathe, it can feel. If the child can cry, it needs. And through that normal process, it understands, remembers and will know love, warmth, care and consideration, as well as doubt, unkindness and deceit; the repayment of which the child will one day have to make.

So if you're late or delinquent in your care and interest, there is no known way to make up for this. The infant mind has already grasped the situation and tucked it away until the rent comes due.

Therefore, the next time you visit the zoo, remember . . . *an elephant isn't the only one.* If you mistreat that knowledge, you have produced two decades from now a troubled child.

This is why in every one of Patti's pregnancies I would ofttimes kiss her belly and talk to my baby, squeaky little laughs, caressing, talking to *him*—"Do you know dat you're gonna come an' live here? Do you know dat I'm not a plumber? I love you already because you're a nice-looking, nifty fella. So don't come out naked. You dress in a shirt, slacks and a tie. . . ."

I know he heard. And nobody in this world is going to convince me that he didn't have a good time, too.

Now, let's move ahead and watch the years melt by, from *The Best Years of Our Lives* to *The Russians Are Coming, The Russians Are Coming.* And there's seventeen-year-old Bob Mathias going out to beat the world's best to win the Olympic decathlon in rainy London, 1948. See it now: "Howdy Doody," "Captain Video," "Hopalong Cassidy," "Kukla, Fran and Ollie" "You Bet Your Life." On they go: "Person to Person," talking about Montgomery Clift, Marlon Brando, Gorgeous George and Jackie Robinson; the Army-McCarthy hearings; long sideburns and blue-suede shoes; the incomparable *Lolita;* the Nixon-Khrushchev kitchen debate; "The Untouchables"—and whoosh!—there go the fifties. "As the World Turns" here came "The Beverly Hillbillies"; and John Glenn, James Brown and Jimmy Brown; the Maharishi; Malcolm X; A. J. Foyt—zoom—*Dr. Strangelove;* and Lyndon Baines Johnson ushering in the Great Society!

In early 1966 President Johnson was in the Philippines attending a high-level conference on Vietnam war operations. Coincidentally, my number-one son arrived there on a tour with The Playboys. That's when I got a call from him, all excited, telling me about Jinky Suzara.

"Well," he said, "I love her . . . and we plan to be married."

He had met Jinky in Hollywood. I recalled my brief introduction to her, one of those special kicks you get upon seeing your kid with his eyes lit because there's a wonderful girl he wants you to meet. A slender, pretty, doe-eyed girl who'd soon be going home to the Philippines where her father worked as chief pilot of Manila Harbor.

And I, the parent of a twenty-year-old boy who little more than a year ago worked as a car park during his school vacation to have money for college. Now, suddenly, the years were advancing at a blinding rate of speed. One phone call coming from halfway round the earth, and I realized it was time to let go.

Then Gary received his notice from the draft board, so all bets were off. The Army had allowed him thirty days to wind up his business affairs.

I'd been filming *The Big Mouth* down in San Diego when Patti phoned to tell me the news. Stony silence, my emotions fluttering like a haywire needle—anger, hate, guilt, terror, heartbreak. In Asian jungles they were sorting the living from the dead while here I was, shooting glamorous scenes around the gardens of Sea World. A sick joke!

I flew home that evening. Whatever agonies Patti had covered during her call were now released by an even greater agony of the unknown. I had never seen her so distraught.

Later, getting up from bed about three in the morning, I found myself at the desk writing a letter to Lyndon B. Johnson, c/o The White House (Personal) (Urgent) (Confidential):

Dear Mr. President:

    Vietnam, although a faraway place, reached out and knocked at our door in Bel Air. Sure, we heard about the trouble, the uncertainty, but like most Americans the feeling at our home was that if we left it alone it would soon go away. Well, it didn't. It's here, and real, and angry, and sticking its ugly arms out to grab our son, our firstborn.

Why? Why any son? And whom do we blame? The bureaucrats? The nasty munition companies? The politicians? The Communists? I don't know, but must we wait till the '68 election year for a white flag that might save our son Gary? And how many years do we have to pray that God will be good to the world and deliver a final, everlasting peace?

Why must men use boys to climb upon to gain their goals?

Can't they find what they have here, instead of such a faraway place?

It was written, but never sent.

That's your American patriot, something they taught me in school: *My country, right or wrong.*

We drove Gary to the airport that January morning in 1967. The good-byes were rough. He climbed aboard the plane, looked back smiling at Jinky, at his brothers and Patti, finally at me. Then they locked the door. He went flying out to Fort Ord, California. A brand-new recruit going to school in the U.S. Army.

I saw him a couple of Sundays during his basic training. He appeared bright-eyed and bushy-tailed, everything rockin', as he said. A lot of other guys in his outfit had the same confident outlook, which made things easier for Patti and myself. Besides, there were wedding bells to think of; as a matter of fact, Patti spent most of her days handling the preparations, going around shopping with Jinky for her bridal gown, coordinating whatever had to be coordinated; a bunch of things beyond my ken. What did I know? I was a comedian, not a caterer.

Anyway, the kids got married March 11, 1967. Beautiful ceremony, champagne toasts to health and happiness . . . mothers and fathers, relatives, friends, everybody seeing them off on their honeymoon.

We prayed he wouldn't be shipped overseas, but our prayers weren't answered.

Two years passed. He came home. I expected the same boy to come home. When he stepped off that plane, I didn't see my son. I saw a beaten old man. He just wanted to know: "Why did it happen? What was it all about?"

Later, months later, sitting in a corner staring at nothing, looking as though he had lived a thousand years and witnessed nothing but madness, he spoke softly, would pause, then find his voice again. . . .

He told me what he could remember. . . . Villages uprooted, swept away by napalm, people with bound hands, babies crying out to their mothers . . . No sleep at night, living with rats the size of cats . . . Two of his buddies wiped out . . . They were having lunch; their bodies splattered on his food. . . . He asked: "How long do you think it's going to take me to sleep, Dad?"

He was on drugs. He hid them in his shoes, his jackets, in the lampshades—Christ knows where! We got him as much help as we could: doctors, hospitals, treatment. Then, after two years, he began to put The Playboys back together again. He felt OK. He was alive.

And I found myself in a continual rage, sounding off in interview after interview and getting into all kinds of controversy—"Stop the war!" (Ha!) But then there were very few in Hollywood who really knew if the war was right or wrong. On one side we had the John Wayne-Bob Hope forces. On the other side, Jane Fonda. Nothing between except apathy; hawks, doves and do-nothings.

"Let's make pictures!"

I made two more after *The Big Mouth*. You may recollect *Don't Raise the Bridge, Lower the River* and *Hook, Line, and Sinker*. Did they have any merit? I'll leave that to you; I hardly knew what my feelings were back then and the kind of work I was turning out. My son Ronnie had reached the draft age. Cornered, perhaps, by Vietnam, his only refuge a classroom seat at the School of Performing Arts. So as far as I was concerned, the government had placed me in a very untenable position. It made me choose.

I was prepared to hire a moving van and start heading towards the water.

[2]

Oh, yes, I was howling like a sonofabitch those days. Not only at the war, or the crap coming down from Washington, but also at the daily violence coming into our homes through television. A murder a minute. Cops and robbers, assassins, arsonists, kidnappers, rapists, homicidal maniacs —a full schedule of devastating ugliness. Whatever happened to "I Remember Mama," "Kraft Theatre," "Playhouse 90" and other shows that had offered up a lot of fine entertainment? Really sad, the kitchen homilies of Mama and the poignant heroism of Marty the butcher were abandoned by the programmers in favor of trash, and good writers like Paddy Chayevsky left television because they finally got tired of being ground up by network bosses whose only concern seemed to be, "Is it ready?" And if not, "Well, what're we gonna do with all these pilots? Oh, let's take the one where the nun has an affair with the llama, that's a good one! Put that in the eight-to-nine slot on Wednesday night!" Years later, Paddy got even by writing his magnificent screenplay *Network*, with its never-to-be-forgotten: "I'm mad as hell, and I'm not going to take it anymore!"

Screaming out the window—Jerry Lewis in the closing years of the sixties.

Things had changed. Values were different. People got to a stage where it became unfashionable to greet one another with, "Have a nice day." It was, "Have a good one," and, "Hi, doc . . ." What's doc? That man busted his hump for thirty-five years and they call him doc. Call him Doctor! And those kids I'm fighting for are not victims of MD. It has a name: muscular dystrophy. It needs to be said and pronounced. It demands attention. Not like, "Hi, sweetie, didja hear about Bert? He's got MD." "Oh, really? Who's his doc?"

Or: "Ol' Johnnie boy beat the big C." No, John Wayne didn't. He died of cancer.

And so did Paul Cohen.

Most of us who banded together in 1950 to implement Paul's cherished dream for the creation of a muscular dystrophy facility were with him when he opened its doors at Columbia University nine years later. Since then, until his death in 1968, the ranks had grown to a virtual army of scientists, doctors, social workers, therapists, volunteers and others, all unified into a solid, totally dedicated organization. There were now 75 new clinics and 350 chapter affiliates located throughout the 50 states. Add to this the financial aid given to scientific studies going on at 100 similar institutions, and you have some idea of how rapidly we sprang from practically nowhere. Just suffice it to say— and this is the essential point—as we spread our wings searching for a cure, the sheer weight of expansion required more and more dollars, and the telethon served as the indispensable catalyst bringing the money in.

Yet if I had known at the beginning what would happen —the dissidence, the flack I would have to take, the pain and slamming of doors, the days and hours and weeks of depression; indeed, all the stuff that would fall on my head

so I could look like Harry Horseshit each Labor Day—
well, the truth is, I'd have never started.

But as old Omar once foretold: The moving finger
writes, and having writ, moves on. . . .

On January 4, 1964, MDA executive director Bob Ross
wrote me the following letter:

> New York City has become a "trouble spot" since
> we stopped doing telethons. Gradually, our image
> is fading and public response is falling off. I've
> knocked myself out trying to come up with new
> ideas that would be rewarding from a fund-raising
> standpoint. When you get down to it, however, there's
> still nothing like a telethon, especially in a city of this
> size.
>
> You've said no a number of times, predicated on
> your feelings about television. But, by now, you've
> made several appearances, so maybe you've softened
> your attitude. What else can I tell you, Jerry, except
> that we really need a New York telethon—and need it
> badly. Will you reconsider? Please?

I told Bob it was out of the question, that I was gun-shy
about going back into television.

And being an instinctive, understanding man, he knew
when to stop asking, Why?

That settled, I proceeded to do what was necessary, using the same alternate routes as before, clocking hundreds
and thousands of air miles over the next ten or twelve
months in behalf of MDA, going around meeting corporate
heads, labor chiefs, the rank and file from pickers and
packers to people in the freezers. I met them all—the fire-
fighters, letter carriers, truckers, machinists, hotel and restaurant workers, the painters, paperhangers, pipefitters,
plumbers, printing pressmen and so forth—I mean the

grass roots of America, those men and women belonging
to the AFL-CIO. They were the real heroes in our fight to
lick the disease. If they didn't give, we would still be on
square one. Because what's amazing in the human condition is how consistently the little guy puts out while the
big guy is taking in.

I remember meeting a wheelchair manufacturer who
said he couldn't bring the price down on his chairs. He said
we weren't ordering enough. I said, "Thank you. I'll go
home tonight and pray that a lot more children will get sick
so we can order more chairs."

Here's the classic of all time: I'm at a meeting with the
president of a major corporation, and after spilling my guts
for a good half-hour, trying to get a contribution out of
his firm, he says, "My business is making autmobiles. I'm
not in the business of working for cripples."

I can't believe that I really heard what he said. But I
know I'm never going to forget it.

So I say, "I'd like to have another meeting with you tomorrow and bring a friend. Would it be all right?"

He says, "Fine."

I brought along a poster child; wheeled in this beautiful
eight-year-old boy and introduced him to the industrialist.
"Now, would you kindly repeat to him what you said to me
yesterday?"

P.S. I nailed the sonofagun. He authorized a fleet of vans
to transport my kids—though we paid for them. But thank
God, at cost.

The things you have to go through.

In mid-1965 I got another letter from Bob Ross:

Some months ago, when I asked you about the New
York telethon, you said you weren't ready to take the
dive back into television yet.
Maybe *now?*

We really need a major telethon this November or early December—or even in January. I realize the magnitude of what I'm asking you. But I also think, very sincerely, that it would benefit all concerned. Your devoted fans here in New York comprise the ideal audience for your "return." What do you think?

We must move quickly because, as you know so well, it takes weeks of preparation to get a telethon organized.

This time I couldn't bring myself to answer him directly. Instead, I sent off a note to Jack Keller, with the letter attached:

Dear Trapper—

I can't do it! My heart and my mind won't allow me the luxury.

I'm sure you understand. Please try to get the MDA boys to understand. Maybe they'll come up with a different plan that won't hurt as much.

So there it stood; no ifs, ands or buts. I wasn't ready for a telethon.

Except—one never knows what tomorrow brings.

Sometime during 1966, Mucio Delgado joined MDA as director of program development. And here I'm telling about a man who provided the sort of leadership you'll seldom find in anyone. He was our Lewis Stone—the judge —and we were his Andy Hardys. One twitch of his eye and I knew when to get the hell off a particular subject, or keep talking because that twitch said, "You're honing in perfectly, my boy." Moose came out of Sasco, Arizona; big, strong, ruddy features, a little touch of shyness behind his smile. Everybody loved him. He was our protector; the recommender. If there were traps or stalemates of any kind, he had the answers.

One afternoon I'm sitting with him and Bob Ross at the New York office. Now, once again, Bob's trying to talk me into a New York telethon.

This time he has WNEW-TV cleared for a shot on Labor Day. I said, "Bob, I'm sorry, but I have to turn it down. I'm not going to stick my neck out and get rapped for doing good stuff."

"So there'll be a few cynics. What is that compared to the millions who've shown their support?" He sighs, looks helplessly at Moose. "I don't know what to do with this guy. He's impossible."

Moose twitches an eye.

I say to Bob, "That's some terrific bargain you got. A Labor Day telethon? Who's gonna watch? Nobody is home; they're all celebrating in parks."

Moose: "Is that a fact?"

"Well, it's a supposition. . . ."

"Quite right, my boy. A mere supposition."

And the rest is history.

Nineteen sixty-six: The first Jerry Lewis Labor Day Telethon (broadcast only to the New York area) raised $1,002,114, the largest total ever in a single fund-raising event for humanitarian purposes. Nineteen sixty-seven: We did even better; $1,126,846 pledged, plus some $50,000 more collected. Nineteen sixty-eight: The first telethon to be networked, five stations combining to help MDA raise $1,401,876.

Then came Labor Day, 1969. On a twenty-station hookup, live from the Imperial Ballroom of New York's Americana Hotel, I watched the tote board hit the $2,000,-000 mark before leaving the stage.

[3]

Almost without my knowing it, three decades of movie-making slipped behind me. The Dean Martin period, the solo years, the vagabond years after Paramount; at work turning out pictures for Columbia, *One More Time* for United Artists, then *Which Way to the Front?*, a 1970 release for Warner Bros. I had seen a lot of growth, but the current Hollywood trend saw selfish, ambitious men who called themselves producers beginning to transfer their poisonous ideas from television to the silver screen. Everybody crying out for happy entertainment, while everything in sight was being tainted by the grime of "realism" and magnified on celluloid. A decaying process, a chipping away like water that hits the rock, century after century, until one of nature's strongest minerals slowly erodes. And that's what they were doing to our industry. It was eroding under a heavy flood of X-rated films. So I backed off. I wouldn't play the game. I'd made forty-one pictures in thirty years; in the next seven years, I made only one.

There weren't too many people in the business who wanted me, anyway. I had a big mouth and usually said what I thought and believed. And there's no place in the corporate structure for a man with convictions, who also happens to be ruthlessly honest. The two archenemies of film corporate enterprises are "conviction" and "honesty." If you have those qualities, you will be labeled "difficult," "egomaniacal," "tough to get along with"—but isn't it interesting that the people who have earned those reputations are generally multifaceted talents who know their craft and care about the product they're making? They won't settle for less than what they know they're capable of. Money be damned; screw the clock!

I'd like to think that my name belongs on the list of "difficult" people, along with, for example: Barbra Streisand, Marlon Brando, George C. Scott, Paul Newman, Robert Redford, Frank Sinatra, Al Pacino, Dustin Hoffman, Robert DeNiro, Jane Fonda. . . .

Now, if you want a list of those who had "great" reputations and were also known to be "pussycats," they were: Myrna Loy, Edward Arnold, Pinky Tomlin, Van Johnson, Deanna Durbin, Smiley Burnette, Roy Rogers, Jean Parker, Tom Brown, Kent Smith, Vera Ralston, Frank McHugh, and Sonja Henie.

So if you're ready to be a puppet by saying yes to whatever the corporate structure wishes you to adhere to, you'll have a hell of a five-day week in Hollywood.

But the worst of it is . . . the little fellow who lives in a two-room cold-water flat goes to a movie to forget his problems and finds the movie is all about a man who lives in a two-room cold-water flat.

[4]

Jack and Emma Keller had been living in British Columbia for some time, in a rustic, old-fashioned house, set back from the stream; comfortable and secluded, a place you could never tire of. It was a perfect spot, with rainbow-trout streams, innumerable lakes and mountains so picturesque they took your breath away. Ironic, how wonderful and ideal this retreat could be from stress and worry, and how terrible that Jack had had the sword of melanoma poised over his head the past five years.

Emma, affectionate and loving Emma, was his main support. She focused all her attention on him. Whether things were happy and good, or bad, or even catastrophic, she never wavered, was always there at his side.

I felt like an oddball with my Gucci bags in hand as

Jack Keller opened the front door. The few days I spent at their house moved like the wind; yet all the joking, the stories and remembrances of other times and places filled me with lingering thoughts, bringing chuckles along with some measure of sadness.

Years before, he had been taken to Cedars of Lebanon Hospital, really sick. I had phoned him from the studio. "Is this the Old Trapper?"

"Yep. Is this Super Jew?"

"Yeah."

"Then get me the hell out of here. You're supposed to be my friend. I can't take it no more! Get me outta here!"

"What's so bad?"

"I can't stand the food. I can handle everything else—"

At seven o'clock that evening I walked up to his floor carrying two full trays of food, followed by the captain of Chasen's Restaurant and three violin players. I walked in saying, "Here—now maybe you'll keep your goddamn mouth shut."

Then we had dinner while the three violinists danced around his bed playing "Clair de Lune," with the captain serving pheasant under glass. I'm sitting on one side of the room, Jack's stuffing his jaws on the bed, and we're hysterical.

He says, "This is terrific. But what band's gonna play for breakfast?"

When I left British Columbia and the world came in again, I thought of Jack and wished he could take off and accompany me to Paris, where my audiences were growing and getting larger and digging everything.

"Ah, life."

An April night at JFK International Airport. Sitting far back on a sofa in the Air France lounge and talking to Joey Stabile, saying things about the upcoming Olympia

Theater engagement and the retrospective showing of Jerry Lewis films at the *Cinémathèque Française* . . . just a lot of talk. Joey doesn't miss a thing. He sees that giveaway look of mine. He says, finally, "Is your neck hurting?"

"Yes, but that's nothing new. That's only the half of it. The other half is Patti."

"What do you mean? She was all smiles when we left Los Angeles."

"I yelled at her at the dinner table last night. I could've cut my tongue out. The pain was so bad, and I couldn't deal with it. So I struck out at her. She confronted me this morning. She said, 'You embarrassed me'—that's all I had to hear. I wanted to drive my car into a wall. Sure, I hurt her. I humiliated her in front of my sons."

"Jerry, why are you so hard on yourself?"

"Because when it comes to telling Patti how much I care, I don't do it enough. I'm very guilty of being complacent when I'm with her. I get so comfortable, not realizing the things she needs."

Joey fingers his lips vacantly. "You don't have to tell me, Jerry. We get our priorities mixed up sometimes. It's the curse of our business."

"Something like that. Anyway, I should serve her more. You know, I'm thrilled I can say this. At least I recognize it. But recognizing is not fixing the problem. Strange. When I'm at home I can work in the next room, knowing she's around. It's cool. I think, 'Well, we're home. Everything is safe; there's nothing to worry about. So if everything is under control, *she* has nothing to worry about. Therefore, she needs nothing.' "

"I guess you have some mending to do."

"Yeah, I better start doing it soon."

Gay Paree—that rare, magnificent city of *joie de vivre*— where you can stroll down the Boulevard des Capucines with its sidewalk cafés and Opera House, lights shining,

neons winking, colored posters and amusement signs plas-
tered on corner kiosks; and Parisians standing in little
groups, smoking, chatting, reading newspapers, reading the
sign: JERRY LEWIS A L'OLYMPIA.

Outside the theatre, on the boulevard in front of it and
on nearby side streets, a double line of limousines was
moving slowly into reserved spaces, while under the huge
marquee a brilliant throng swarmed through the entrance,
crowding into far corners of the hall, packing its two
thousand seats. An extraordinary night, the first time any
American comedian had appeared on the Olympia stage—

I dished up the same brand of foolishness in slow English
with a butchered French accent: "Ladeees and gentlemen,
I am now goeeng to play for you zee famoos muzeeek called
zee second movement of Handel's fifth symphoneee in
D Minor," which seemed reasonable enough to the crowd
who really didn't care what language I spoke. They were
laughing at the silly stuff, like getting my hand caught in
the music stand, being startled by the crash of a cymbal and
taking pratfalls in my seven-hundred-dollar tuxedo. Everything worked—every second, every wild beautiful minute
—before the most enthusiastic and loving audience I'd
ever played to.

I slept like a log that night and woke up to keep a breakfast engagement with Geraldine Chaplin. Over rolls and
coffee, she complimented my performance. I was flattered
and pleased by this charming young lady, whose father
happened to be the "little tramp" and undisputed king of
comedy.

I asked politely, "How is your dad?"

"Simply marvelous. He's thoroughly enjoying himself in
Paris."

"Oh?" A sudden letdown. I tried to hide it. Maybe
Charlie would catch the show tonight. I wouldn't ask Geraldine what his plans were.

"As a matter of fact," she said, very near to releasing a

laugh, "we stayed up half the night talking of no one but you."

"Really?"

"Of course. He thought you were superb."

I was shocked. "You mean he saw me at the Olympia?"

"Yes."

"So why didn't he come backstage? My God, Geraldine, I revere that man."

"Well, the truth is, Dad was up in the light booth. He preferred the anonymity."

"Why?"

"Because he didn't want to steal your thunder."

As it turned out, I didn't get to meet Charlie Chaplin during my stay in Paris. Ten days later I was in Germany, researching material on the Third Reich for a projected film, and Chaplin had gone back to his estate in Corsier, Switzerland. By then, 1971, he had passed his eighty-second birthday; the clock would not allow him the luxury of finishing a number of projects that were in various stages of development.

I saw him briefly that summer, at dinner in Corsier. We talked intently about the industry, of the great silent funny men—Buster Keaton, Harry Langdon, Charlie Chase, Harold Lloyd, Chester Conklin, Ham Hamilton, Stan—and no less of the modern comic artists such as W. C. Fields, Red Skelton and Jackie Gleason. Each of them, Chaplin maintained, was a visual genius who would have done equally well in either silent or talking pictures. He said, "I believe the camera should be pointed at talking people who are doing something. If they are not doing it, it won't be funny."

His recall was sure and incisive as the old days flooded back. I listened as though his voice came down from a mountain (though I towered over him by at least a foot). "The most vivid impression I have of Mack Sennett," he said, "is that he was filled with excitement. His Keystone Company served as a playground, and he enjoyed playing in it more than anyone. There were only two things he required from the actors—put on makeup and get going with the rough-and-tumble."

During our discussion, Chaplin also made no bones of the fact that his last film lacked the essential qualities embodied in his former work. "I guess it happens to all of us," he mused. "We fall in love with an idea but sometimes overlook the substance. This was the case when I made *Countess From Hong Kong.* Marvelous actors—how could you not adore Sophia Loren and Marlon Brando? Nonetheless, the script was thin. It's a regret."

Chaplin. At that moment all his energies seemed dissipated. The years were etched deeply on his face, which no longer made him appear pixyish, devilish, carefree. He looked old and knew it.

Seeing him then, I remembered watching a television documentary on the great champion sprinter Jesse Owens. There were shots of him running in the Berlin Olympic Games of 1936, and shots of him walking in 1968; slow, deliberate, one spot to the next. It was frightening.

And the same thing happened to Charlie Chaplin. He made *Modern Times* in 1936 and *Countess* some thirty-one years later, tackling the same problems in a wholly different world at a different speed. His juices had dried. There was no way for his creative mind to cook.

[5]

At 6 A.M. the Rodriguez child is born. Three minutes later the Cohen baby arrives. Five minutes after that we hear the cry of the McPherson girl. And by 8 A.M. the nursery is filled. These are the heirs of Schultz, Brody, Capper, Smith, Aparicio, Fiore, Glick, Robison, Tzvaras, Ostrowski, Chan and so forth. They are cuddled in their respective blankets, sound asleep, all in one room. Now, wouldn't it be nice to have these babies meet twenty-one years later for a reunion, when each and every one of them can sleep in the same room again?

You must be kidding, say the cynics. Whoever heard of such a thing? It's dumb, stupid and wrong.

To those cynics I say: Please define wrong. When you do . . . color it hate.

Six years before my dinner with Chaplin, in 1965, my agent brought me a Joan O'Brien script titled *The Day the Clown Cried,* and I said, "I'm not ready for that." But it kept coming back, popping up regularly. The central character is a clown named Helmut Doork—Helmut the Great, once a very famous clown in Germany. But he had aged, his talent wasting away through drink, through an abhorrence of the Nazi regime. A despondent, degraded and broken-hearted reject consigned to the scrap heap, he's arrested by the Gestapo, interned in a concentration camp and used to march Jewish children into the "showers"; that is, the ovens. He had to clown to keep the children from screaming and crying, "Mama, Mama, Mama . . ."

Something you don't forget.

Then 1971, and this French producer, seated in my dressing room at the Olympia Theatre, pulled the script from his briefcase. "I have made a deal with Joan," he said. "Yes. We absolutely agree that you are the only one who can play Helmut exactly as she envisioned him." And here Nathan Wachsberger leaned forward eagerly. "What do you say? Can I have your approval to be the star and director? If it's yes, all the necessary financing is available."

I didn't answer right away. The thought of portraying

Helmut still scared the hell out of me. I knew the loneliness in him, the fear, the desperation that lay deep in his soul. I knew that to play him would be no casual affair, but the greatest artistic wrench of my life.

"Who's financing the picture?" I asked Wachsberger.

"Myself, of course, and Europa Films in Stockholm. They will provide half the money, including the facilities of their studio. You'll see, they have some of the best actors in Europe. Jerry, say you'll do it. It will be the strongest statement you can make to the world. Say I'm right."

"I don't know if you're right. Why don't you try getting Sir Laurence Olivier? I mean, he doesn't find it too difficult to choke to death playing Hamlet. My bag is comedy, Mr. Wachsberger, and you're asking me if I'm prepared to deliver helpless kids into a gas chamber. Ho-ho. Some laugh—how do I pull it off?"

He shrugged and sat back.

After a long moment of silence, I picked up the script.

"What a horror . . . It must be told."

Wachsberger looked at me cautiously. "Jerry, nobody else can tell it the same as you."

"You never know. Well, give me some time. I might just do it."

In spite of my knowledge, my awareness and understanding of the Holocaust and the beady-eyed lunatic with the comic mustache who had started it all, I couldn't for the life of me grasp how it was possible for the whole world to stand by without halting the destruction of six million Jews.

So I proceeded to research. I went to Belsen, Dachau and Auschwitz. I saw the killing camps, the sprinklers which unleashed Zyklon B, and I saw the nail scratchings on the walls; the initials, the writings. Hans Geibler showed me around, this seventy-year-old man who was doing penance for pulling the plug in the gas chambers. Full of self-reproach, he would wipe his eyes, and wince, as we examined the ovens. He became my technical adviser when we began filming *The Day the Clown Cried*.

To prepare for my role I dropped thirty-five pounds in six weeks by eating nothing but grapefruit. So that if you looked at me you'd see a bag of bones walking about, wearing an oversized concentration-camp outfit.

The camp scenes were filmed at a Swedish military compound. Whatever visions you may have of the real thing, this was as near to it as anyone can get—belching smokestacks and all.

In one of the sequences, Helmut is bunked up with his fellow political prisoners. Suddenly they rouse him from his cot to give a performance—"We don't expect a whole routine, Helmut. Just a little something to make us laugh." Helmut quietly tolerates the imposition, but that only drives the inmates into further entreaties, and finally angry verbal assaults—"Why don't you do something?" "Ach, you have forgotten to be a clown." "Are you trying to fool us?" "Come on, Doork, we want to see what makes you so great." "All right, that's enough. Leave him alone." "Stay out of this!" "You stay out!" *"No! We need a laugh!!"*

Helmut: "Can't you get it through your heads, I don't feel like—"

They pounce upon him, seething with hatred, everybody fixed on strangling him right then and there. As he lies on the floor, barely conscious, an SS officer comes swaggering in. "What is going on here!"

"Nothing. We were just showing this fellow a clown routine—"

The SS officer screams at Helmut, *"On your feet!"*

That officer, a servant of the state—he's the victim, not the clown on the floor, or the prisoners hovering over him. Free the prisoners and chances are they'll adjust, they'll get back into the mainstream. But the officer is scarred for life. Take away his uniform, put him into civilian clothes, it doesn't matter; he's still got the poison inside. That never gets extracted. The natural resources of spirit, soul, sensitivity, sensuality, adulation, adoration, love—that SS officer had nothing, none of it. So he doesn't know he's the victim, that what he did was bad. And I contend he'll never know. History tells me I'm right.

I thought *The Day the Clown Cried* would be a way to show we don't have to tremble and give up in the darkness. Helmut would teach us this lesson. It was all I wanted to establish; just a reminder.

Instead, I got crossed.

Two weeks into the production, we began having financial problems. The suppliers were getting impatient, asking again and again when they'd be paid. What could I tell them? That was Nathan Wachsberger's end of the deal, handling the money, paying the bills as they came due. Yet the French Eastman Company, which shipped the film stock, for example, had received no money at all. Even worse, members of the crew and some of the actors had been stiffed by checks that were bouncing higher than the proverbial kite. I was in Stockholm, frantically placing phone calls to the South of France, with Wachsberger assuring me the checks were forthcoming, saying not to worry, they had gone out. . . . . "And, Jerry, if you write a few checks to cover mine—they're in the mail—without question you'll be reimbursed, *mon ami.*"

So I kept shelling out my own dough while waiting for those forthcoming checks. But they never came. Wachsberger was elsewhere. In fact, I didn't see hide nor hair of him during the entire shooting.

As the situation grew more desperate, there were days when I would order four hundred feet of film from a local supplier, have it rushed to me on the set and pay for it

with Swedish krona. Otherwise, we couldn't shoot. It became a bottomless pit, trying to make the picture, trying to
raise money and getting on the phone trying to hunt down
Wachsberger. The man almost gave me a coronary. But I
turned all of my pain into the performance.

That last scene. Helmut in full clown makeup, walking
the children through the compound, past the barbed-wire
fence and the towers. They follow him like he's the Pied
Piper. . . .

When I thought of doing the scene, I was petrified. I
stood rooted in my clown's costume, waiting for a take.
Then the children came running toward me, unasked, un-
directed, clinging to my arms and legs, looking up so trust-
ingly. I forgot about being an actor. I began to walk with
them, and they went laughing and singing straight into the
gas chamber.

And the door closed behind us.

As of now, *The Day the Clown Cried* has not yet been
released. It sits in Stockholm, tied up in litigation. Until
the courts finally decide on the merits of Joan O'Brien's
and my case against Nathan Wachsberger, the film stays
there under lock and key. The last three scenes are all I'm
holding; they're my protection. Meanwhile, I'm still hoping
to get the litigation cleared away so I can go back to Stockholm and shoot three or four more scenes. I also have to
dub and score, maybe even do a re-cut. Fortunately, though,
the story is timeless. I can release it ten years from now, and
it will hold up.

One way or another, I'll get it done. The picture must
be seen, and if by no one else, at least by every kid in the
world who's only heard there was such a thing as the
Holocaust.

BOOK EIGHT

My father was seventy. Tired of California, he now lived in Miami Beach with his memories and Mom to lean upon for the daily necessities. Among his many neighbors were a few old-time vaudeville people who'd occasionally visit and bring a little extra cheer into his life. Other than that, he hardly went out or saw anyone, content to sit around the apartment whole afternoons until Mom had his dinner ready.

So it went.

While playing the Westbury Music Fair on Long Island, I received a phone call from Mom. "Please get down here—Dad's had a stroke."

"Oh, God. How bad is he?"

"He's breathing. But please, Jerry, hurry."

I chartered a private jet and flew out that night. At the hospital, walking into his room, I saw him lying still and motionless, his eyes half-closed; frightened.

He was hanging on to his poor life, not knowing whether he was there or anywhere else in the world. He just wanted to be in it a while longer.

After some weeks, the doctors allowed him to go home. Mom took care of him as though he were a baby, giving so much of herself, trying to put a spark back into his eyes and that old happy-go-lucky feeling back into his heart again.

My father, my first real hero. I used to see him as a hero in everything—science, sports, politics, the very White House itself—and was especially glad to have him as a hero in show business. I loved to sit in the front row of any theatre and watch him put on a straw hat—man, I'd come away from the experience puffed up like a theatrical Rhodes scholar!

So what happened?

I got angry at this hero of mine. He settled. He lost his drive. He had no desire to be anything other than what he was, a big fish in a small pond.

"Hey, as long as I can feed my family, I'm satisfied."

Sure. But when I reached twenty, somehow things got turned around. I began to feel more like a father to him than a son. There were reasons, of course. Mainly, if we didn't talk show business, forget the rest; no discussion, it was over. For instance, I'd point to a newspaper headline: "What do you think about this, Dad?"

"I don't."

"Well, you should get interested, be aware, have a point of view. I mean, you oughta know about what's going on with civil rights, the Vietnam War, the ERA issue—whatever. Dad, there are other things, you know, beside Johnny Carson and how your boy is doing in the movies."

He'd shrug it off, then pick up the paper and impassively turn to the theatrical page.

It was that kind of battle. It never seemed to end.

One time I remember, we were shmoozing in my Paramount office when suddenly the mood felt right to show him something I had written—*An Elephant Isn't the Only One*—

thinking possibly he would understand its meaning, even sense my need to get closer to him . . . .

"Dad, please read this carefully. I want your honest opinion. Tell me what you think, OK?"

He peered at it for a few moments, then looked up, a blank expression on his face.

"Well?"

"Well, what?"

"Can't you do any better than that!" And exasperated, steaming mad, I hollered, "Goddamn it, I'll write a check this minute for fifty thousand dollars if you'll just get up and smack me across the room!"

"I can't do that," he said, looking around with stunned amazement.

"Why?"

"Because I love you."

"No! You don't love me! If you did, you'd smack me!"

"Oh," he said. "You're getting into the psychological crap again."

I stormed out of the office, went reeling halfway down a back stairwell, sat there for I don't know how long in shame and anger, and then wept.

[2]

Going back to New York was like going back to the source where everything began, where all that's felt or dreamed is carried by the pulse beat of eight million souls in this incredible city. Here, on September 3, 1972, I went into action with a twenty-hour muscular dystrophy telethon, presenting a full range of stars including Carol Burnett, Stevie Wonder, Wayne Newton, Sarah Vaughan, Sammy Davis, Jimmy Durante, Art Carney, Johnny Cash, Sonny and Cher, Julius LaRosa, Carroll O'Connor and countless others in a continuous flow from hour one to the sign-off. It was by far the most successful telethon to date, with a record $9,000,000 in pledges. Significantly, too, we were seen for the first time outside the continental United States, a total of 140 stations carrying us live to nearly 70,000,000 viewers. But the key was New York—the key to everything. Its generosity had once again triggered a strong response across the nation, so the idea of shifting our base would have been unthinkable. I felt loyal to New York. Things like considerations for logistics notwithstanding, it just didn't cross my mind to leave. I had a lifetime love affair going on with this town. Why change my luck?

Except—except for the fact that the major show business names were not here. On the opening segments (where you either win or lose an audience) I introduced through split-screen two-way conversation the heavyweights I needed, and they were in Las Vegas, or Los Angeles, which is only a short drive away.

A sign of the times. A matter of survival. I guess that's how Walter O'Malley felt before he took the Dodgers out of Brooklyn.

So after seven years and now a great deal of talking and planning the next Labor Day telecast, I decided to make a switch to Vegas. It had the glittering casinos and all those stage shows headlining the magical names. And this was my primary motivation for relocating the telethon into Del Webb's Hotel Sahara.

That first year, 1973, a whole new family of corporate sponsors climbed on our bandwagon. My tired old legs were caving in from shoving some of them aboard. I remember how it was with the Southland Corporation. Those people are something else entirely. I mean, they are one big outfit—more than a billion customers buying everything from Hot-to-Go fast foods to dips, eggnogs and Slurpees at their franchised and company-operated 7-11 Stores. That's what I call American enterprise!

So I went after them. About forty-seven times, traveling from Los Angeles or New York, Chicago, Honolulu, Tokyo—whatever—to their corporate headquarters in Dallas. When I finally had them in my pocket, the real work began. Do you know how many divisions they have? How many stores? Maybe you do, but I couldn't keep track. They've got sixty-three 7-11 Stores in Vegas alone, so I'm always showing up late at the golf course just by stopping at all the stores. One more Slurpee and I'll have the runs for four years.

And do you know what it is to stuff yourself solid with Sara Lee cakes, not to mention a truckload of McDonald's hamburgers, an ocean of Budweiser beer and a whole island of Hickory Farms sausage and cheese products—huh?

Suffice to say, those sponsors and many more of the same caliber play a vital role in generating funds for MDA. They believe, they go out and work; and one fund-raising campaign creates still another. Then, each Labor Day, it all comes together on the Love Network. People feeling good about what they're doing, feeling good about themselves.

It's like a party.

But when the party's over, when everybody goes home, I'm all fired up and ready to get them excited and participating again for the next one . . . always hoping it'll be the last, hoping that by next year we'll have found the cure.

Meanwhile, things happen which cannot be foreseen: I would find myself attacked for wanting to wipe muscular dystrophy off the face of the earth. I'll draw a picture of that. A picture of me standing onstage during the telethon, making my pitch, making it through fifteen or sixteen hours, all the while noodging, scolding, pleading, looking up at the tote board and praying for the numbers to climb. . . . No one knows that something else is also flashing in my head. I see the stage suddenly turn to sawdust, my tux change to a tramp's outfit, and I feel as though people are

looking at me like I'm some kind of freak in a sideshow . . .
I'm remembering the guy in Cleveland going on the air a
couple of days ago. . . .

"Good morning, WHK. You're on the air."
"I'd like to ask if you have any knowledge whether Jerry
Lewis gets paid for his work on the telethon."
"You better believe he gets paid."
"Do you have any idea how much he gets paid?"
"We went through this last year because I wasn't going
to appear, and I think with all the money that goes in,
about sixty percent goes to MD and forty percent goes to
Jerry Lee Lewis—I mean Jerry Lewis."
"We're talking about millions of dollars, right?"
"Oh, yeah. . . ."
"And he gets *that* much of it?"
"Yes. And we all know he's a no-talent. He hasn't
had . . ."
"That's beside the point."
"Sir, it's a fact. He couldn't get a job at WHK. You
know that?"
"Right on!"

"Good morning, WHK. You're on the air."
"What proof do you have that Jerry Lewis gets forty
percent from the telethon?"
"That's what they told me before I appeared last year.
I think some spokesman from Channel Eight gave me the
information. . . . It didn't all go to MD, I'll tell you that
for sure. And sixty percent is pretty good. . . ."
"Is there any way of finding out how the funds are
broken down?"
"Yeah, I think if you're not a dullard and a dummy. I
always ask before I give a dime to charity. Charity for me
begins with my family, and the hell with everybody else.

But if you want to give your hard-earned money to charity, that's your business. OK?"

"Sounds good."

"Good morning, WHK. You're on the air."

"Yeah . . . I'm fully aware that Jerry Lewis is an ass. But if your new child was born with multiple sclerosis, you'd probably—"

"Get out of here, you lily-livered, yellow-bellied, pinko Commie, egg-suckin' dog. . . ."

It sounds unbelievable, but it happened, on the air, word for word.

I'm up in my suite at the Hotel Sahara talking with Artie Forrest, the telethon's producer-director. We're preparing for a production meeting when the phone rings. It's Moose Delgado, calling from his room across the hall.

"Jerry, you got hammered this morning by a talk-show guy in Cleveland."

"Really?"

"Yes. He made you a multimillionaire. Said you're skimming forty percent from the telethon pledges."

"What? You mean he said that on the air?"

"I'm afraid so, my boy."

"Well, Moose," I finally say, "I'm gonna catch a plane to Cleveland and kill him." It's a knife to the heart, knowing all these years I've never asked, nor taken, one quarter from MDA for the work I've done.

He says, "Bob Ross will handle it the right way. He's been in contact with the station and is preparing to sue them unless they make a retraction."

"What good will that do? The damage is done. I tell you, I'm gonna go down there—"

"Please reconsider. At least, wait till after the telethon.

And if you still want to go, I'll help you to blow his head off."

That's all I have to hear. "OK, Moose. . . . Don't worry about it. I'm not going anywhere."

"Thank you, my boy. I thought that would do it."

Ten days later I booked a three-day weekend at the Front Row Theatre in Cleveland, itching to stroll over and come face-to-face with WHK's talk-show host.

He was in his studio, taking calls as MDA attorney Milton Small and I walked through the door. Swiveling his neck around to see who it is—"I-I can't believe that Jerry Lewis is here in the booth with me—"

"Hi, there. I just thought I'd stop by to say hello."

"I-I gotta tell ya, Jer, I made a big mistake."

"You sure did."

The full-page ad, as it appeared in the *Cleveland Plain Dealer* and the *Cleveland Press,* same day, November 8, 1977:

Editor:

AN APOLOGY TO THE MUSCULAR DYSTROPHY ASSOCIATION AND JERRY LEWIS
An Open Letter to Clevelanders:

At some time between 8 and 10 A.M., on Friday, September 2, just two days preceding the broadcast of the annual Jerry Lewis Labor Day Telethon to benefit the Muscular Dystrophy Association, the morning personality of WHK Radio irresponsibly made some very serious misstatements on WHK/1420 about the Muscular Dystrophy Association and Jerry Lewis and his telethon broadcast over WJKW-TV.

In response to comments phoned in by listeners, our morning personality stated that all he cared about was "to get you people the truth" and that, if what he said could be proved wrong, he'd eat his words. He was absolutely wrong and was proved so beyond all question. The purpose of this message from WHK is to acknowledge publicly the error of our morning personality.

The most reprehensible remark made by him was his statement about the telethon that ". . . with all the money that goes in, about 60 percent of it goes to Muscular Dystrophy and 40 percent goes to Jerry . . ." That remark was and is entirely in error. WHK and its morning personality categorically state that Jerry Lewis is not paid one cent in personal income as a result of his hosting the telethon. Nor is he paid for any of his extensive year-round activities as Muscular Dystrophy Association National Chairman. WHK's morning personality further apologizes for the insulting remarks made about Jerry Lewis' motives in connection with the wholly false claim that Jerry Lewis derives personal income from the telethon. We regret that our morning personality misused whatever influence he may have over members of his radio audience. WHK and its morning personality acknowledge the telethon to be a charitable effort founded solidly on the principle of voluntary action, and conducted with high standards of fiscal and administrative integrity—standards which equally characterize the operations of the telethon's beneficiary, the Muscular Dystrophy Association, as well as Jerry Lewis' conduct as the Muscular Dystrophy Association National Chairman.

WHK paid for this space so its morning personality may apologize to the Muscular Dystrophy Association and Jerry Lewis for the injustice done to them.

WHK Radio endorsed and fully supported the Jerry Lewis Telethon and the Muscular Dystrophy Association.

Thanks.

And if I ever take advantage, then rap me. I'm sure there's plenty to rap me for. I used to tell Patti, "I'll give the critics a memo listing a hundred things that I did which literally hurt people unintentionally. Only, why do they have to make up crap?"

When I'm attacked for something I've done wrong, I'll usually write a note to the guy and say I'm sorry, because he was telling the truth. But let him tell a lie, he'll hear from me also. And I can't count the number of editorial offices I've visited during the past twenty-five years. Quiet. Very nice.

"How do you do? I just want to look at you. Don't worry, I'm not going to hit you. I'm not going to do a thing. . . ."

On the 1976 telethon I caught it from nearly everybody by saying that God goofed. I said, "Do you think it's normal for God to put children in steel cages? If it is, then I say He goofed."

I said it in front of 85,000,000 viewers. And do you know what kind of static I got? Plenty! I mean within seconds we were losing stations left and right. I had no idea what was happening until Bob Ross gave me a frantic wigwag while I was still expounding on the subject. So I kinda slipped within hearing distance. He cupped his hands around his mouth and said, "You just lost six states. It's gonna hurt. You'd better apologize."

"Ah, come on, Bob . . . *apologize?*"

He said, "You have to."

So I came back after the station break.

"I've been told that I have offended a lot of people. Therefore, I humbly apologize. It was not my intention to offend anyone . . . but I still think *God goofed."*

I believed it. And I wasn't going to backwater, no matter who got offended.

Why can't God goof? You mean to say the San Andreas Fault isn't a goof? You mean He put a split in the earth so people would get swallowed up by an earthquake? I think God had some other things in mind, and I really believe He invented hurricanes and tornadoes to give us some air during the hot summer months. So God goofed. But why blame Him? He did a lot of good stuff, you know, starting from embryos to Mount Everest. And let's not forget that He parted the Red Sea and led Noah aboard the boat with all his couples. He made sure Reggie Jackson hit .280 so he could stay in the major leagues. . . . You see, God has a lot of things to worry about. A whole world! How can you expect Him to remember everything? You can't tell me that God meant to bury Pompeii. Not at all. He was meaning to build a nice highway past the town but didn't figure on the tar melting and sliding over to the right a little. How did He know three hundred people would come running out of their huts yelling, "Ugg uggghhh glnk glunnnk"? No, He didn't mean to bury Pompeii. There were some swell things there. There was a McDonald's and a Häagen-Daz, and they had a Wendy's. . . . Why would He cover that? To use a country and a whole population for fertilizer? Someone goofed! I mean, the Chicago Fire had to happen. Sure, He was watching the Tammany Hall boys in New York at the time—He's going to keep His eye on a cow? Why bother? The cow's only got a few weeks anyway before it winds up on a plate at Delmonico's. So why watch the cow? Better to watch all those schmucks and hookers down in the Loop. Meanwhile, the cow goes,

Brrrrrrrr . . . knocks over the lantern and destroys an entire city!

I can tell you plenty of stories about God. I'm entitled. After all, George Burns is a personal friend of mine.

So don't be offended.

Back on stage Labor Day, 1976. No fuss, no bother, no "How come you didn't call me?" Frank Sinatra was *there,* working for my kids with his music, his talent and his great heart. Through the years, ever since our paths crossed at the Copa in 1948, he's always extended himself generously, trying to make things a little better in this world by word and action. That's the manner of man Frank is. . . . He had his hand on my shoulder, turning me toward the wings, saying with a matter-of-fact smile, "I have a friend backstage who wants to say hello."

I couldn't imagine. And, for a moment, I stood gape-jawed in astonishment as Dean walked out, nodding warmly, his arms coming up slowly. . . . We hugged. Suddenly everything washed, there was no past or bad, everything was good. I looked up and said to God, "Give me a line. Help me to say something . . . I don't know what to do." I looked at him:

"Ya workin'?"

"Yeah, I get a few weeks at the MGM Grand."

For all I knew, there could have been tears all over the place. I had visions; they sped through my mind in a microsecond. We'd play golf together; we'd talk and reminisce, catch up on the last twenty years, maybe look forward to better times ahead, to a friendship we never had before. And now that we were older, perhaps a little wiser, there would be so much more to learn about each other.

The show sped on. I got busy calling the affiliate stations, introducing the acts, doing turns with anchorman Ed Mc-Mahon, then going off to change my clothes during the cutaways. All night it went; a performance, a tumultuous celebration, an outpouring of help from everywhere around the country. Then came late afternoon when Ed called for a final timpani roll—

And the board hit $21,723,873.

I wanted to sleep a whole day. But tired as I was, before going to bed I wrote Dean a letter and had it hand-delivered to his hotel. No reply. A few weeks passed and I sent off another letter, enclosing a twenty-dollar gold piece with the telethon symbol embossed on one side, a love inscription composed specially for him and Frank on the other. Frank responded immediately. As for Dean, not a word.

The following August, when Dean was working Vegas, I picked up the phone and called his hotel. The operator said he wasn't in. I left a message, waited, waited some more. Finally, I asked Joey Stabile to go see him. "Just tell Dean he's invited back on the telethon, and remind him we're getting close to Labor Day. But whatever he decides, make sure he knows I want a meeting."

So Joey drove to the MGM Grand. Dean greeted him pleasantly; as charming as ever. Everything worked out fine, and Joey set a date for the next day. "Jerry will come to your hotel," he said.

"No, no," Dean insisted. "I'll come and meet Jerry at the Sahara at four o'clock."

I'm still waiting.

[3]

At the age of eight I believed in the power and invincibility of heavyweight champion Max Baer. I felt he would hold his crown a hundred years. At the age of nine I sat in my grandmother's house, listening to a radio account of his defeat at the hands of James J. Braddock. To me that was an indignity. A fake. The announcer had lied.

So a week after the fight I went to the Rex Theatre with Herbie Diamond, and we watched Max get beaten again on film.

"Do you believe it now?" asked Herbie as we came out into the sunlight.

"Not yet," I answered. "Max Baer is fighting at the Adams Theatre. I bet he won there."

Well, just as my boyish belief in heroes has been altered by the process of age and experience, so my wildest fantasies have diminished in the light of present-day reality, without vanishing entirely. At fifty-five, I no longer dream of fixing the world, of making all the hurt go away. The lonely, skinny, monkey-faced kid has come too far and over too many hurdles for that. But I can still find him. I have only to reach down and he's there whenever I need him for a laugh, recognition, ego, self-esteem . . . and solace.

The laugh. It's carried me around the globe to places where millions of people are starving for laughter. Where a pratfall or a silly joke is all that it takes to make them forget their bellies are empty. . . . In Africa, South America and the Far East. It's earned me film-director awards in France, Belgium, Italy, Germany, The Netherlands and Spain. It's opened windows behind the Iron Curtain. . . . No matter what I thought politically, whatever the mood or time of day, the laugh has been there, and I've loved every cockeyed minute of it. You can bet I want more.

But who's to guarantee when you go to bed laughing you won't wake up crying?

During January 1977, only forty-eight hours from fulfilling a dream to go all the way from stardom in nightclubs, television and motion pictures to stardom on a Broadway

legitimate stage, I awakened one Sunday morning in Boston
finding the dream unfulfilled. I had been signed into a
"can't miss" show, the revamped 1938 *Hellzapoppin*. The
new version didn't pan out. Technical and artistic difficulties dogged our heels all through our tryout run in Washington, D.C., got worse when we played Baltimore and
finished us altogether after the final curtain at Boston's
Colonial Theatre, with me and producer Alexander Cohen
moaning and foaming at the mouth and at one another over
what the hell went wrong—

So I said "Good-bye, Broadway, see you another day."

Meanwhile, poof, there went the dream.

[4]

Besides, there were more problems.

Mostly, my dependence on the painkiller drug Percodan.
I was taking anywhere from ten to fifteen a day, enough to
knock out a horse. Stupid, yes, and dangerous, but I
couldn't get along without them. The pain in my spine was
that bad, compounded by debilitating side effects, a numb-
ness of the fingers, impaired vision, the shame of bowel
irregularities and the depressing realization that I had become impotent. Pain, indeed—for the best neurosurgeons
in New York, London, Paris, Stockholm, and as far away
as Tokyo, had decided against an operation; though one of
them indicated he might risk it, looking at me and saying,
"First, I'll tell you the odds. There's a fifty percent chance
you'll come out no worse than before. Of course, anything
is possible. However, you could end up paralyzed the rest
of your life."

With those odds, my intake of Percodan immediately
increased.

Now, during that period (1975–1978) I was working, extending the same energy as always. And nobody, not even Patti, knew how many Percodans I had been sneaking into my system. They saw only that I had become terribly jumpy, irritable, impatient and sometimes meaner than hell.

What Patti didn't see were the pathetic moments on the road. Once, while taking a shower, my left side went numb, my legs folded and I collapsed under a steaming-hot spray of water. If Lou Brown hadn't come to my aid when he did, God knows what would have happened.

Then one night I played a benefit for the Italian Boys' Home at the Chicago Garden. Before going on, I swallowed three Percodans. It helped a little. After the benefit there was a party, a great bunch of people eating hors d'oeuvres and drinking champagne. I treated myself to a few sips, placed the glass on a table and felt an explosion of pain. I hit the floor, smack against it, in a convulsion, the ceiling roaring over me. And came to in my suite at the Ambassador East. A doctor had given me a shot of something, was standing there saying, "This will hold you for a while . . . I'll write a prescription."

So now, September 27, 1978, I'm at the Hotel Sahara, gabbing with entertainment director Jack Eglash. He has a headache. No secret to that; he's been suffering from migraines ever since I've known him. Still and all, tonight Jack's been complaining that his headache is really wicked. "Well, Jack, you should have a specialist check you out. As a matter of fact, there's a top medical team at Methodist Hospital. I can call and make the arrangements." And Jack says, "Forget it. I'm scared to death of doctors."

The next day, with a strange premonition, I telephoned my friend Dr. Michael DeBakey at Methodist Hospital, Houston, who is also a member of the MDA Scientific Advisory Committee. It all began in 1970. . . . The organization needed some prestigious people on the com-

mittee, which made me think, "Let's get Dr. DeBakey
involved. I'm sure he can help us one way or another." Well,
this most important heart specialist turned out to be 170
pounds of total heart. I've seen him at work, watched his
skills under severe pressure when it meant life or death
for the patient. I've been at his home in Houston, where I
have discovered time and time again how much he cares
about people. "When a patient dies, I am diminished," he
said one night after a successful seven-hour operation in
which a young girl had arrested twice on the table. I was
there, saw Michael's face as he removed his mask, a
trembling smile playing on his lips. . . . He's no Robert
Redford, but right then he looked like the handsomest man
you could find anywhere on this earth. This man . . . if
he hears of a blatant case of malpractice, it shatters him.
I'd say, "Michael, it happened in North Dakota," and he'd
shake his head. "No, it didn't. It happened in my home,
near my child, here where I live and breathe." DeBakey—
one of the Originals. He could tell me to walk in the street
and get hit by a truck, and I would let it hit me . . . need
I say more?

And so now, talking with him about Jack Eglash's problem, valuing the preciseness of his advice, I decide to make
arrangements anyhow and have a room set aside for Jack
at the hospital.

I go to him and say, "Everything's in order. Dr. De-
Bakey's got a team of specialists waiting in Houston."

"I'm sorry, Jerry. I can't do it. I'm not going."

"*Jack,* they're waiting. Don't be a baby. I'll take you
there."

Next afternoon we're at the hospital. Jack's got his bed,
and they're doing a workup on him. Meanwhile, Dr. De-
Bakey and Sylvia Farrell—his right arm—are walking down
the hall with me. Fifty feet from Jack's room, I keel over and
wind up in a bed on the same floor with Jack.

Michael thought I had had a heart attack. The symptoms were there: excruciating pain, legs doubled against my chest like in the embryo stage. When they lifted me onto a stretcher, it must've looked as though they had picked up a piece of petrified wood.

After they ruled out the possibility of a heart attack, came an X-ray plate of my abdomen, showing an ulcer the size of a lemon. There was no telling how long it had been there because the Percodans had disguised its symptoms. Anyway, Michael maintains that if the ulcer had gone undetected two more weeks, I probably would have bled to death.

He knew I had been on Percodan but had no idea to what extent. He thought maybe two or three a day; not a lot, considering the pain. He was stunned when I spilled the whole story, all the gruesome details. Eventually, Dr. Arthur Errickson and his staff associates came around and consulted Michael on procedures. That's when I realized I wouldn't be going home right away. Eglash did, still harboring his migraines, while I stayed behind at Methodist Hospital, placed under heavy sedation (dosages of belladonna) with steroids injected regularly into my spine. A merciful release. I slept in a sort of twilight zone, nothing save flickers and shadows for practically ten days.

The ulcer was gone, so Michael said I could go home. Before leaving, I listened carefully, forewarned, understanding that my craving for Percodan had been touched off not only by the pain but also by my craving for *Coca-Cola:* I never took a Percodan without guzzling it down with a Coke; and the two had become associated in my brain, the way coffee and cigarettes are associated for some people. To stay off Percodan, I'd have to stay away from Coke.

Riding to the airport—my head clear, the air pure; everything's great, sane, absolutely remarkable. All's well in this wonderful world again—

From that day on I haven't as much as looked at a Percodan, or any other narcotic. The pain is still there, of course, and always will be, as nobody in my lifetime is gonna figure out how to replace a degenerated spinal cord. Unless—just maybe there's somebody around with the same kind of pioneering genius that Michael DeBakey has.

If there is, I got hope.

[5]

"Camera rolling!"

"OK, shoot—light a single on Harold Stone—'A' camera mark—'B' camera mark—all right, roll—speed—and *action!*"

"Hooper, I want to see you in my office right now!"

"Oop. Cut! Hold it a sec, we need another prop."

That's me, on the set of *Hardly Working,* directing a scene at the West Palm Beach post office. I was back doing my thing again, seven years after *The Day the Clown Cried.*

Once again, it was a financial cliff-hanger. Our producer had been playing in Nathan Wachsberger's league, owing money to everybody and skipping town when we discovered the extent of his chicanery. Fortunately, Jim McNamara, a thirty-two-year-old Palm Beach resident, brought in a group of angels who bankrolled the picture. Jim assumed the job of executive producer, and we finished principal photography under budget, three days ahead of schedule.

Hardly Working earned about $25 million abroad before opening here in the spring of 1981 at 704 first-run theatres. It was a box-office bonanza, despite some wagging heads among the critics.

Whatever, the trades and dailies alike gave me credit for

staging a remarkable comeback. Funny, because I never felt I had been away.

To top it off, two months after the opening, I came into New York to co-star with Robert DiNiro in a Martin Scorsese film titled *King of Comedy*. It is the story of Rupert Pupkin (DeNiro), a fan-a-tical would-be comic who kidnaps number-one night-show host Jerry Langford; the plan is for Rupert to get on the show and do a stand-up routine while I'm held captive, bound to a chair with a gun at my back.

We made the film at various locations around Manhattan and shot one sequence on Long Island Sound. After completing my part I flew out to Las Vegas, particularly satisfied over the combination of playing a dramatic role and working with Bobby and Marty. From the very first day, we hit it off. What's important, they didn't treat me as a Hollywood celebrity or as the idiot kid; they showed a high respect for my talent as an actor and a fllmmaker. Which made us even, because they are brilliant professionals, a delight to work with and to know.

BOOK NINE

I T ' S easy to say, "I'm going to write a book, and I'm going to tell the truth, the whole truth and nothing but the truth." It's not so easy to do. Before you know it, all those fine resolutions about being honest come up against things in your past that you'd just as soon not talk about, things you'd like to skip over or lie about; shame, embarrassment, foolishness, inadequacies, sorrows. And—you say to yourself—what's the harm? Who's to say what really happened? What is truth, anyhow?

Well, whatever it is, I've tried to tell it all and go on a bit more, knowing that everyone has to have a finish.

I'm doing what I want to do, and I'm sensing all that's ahead of me. Tomorrow I'll be in Los Angeles to begin work on the forty-fourth film of my career: *Slapstick,* a script written by Kurt Vonnegut (from his novel), being produced and directed by *wunderkind* Steven Paul, a feisty twenty-two-year-old with tremendous energy, drive and excitement for what he does. Come to think of it, he reminds me of me at that age. He knows what he's doing; he cares and loves his work; and I know whatever he does will be good because he's good.

I'm pretty lucky; within two years a film with Martin Scorsese, now Steven and later with Peter Bogdonovich. We need the Scorseses, Pauls and Bogdonoviches today more than ever. We need directors and producers who really care, who get things done for all the right reasons. No egos, no self-indulging; just good filmmaking to complement the art and give something to the theatregoing public—their money's worth, rather than embarrassment and the feeling of being had.

So I'm looking forward to tomorrow. Yet, at the same time, I'm thinking of yesterday, of that skinny, lonely little kid who wanted to grow up to be a clown because he felt so inadequate, felt that by hiding behind greasepaint he would not be just a sad face in a huge crowd. And I did grow up . . . and so did millions of others right along with me. There isn't a day that someone doesn't come up to me and say, "I've grown up with you and your humor!" That makes it all worthwhile. I've been fortunate enough to play to four generations, which I hadn't realized until one night after my show at the Sahara. Backstage, a lady had somehow talked her way past the security guard. Moments later in she walks, a most dignified, lovely, classy woman who I'm sure had enjoyed at least sixty birthdays. With her, another beautiful woman about fortyish, and a pretty lady about twenty-two holding the hand of the sweetest four-year-old little Dresden doll. . . . I welcomed them, asked them to have a seat, and the elderly woman spoke. "Jerry, I felt compelled to see you and thank you for the many years of joy, fun and laughter you've given me, my daughter, her daughter and now her daughter. . . ." And as she spoke my eyes wandered over the pretty faces. The largest smile belonged to the four-year-old. And as the lady went on, she made it clear that the youngest was as big a fan as the eldest.

Alone in the dressing room I thought to myself, "I've done some good stuff." I felt satisfied and deeply humbled by what had just happened. It made me understand that you can do a great deal in three-quarters of a lifetime and never really know the impact you've had on so many.

Couple all that with my home life and it has been full, to say the least. I married a great lady who gave me six great sons, and we had thirty-five years of all kinds of stuff . . . good, bad, painful, anxious, wearying, troubled, ecstatic, not really very different from most people. . . . Only because everything is relative (no pun intended).

Now Patti and I are getting a divorce. Of all the lines in this book, that one is the hardest to write. I have never believed in garbage like "stay together for the children"; we stayed together (and I'll never know how she put up with some of the stunts I pulled) because we wanted to, because we really cared, because we both believe that if you do your honest best to do what's best for you, everyone will benefit, directly or indirectly.

Gradually, I had come to know that my staying would be worse—for me, for her—than my leaving. I don't ask for sympathy or for a judgment, good or bad. Patti stayed with me over some pretty rough roads, and I'll always love her for that. Then our own road got rocky, and it was time to go our separate ways. It's a cliché, but it's true: my life has extra meaning for me now; I'm happier than I've ever been, enjoying a peace of mind I had all but forgotten. I feel as if I'm on a smooth highway, and the ride is terrific.

⌈ 2 ⌉

In the Congo Room of the Hotel Sahara I was rehearsing a Jolson medley when a phone call came from an Associated Press reporter. He needed a comment about something or other. I told Joey Stabile I'd get back to the guy and went on rehearsing.

The next day it was in all the papers:

JERRY LEWIS NOMINATED
FOR NOBEL PEACE PRIZE

"Just to be in that company is magnificent," said Jerry Lewis on learning that Rep. Les Aspin, D. Wisc., had nominated him for the Nobel Peace Prize, in recognition of his work in behalf of the Muscular Dystrophy Association. In 11 years, Mr. Aspin noted, Mr. Lewis' Labor Day Telethons have raised more than $95 million for the muscular dystrophy organizations. The nomination has been accepted by the Nobel Prize Committee of the Norwegian Parliament for the 1978 award. The nomination cites Lewis' sensitivity and commitment which have enabled millions "to express their innate desire to help their fellow man."

As it's been said: the things you keep you lose; the things you give away you keep forever.

So this is for my father, after all. . . .
I wanted to tell him that he had given me the tools of my trade. But, instead, he found out through others. My old man, he saw things his way, the things that were made up in sweet songs and a tip of the old straw hat and a cane; and he saw that his kid had a chance to do them the same way. So he taught him. Then all the sweetness and beauty of what he taught were put together by his kid and made to go a little further than the sounds he could hear. . . .
One early November day in 1980 I arrived at the hospital with Mom and my Las Vegas golf pal Benny Benigas. Too late. The doctor said my father had just passed away. I went in and stayed awhile; then came out, took Mom around and held her close. She said, "All this time, all those years, but where did they go?"
And all I could do was hug her a little closer.

EPILOGUE

MORE times than not, once the last page of a book is written, the cover closes, the reader likes or dislikes what he's read, and you've done a book. . . . Well, I've hardly been the kind of man that's been referred to as a conformist, so why should this be any different?

As I scanned the pages of my life and I relived much of that life that's now pressed between two covers, I realized that everything could never be said—so why not a p.s., an afterthought, the epilogue. Who said I couldn't?

So I will!

I have no regrets. I wouldn't change a minute of any of it. I feel I've done more than most men ever get a chance to do. I'm very fortunate and deeply grateful that I didn't wind up one of the many drummers in the parade. I was chosen to carry the baton . . . and that makes me feel very special.

And now that my life goes into part two I must say it's as exciting as, if not more so, than part one—probably because the changes that have taken place give me a freshness and a vitality and energy that men rarely get a shot at this

late in life. But that should act as an inspiration to everyone who can identify with the magic I'm lucky enough to
be encountering. . . . Her name is Sam (short for Sandee)
—a lovely, warm, sensitive, caring, loving human being,
who stepped into my life right on cue. The merry-go-round
wasn't fun anymore. I caught the brass ring many times,
and how long can you go around in circles? She helped me
off, held my hand, walked me towards the sunset, and
showed me there was much more—that life was *still* a
party and I should get dressed and go. . . .